Case Studies in Coaching Ethics

Coaches are placed in a myriad of ethical decision-making situations. Making decisions such as playing time, boosters, parents, social media, power differentials, scholarships, and relationships are just a few examples of what a coach may need to navigate. While many day-to-day situations are easily resolved, some are not. Therefore, how and by what process should a coach make these decisions? This book presents a variety of cases based on true stories that present some of the ethical decisions coaches must make across high school, collegiate, and professional sports.

Using a sequential system of less to more complicated, 40 case studies are presented across the sports spectrum that coaches have experienced. This is a key component of the book. Although names and situations have been changed, these cases have happened and provide real applicability to coaches. In addition, each case may contain multiple situations perhaps with no "right" answer that test a coach's value system and ability to prioritize actions. Questions are provided at the end of each case that allow for reflection.

The primary audience for this book includes current coaches as well as students in coach education programs at both the undergraduate and graduate levels.

Timothy M. Baghurst is Professor of Education and the Director of FSU COACH: Interdisciplinary Center for Athletic Coaching at Florida State University, USA. His scholarly work has been recognized with a Board of Regents Research Award and state and national awards, and he has been honored with Fellow status by SHAPE America and the National Academy of Kinesiology. Tim has served the larger community through many organizations, including the National Association for Kinesiology in Higher Education as President. He serves on the Board of Directors for the Ladies Professional Racquetball Tour and is the current Head Coach of the USA Racquetball Junior National Team.

Anthony Parish is Associate Professor in the Waters College of Health Professions at Georgia Southern University, USA. He has over two dozen article publications in both national and international peer-reviewed journals. Anthony currently serves as Editor for *Strategies*, a National Association for Sport and Physical Education's (NASPE's) physical education and coaching journal. Anthony has more than 25 years of teaching experience at all educational levels. He has actively coached a variety of sports for over 20 years. He has also worked both as a strength and training coordinator and as a certified personal trainer.

Case Studies in Coaching Ethics

Real Dilemmas in High School, College, and Professional Sports

Second Edition

Edited by
Timothy M. Baghurst
and Anthony Parish

Routledge
Taylor & Francis Group
NEW YORK AND LONDON

Designed cover image: Getty images

Second edition published 2023
by Routledge
605 Third Avenue, New York, NY 10158

and by Routledge
4 Park Square, Milton Park, Abingdon, Oxon, OX14 4RN

Routledge is an imprint of the Taylor & Francis Group, an informa business

First edition published by Routledge 2010

ISBN: 978-1-032-45113-8 (hbk)
ISBN: 978-1-032-45105-3 (pbk)
ISBN: 978-1-003-37544-9 (ebk)

DOI: 10.4324/9781003375449

Typeset in Garmond
by Apex CoVantage, LLC

Contents

About the Editors *viii*
About the Contributors *ix*
Foreword *x*
Preface *xii*
Acknowledgments *xiv*
How to Make Sound Ethical Decisions *xv*

PART I
High School Sports 1

1 Coaching Styles 3
2 Scheduling and Use of Facilities 8
3 Academic Ineligibility 12
4 Running Up the Score 16
5 Juggling Jobs, Juggling Life 19
6 Coaching Girls Versus Boys 22
7 Coach Relationships: Know Your Role 25
8 Booster Pressure 29
9 Athlete Injuries 32
10 Crippling Success 37
11 The Importance of Policies and Procedures 41
12 Parents and Principals 45
13 Winning Versus Player Development 49
14 The Unsupportive Parent 53

15 Stretching the Rules 59
16 Age and Competition 64
17 Eating Disorders: Watch What You Say 69
18 Coach–Athlete Relationships 74
19 The Importance of Athlete Equality 80
20 Accusations: It Takes Just One 85
21 In Loco Parentis 89
22 Cash Is King 93

PART II
College Sports 97

23 Scholarships: Who Gets What? 99
24 Less Than Four 104
25 Stats Get Me Drafted 108
26 Self Over Team 113
27 The Job Carousel 117
28 The Transfer Portal: Decisions, Decisions, Decisions 122
29 If We Can Buy It, Why Can't We Use It? 127
30 It's Not Who I Am 132

PART III
Professional Sports 137

31 The Salary Cap and the Boss 139
32 Drafts, Management, and the Coach 144
33 I've Got the Power: Or Do I? 148
34 The Assistant 153
35 To Coach or Not to Coach, That Is the Question 158
36 Titles Versus $ 162

37 A Clash of Ideologies: Personal Perspectives From a Journal 167

38 Who Do You Work For? 174

39 Not My Fault 179

40 Forgive and Forget? 185

Index *190*

About the Editors

Timothy M. Baghurst is Professor of Education and the Director of FSU COACH: Interdisciplinary Center for Athletic Coaching at Florida State University. He earned his doctorate in kinesiology from the University of Arkansas and has four additional degrees achieved in three different countries.

Tim's research focuses on coaching education and development, with specific interests in coaching ethics and coach health and well-being. He has had more than 125 peer-reviewed articles published in addition to many book chapters and several books. His scholarly work has been recognized with a Board of Regents Research Award and state and national awards, and he has been honored with Fellow status by SHAPE America. He has worked with many organizations such as those affiliated with the National Collegiate Athletic Association (NCAA), United States Olympic Committee (USOC), and International Olympic Committee (IOC).

Tim has served the larger community through many organizations, including the National Association for Kinesiology in Higher Education as President. He serves on the Board of Directors for the Ladies Professional Racquetball Tour and is the current Head Coach of the USA Racquetball Junior National Team. He is a competitive racquetball, squash 57, and pickleball player and has represented England at multiple world and senior world championships.

Anthony Parish is Associate Professor in the Waters College of Health Professions at Georgia Southern University. He earned his doctorate in Kinesiology at the University of Arkansas. Before that he earned an MS at Columbia University in New York City.

Anthony's research interest centers on a variety of topics, including intrinsic and extrinsic motivations within athletes and coaching ethics. He has over two dozen article publications in both national and international peer-reviewed journals. Anthony currently serves as Editor for *Strategies*, a National Association for Sport and Physical Education's (NASPE's) physical education and coaching journal.

Anthony has more than 25 years of teaching experience at all educational levels. He has actively coached a variety of sports for over 20 years. He has also worked both as a strength and training coordinator and as a certified personal trainer. In addition, he is a former competitive bodybuilder.

About the Contributors

The authors of these stories and contributors to this book come from diverse backgrounds and have experienced a wealth of coaching experiences. They include teachers, coaches, professors, and athletic trainers from across the United States and globally. Many currently serve as coaches. The experiences this broad group gives to the book provide a real perspective of what goes on in the athletic environment of schools, colleges, as well as international and professional sports. Their diverse expertise allows readers to appreciate a variety of sports examples and experiences. We would like to say thank you to these contributors: Daniel Burt, Jeremy Davis, Carrie Barber, Paige Rollins, Aaron Gisler, Bo Mabry, Max Washausen, Jonathan Elrod, Brandon Lynch, Jimmy Bullington, Brooks Hunter, Austin Winters, Beth Fahey, Nathan Bodenstein, Lindsey Fox, John Proffitt, Meagan Thompson, Brooke Niles, Michael Granato, Clara Robbins, and Omar Badran.

Foreword

Coaches are perhaps the most visible individuals in a community. Success and failure are public, and as coaches we must learn from both. Great coaches are likely to be great teachers and vice versa. However, although we may feel that we have all that we need to be a good, if not great, coach, the reality is that our successful and unsuccessful experiences mold us as coaches; some things and experiences cannot be directly taught in the classroom, clinic, or book.

Each one of us has our own internal moral compass comprising layer upon layer of experiences over year upon year in every aspect of our lives. This book of coaching case studies aims to strengthen the direction of this compass by allowing you to consider and avoid some of the potential pitfalls that may occur in your coaching career. Crossing the boundaries of gender, sports, age, skill level, environment, and culture, this book gives you a unique perspective on what being a high school, collegiate, or professional coach will entail. It helps you to tackle issues head-on; to think beyond the world of your own firsthand experiences, assumptions, and understandings; and to dare you to develop a more comprehensive and cohesive coaching philosophy that will guide your future career.

This is not a "how to coach" book. This book serves as a catalyst in providing you with further thought and discussion. It allows you to learn via a mix of the common and the unique real-life experiences of coaches already in the field. As you progress through the scenarios in these pages, remember that these situations are real, have happened, and do happen. Each coach was faced with a situation that had to be dealt with, either effectively or poorly.

This book is straightforward and can be used very effectively not only by those in a structured learning situation but also by those who are already out in the field. The key to how much you take away from each case study is how much thought and effort you are willing to invest in answering the questions at the end of each case. This book helps you to fill in some of the gaps in your coaching preparation that no strategy or "how to" book can do. Some of the case studies may make you feel uncomfortable. This is a good thing! It will dare you to take a stand and then be able to explain your reasons logically and rationally for doing so to others who might not agree.

Within these case studies you will find very little that is black and white. Most coaching requires decision making in gray areas, and it is these gray-area decisions that can strengthen and display your character as a coach. We do not know any coaches who don't replay every practice and every game repeatedly in their mind trying to grasp what happened, when, where, to whom, and how to better themselves and expand their awareness of what their next coaching step should be. Read these cases with an open mind, put yourself in the shoes of the coach, and consider the implications of your actions. Happy discussions!

Betty Kelley, Ph.D.

Preface

Within the coaching profession there are numerous ethical scenarios that may and often do occur. The focus of this book is on adolescent and youth coaching, but we have included collegiate and professional coaching within this second edition. Frequently, coaches are placed in unique situations that are rarely experienced by others who work with them. How the coach responds to these situations can lead to a variety of outcomes. They may become more successful and effective by using strategies to avoid or overcome obstacles. Or, more unfortunately, failing to avoid potential pitfalls or making poor choices could lead to poor performances, unemployment, or worse.

If you are reading this book, it is likely that you either are currently coaching or intend to coach at some point in your future career. The purpose of this book, therefore, is to provide you with a variety of case studies that will encourage you to become more aware of the necessity to remain professional and consider the ethical implications of your actions as a coach.

Case studies involve an in-depth investigation of a topic, a person, a group, or an event. Rather than provide just a snippet of information, they provide a case that helps to identify context and force you, the reader, to make decisions based on the situation.

To successfully progress through these cases, several steps must be taken. First, read the case with an open mind. Some cases may be moving toward an obvious conclusion, whereas others may not. Recognize that by forming an opinion early in the case, you may miss important facts or subtle changes. Second, place yourself in the position of the "stakeholder," a term used in the questions at the end of the case studies. Stakeholders are those individuals who are affected by the situation and decisions made. However, also recognize that a stakeholder may not necessarily be only one individual; a school or an athletic department can also be considered a stakeholder. Many times, there will be more than one stakeholder, and the outcomes or decisions that you might make as one individual may significantly impact others or even the school or community. Third, use the questions at the end of each case study to provide a starting point for your analysis. References for further reading are provided to assist you in answering the questions. However, recognize that the questions are not comprehensive, and you may be able to formulate your own from what you have read. The course instructor is provided with suggested responses to these questions with supporting references.

These case studies have been written by a variety of people, are based on a variety of sports, and cover a variety of topics. They are based on true stories, many of which have been nationally publicized. The topics are presented in order of complexity. Thus, latter case studies will require greater analysis and may lead to more serious consequences. Earlier studies, although not as complicated, are likely to occur more frequently.

We trust that you will enjoy this book and find the case studies meaningful and beneficial. Most of all, we hope that they will foster the tools needed to carefully consider the situations and decisions that you will face in your coaching career.

Acknowledgments

First, we would like to thank our families for allowing us the time and opportunity to accomplish this task. It was a protracted process that took many, many hours as well as the willingness of our spouses to entertain our ideas and understand our frustrations. Second, we would like to thank all of those who contributed to the book. The many varied backgrounds and experiences of the authors of each chapter have allowed for a very diverse and highly readable textbook full of real-life stories. Finally, we would like to thank all those educators out there who are using this textbook. Its use is a testament to us that not only is our book a useful resource, but an assurance that current and prospective coaches are receiving what we believe to be a vital component necessary for their future successes in the coaching profession.

How to Make Sound Ethical Decisions

"Why is this even important?" you may be asking yourself. While one would hope that all of us do make sound ethical decisions, let's recognize that it doesn't always happen. We all make mistakes, make bad choices, and sometimes suffer their consequences. Why is it important? Well, a recent search of the words "coach scandal" on a search engine revealed 1.6 million hits. That's why it's important, because coaches, whether accidentally or not, sometimes make poor ethical decisions that put them in trouble.

Without getting too deep into the philosophy, recognize that how we make decisions is based on what we observe, what we know, and our analytical ability to decide accordingly. According to Kretchmar (2005), to analyze a given situation we must first develop a "thesis." This means we collect information, and we listen to arguments and opinions. Second, we must clarify the problem. We do this by declaring our assumptions, evaluating the merits of the arguments, and defining what we know. Third, we search for arguments for or against what we know. We do this through inductive, deductive, and intuitive reasoning.

Inductive reasoning means we take a specific example and make broader conclusions from it. For example, if I see a coach verbally abusing a player, I might make the conclusion that the coach has probably done the same to other players. Deductive reasoning moves from a general or several broad premises to a few concrete conclusions. For example, I might have heard multiple complaints from players and parents about a coach's verbal abuse of a player, so I make the conclusion that the coach must be verbally abusive. Intuitive reason relies on what we know to decide using our intuition. For example, whether I've seen the coach verbally abuse a player or heard the parents complain of it, I might use my intuition on to determine that the coach is likely abusive.

What does this all mean? Simply this: situations are complex, and our own interpretation as well as analysis of them will affect how we view them and consequently make a decision. We must be diligent to recognize our own approach to the problem and perhaps even our biases that might affect how we acquire, retain, and interpret.

As decision makers, we must recognize that while we might be able to recognize our own faults, there are likely biases and mistakes made by the witnesses. For example, to illustrate this, I ask my class to answer a series of questions about me that day. What color are my pants? Am I wearing glasses? How much do I weigh? Is my watch on the right or left hand? Invariably, no one gets them all right, even though these are simple factual questions. Now imagine what I might get if I were to ask them for more opinionated responses such as my mood state. As a decision maker, you must take all of this into account to decide.

How, then, do you make a sound ethical decision? Well, there's no right answer or quick fix, but we have found that following these steps will help.

1. Establish a clear description of the situation. Gain as much information from as many people as possible.
2. Who are the stakeholders? Consider who is impacted by this situation.
3. Develop an accurate account of where each stakeholder stands. Recognize that a stakeholder may withhold information or even, knowingly or unknowingly, skew information based on their perspective or what they want to happen.
4. Are there any relevant policies? Many organizations have policies and procedures that exist to help resolve situations that might arise.
5. What does the law say? Likewise, there are legal rules that might supersede policies or make decision making simpler.
6. What options are available? What choices do you have when making the decision? Some will be more severe than others.
7. What will be the consequences to the stakeholders for each option available? Making a decision will impact all your stakeholders in some way. For some, the consequences will be greater than others. You must evaluate whether these consequences are acceptable, just, and fair.

Gaining as much accurate information as possible is imperative to making a sound ethical decision. Remember that if you are using any kind of reasoning within your decision, missing a key piece of that information might cause you to induce or deduct, incorrectly resulting in an even worse situation!

Cognitive interviewing is a skill useful in eliciting as much information as possible. While this requires extensive training (e.g., it's used by law enforcement), the general concept can be useful to help gather information. It generally follows the following process:

1. Establishing group rules with the witness.
2. Explaining to the individual what you're doing.
3. Asking the participant to create a narrative of the event.
4. Forming a mental picture of the situation (using all the senses).
5. Describing their mental state during the event.
6. Asking them to redescribe the event from another witness's perspective (e.g., "What do you think your coach saw?").

In general, when using cognitive interviewing, it is best not to interrupt the witness's train of thought. However, make notes for further reference or follow-up. Sometimes a small item (e.g., "What color was it? How did it sound?") can trigger new memories.

Summary

Making sound ethical decisions may seem simple at first, but getting the right decision, or as right as you possible can, requires considerable time and effort. For example, when Lance Armstrong was investigated by the US Anti-Doping Agency (USADA), their report was 202 pages long! A simple case of a football coach accused of slapping a player turned out to not be as simple as you might think. It took 62 pages to reach a conclusion, and that didn't include any transcriptions! So, understand that making a sound ethical decision is complex and requires time, resources, and careful analysis. Using the process outlined in this section will certainly help.

References and Further Readings

Collins, D. (2014). *Cognitive interviewing practice.* Sage.

Kretchmar, R. S. (2005). *Practical philosophy of sport and physical activity.* Human Kinetics.

Part I

High School Sports

1 Coaching Styles

Athletic Director Alton Hill sits at his desk staring at two names written on the piece of paper before him. They represent the finalists for his new head coach of lacrosse. This is no small decision, as Wilmer High in Newton, New Jersey, is something of a phenomenon in men's lacrosse. A dozen state titles over the past three decades make it the benchmark to which all other nationally recognized programs aspire.

Behind Wilmer's stellar success was the legendary coach, Eddie Bryan. Coach Bryan created a lacrosse machine at Wilmer, producing star after star and title after title. At one point his teams went undefeated for three straight years, and the trophy cabinets glitter from the many awards and titles the team won. Coach Bryan achieved his success through ardent preparation and strong relationships with his players, making him the epitome of a player's coach. Many former players have stayed in touch with Coach Bryan for years after graduating, and many went on to play college lacrosse. In fact, many of the players now successful in work and politics attribute their success to the lessons learned under "Coach B."

Coach Bryan had an infectious personality. Players loved playing for him because he joked around so much. Occasionally he would even participate in a play or two during scrimmage. He ran an up-tempo style of play with his lacrosse teams by having them press their opponents and force mistakes. He relied on the fact that he had more athletic players than the teams he faced and used this to his advantage. In more balanced matchups his team simply outscored the other team. This high-scoring, run-and-gun approach had its critics. A few admonished the fact that defense was not the focus and that at times the players seemed undisciplined. However, despite this limited criticism, the reputation of the program was sound, and players wanted to be a part of it. It was common for the family of a prospective star recruit to move into the Wilmer school district just so their child could have the opportunity to be under Coach Bryan's tutelage.

Athletic Director Hill shakes himself out of his nostalgic reverie and returns to the more pressing matter at hand. "No matter how I look at it I've gotta go with Bobby Dristol," he says to himself. "He's just got so much more experience than anyone else we've interviewed."

Coach Bobby Dristol is the hot new up-and-comer in the coaching community. He has no state titles to his name but has accrued a surprising amount of playoff experience during his time at a smaller school, with not nearly the number and quality of athletes as Wilmer. He is also incredibly respected in the coaching community.

DOI: 10.4324/9781003375449-2

Coach Dristol used solid fundamentals and hard-nosed defense to create a winning program at Teterboro, the small high school where he is presently coaching. His players are relentless, and they are solid citizens in the community. You could not find a soul who would have anything bad to say about Coach Dristol.

Although the other candidates Athletic Director Hill is considering have strong qualifications, Coach Dristol stands out. After a final conference with administrators, Athletic Director Hill makes a contract offer to Coach Dristol, which he quickly and excitedly accepts.

The Coach Dristol era starts off well. At a preseason athletic dinner that includes parents and Parent Teacher Association members, Coach Dristol graciously accepts the responsibilities associated with the Wilmer coaching position. He promises that he will work hard to continue the winning tradition that the program has garnered over the past three decades. He also states that discipline and focus on fundamentals will be the cornerstone of what he hopes to instill in his team. Everything seems to be in place for a smooth, seamless transition.

As lacrosse season approaches, Coach Dristol begins his preseason preparations. This includes conditioning and tactical drills designed to improve fundamentals. Although his predecessor's old high-paced style of play is not going to be totally abandoned, Coach Dristol decides to shift more attention to defensive play and taking care of the ball. He does this because he noticed through past game film that, despite Wilmer's immense offensive output, there were a high number of turnovers in games and the players allowed a lot of easy scores that would not happen with an organized and disciplined defense.

The first day of practice Coach Dristol collects the players and lines them up for drills. In the past Coach Bryan would occasionally jump in with them and run. However, that is not something Coach Dristol does.

"Let's go guys!" Dristol yells. "We're not going to stop running lines till I feel everyone is giving it 100 percent."

After several rounds of line drills the players are exhausted.

"Haven't we run enough yet, Coach D?" asks Tim Schultz, a starting senior player. "We're all tired and this is getting a little boring."

Coach Dristol glares at Tim and stops practice. He gathers all the players and angrily addresses them.

"Here's how it's going to work," Dristol says. "I know that a lot of you loved Coach Bryan. There's no question that he's a great coach and a great man. But he and I are different in our approach. I know in the past you were buddies with Coach Bryan and joked around a lot. I am here to tell you that I am not your buddy. I am your *coach*. You will address me as Coach Dristol, not Coach D or any other nickname you've created. You will also never question my practice methods or game plans. You may not love me, but you will respect me, and that will breed success come game time. Does everyone understand that?"

The players give a low hummed response of "Yes, Coach Dristol."

"I'm sorry, I didn't hear you," Coach Dristol retorts.

"Yes, Coach Dristol!" the team loudly responds.

"Good," Dristol says. "Now let's get back to work."

The season gets underway and starts relatively well. The team has its growing pains adapting to the new style of play, but the players continue to play well and win their first several games. Coach Dristol continues to work the team hard on nongame days, which, again, is in sharp contrast to the previous coaching style. The team members continue to actively participate, although their grumblings begin to get louder in and out of practice.

The contrast of coaching styles comes to a head one evening after a game against a fairly weak opponent. Although Wilmer wins the game, Coach Dristol is disappointed with the effort his team gave. He feels the team took the game for granted and goofed off at times. This is not a big deal against a weaker opponent, but this apathy and carelessness could really get his players into trouble when playing a more talented team.

As the team begins changing out of their uniforms in the locker room, Coach Dristol stomps in. "Hold on, gentlemen," he bellows. "You're not going anywhere."

The team is taken aback by his loud, aggressive voice and freezes half-dressed.

"I don't know what was going on tonight," he continues, "but playing like that is unacceptable! You might think the win is all that matters, but in my book, you'd be wrong! I've told you all since day one that you will always give 100 percent complete focus and effort. Tonight, you didn't do that, so get dressed and meet me back on the field. *Now!*" With that, he walks out.

The players stand in stunned silence. Slowly they redress and then walk back out onto the field.

Coach Dristol loudly blows his whistle. "Line up in one solid line for line drills, gentlemen," he yells. "On my mark, go!"

Many of the parents standing on the field's edges waiting for their kids are shocked.

For the next 20 minutes the team runs lines. Afterward, back in the locker room, Dristol readdresses the team. "Guys, many of you might think that tonight was extreme, but you must get it in your heads that if you take a night off against a real-quality opponent you're gonna lose despite how much talent you might possess. Do you all understand that?"

The team collectively yells, "Yes, Coach Dristol!"

"Good. Have a nice weekend and I'll see you on Monday," he says.

The players quickly change and leave the locker room giving one another furtive glances.

Coach Dristol feels good about what happened. No, he did not like that he was forced to make his players run lines, but it gave him the opportunity to teach them a valuable lesson about effort and focus that will pay off later when they get to the playoffs. He turns off the lights and heads home.

On Monday Coach Dristol is about to go to lunch when he hears a knock on his office door. The principal, Athletic Director Hill, and a member of the Parent Teacher Association walk into his office.

"Coach, we need to talk," Athletic Director Hill says soberly.

"Okay, talk about what?" Coach Dristol retorts.

"Well, there have been a number of complaints about your practice methods with the team," Athletic Director Hill says. "The parents are pretty upset too. Why did you have them run after a win on Friday night?"

"Look, Hill," says Coach Dristol, "I know that it might have seemed a little radical, but the kids are very undisciplined and need a little more structure if we're going to excel in the playoffs this year. You need to trust me on this. There *is* method to my madness. They will all thank me later when we win it all."

"Well, that's the thing, Coach Dristol," Athletic Director Hill continues. "I don't think you're going to get the chance to win it all."

"What are you talking about?" Coach Dristol angrily asks. "Are you firing me?"

"No, not yet anyway," Athletic Director Hill replies. "But this morning, the players handed me a petition saying that they are all quitting; they said that playing isn't fun anymore. Some of the parents are going to the next school board meeting to relay how upset they are with you. Coach Dristol, we have a very sticky situation on our hands."

Coach Dristol replays all the events of the past several months over in his head. He cannot see what he has done that is so terribly wrong. Now what is he going to do?

Questions for Consideration

1. Who are the stakeholders in this case?
2. Explain the two different coaching styles presented. What are the advantages and disadvantages of each?
3. What were some of the mistakes that Coach Dristol made at the beginning of his coaching job at Wilmer?
4. What could Coach Dristol have done to make the transition between himself and Coach Bryan more acceptable to everyone?
5. Could Athletic Director Hill have done anything differently to make the situation less problematic?
6. Is there a place in modern-day athletics for a more authoritarian type of coach like Coach Dristol?
7. Should a coach create a system that caters to his players or have players conform to his system?
8. What would you do if you were faced with angry parents and players?

Further Readings

Grasso B. (2007). Coaching styles and methods. *Brianmac*. www.brianmac.co.uk/articles/article003.htm

Hackenberg, D. (2021, June 17). Rodriguez optimistic in Michigan rebound. *Morning Sun*. www.themorningsun.com/2009/08/11/rodriguez-optimistic-in-michigan-rebound/

Rudder, P. (2022, August 9). Durant wants Nash out: What other NBA players got their coaches fired? *AS*. https://en.as.com/nba/durant-wants-nash-out-what-other-nba-players-got-their-coaches-fired-n/

Schmidt, C. (2022, July 5). Former UA soccer players detail struggles under ex-coach Tony Amato. *Tuscson.com*. https://tucson.com/sports/arizonawildcats/former-ua-soccer-players-detail-struggles-under-ex-coach-tony-amato/article_621f4030-eb48–11ec-8298-e756a268e79a.html

Wachsmuth, S., Jowett, S., & Harwood, C. G. (2017). Conflict among athletes and their coaches: What is the theory and research so far? *International Review of Sport and Exercise Psychology*, *10*(1), 84–107. https://doi.org/10.1080/1750984X.2016.1184698

Wachsmuth, S., Jowett, S., & Harwood, C. G. (2018). Managing conflict in coach—Athlete relationships. *Sport, Exercise, and Performance Psychology*, *7*(4), 371–391. https://doi.org/10.1037/spy0000129.supp

Walinga, J., Obee, P., Cunningham, B., & Cyr, D. (2021). The role of leadership and team culture in enhancing sport performance outcomes. *The International Journal of Sport and Society*, *12*(2), 81–104. https://doi.org/10.18848/2152-7857/CGP/v12i02/81-104

2 Scheduling and Use of Facilities

Kristin Brighten stares out the window of her small office; snow drifts down and makes the mountainous Colorado landscape almost perfect this morning. The beautiful area is one of the reasons she and her husband moved here. But as great as this would look on a greeting card, Kristin knows the weather is going to create problems with her track team this afternoon. Although the team has a weather plan to deal with problematic weather later in the season, this snowfall so early is unexpected. Sighing, Kristin picks up her schedule and heads out of her office to see the athletic director (AD). She expects that this meeting with her AD is not going to work out in her favor since the AD is also the men's head basketball coach, and he is prepping the team for a big game this weekend.

Knocking on his office door, she hears his raspy, distinctive voice call out, "Come on in." As she walks in, she sees the AD, Coach Tanner, standing behind his desk. He gestures with his hand for her to sit in the wooden seat reserved for coaches, problematic athletes, and complaining parents. The office itself seems to bring all the focus on Coach Tanner. It is littered with the awards and plaques he has earned while coaching at the school for the past 20 years.

Coach Tanner straightens his tie and suit before sitting in his leather office chair. Smiling, he begins the conversation, "So how's your day going?"

Kristin smiles in return. "Not as well as I hoped. Judging by the weather I'm going to have to move practice inside. From what I understand this snowfall is going to last for several days." She can tell that Coach Tanner already knows what she is going to ask since he is already leaning back a bit in his chair and has folded his arms.

"Well, that's problematic," Tanner replies, "especially since we just constructed that new track for your team this summer. Seems like you barely got to use it. What were you thinking for your practice?"

Kristin's smile falters a bit. Coaching she feels comfortable with, but politics is not something she feels even close to being prepared for. "I was hoping that we might be able to use the main gym for an hour or two this afternoon for practice, and possibly for the next few days. We should easily be out of there before your boys come in," she says.

Coach Tanner sympathetically shakes his head. "Unfortunately, that's not something that can happen today or for the rest of the week. Coach Grayson and the volleyball team are using that space right before we do."

DOI: 10.4324/9781003375449-3

"But don't they have a pretty much permanent setup in the auxiliary gym?" asks Kristin. She knows that Coach Grayson has been here almost as long as Coach Tanner and that, because of the two men's longtime friendship, Coach Grayson usually gets what he asks for.

Nodding his head, Coach Tanner replies, "That's the regular situation, but there's some stuff going on in that gym, so they'd already requested the main gym before the basketball team comes in."

"For all four hours, though? Surely, they can share it a little while. We could easily fit both practices in for two hours each," pleads Kristin.

Coach Tanner raises his eyebrows a little. "That might be possible, but I think you should mention that with Coach Grayson. Give him a call. I'm sure he'd understand, but I did promise him that gym time and it's a bit of a first-come, first-served situation."

At that, Tanner stands up, implying that his decision is made. As Kristin stands up, Tanner politely moves toward the door to open it for her.

"Don't worry, I'm sure we can work this out," he says, smiling widely.

Kristin knows there is no "we" involved in this situation. She nods her head and smiles, gives him a polite "thank you," and exits the office.

As she walks back to her own office, Kristin can hardly even look at all the "Ol' Boys'" offices littered along the hall. As she closes the door to her small office, she decides to call Coach Grayson, even though she is fairly sure how it is going to turn out. Hearing him answer with a boisterous "Hello," Kristin begins her request.

"How's it going, Coach Grayson?" she asks.

"Quite well actually, Coach Brighten. Good to hear from you. It looks like my team might be going to state this year."

A half smile plays on Kristin's lips; she knows this ego game well. "I've seen you with your team. You've turned those girls from last year into excellent players. It's amazing that it's only their second year. I believe they'll prove more than a match against several of your competitors."

"Thanks, and I sure hope so. A lot of time has gone into the team," he says with a slight laugh. "To top it all off, it looks like we'll definitely be having snow for Christmas this year."

"Actually, that is what I am calling you about. I need to move my practice indoors because of the snow. I know you've had to move your practice to the main gym, but I'm wondering if we could split those four hours of practice between us—two hours for my track team and two for your volleyball team." She crosses her fingers in hope.

Coach Grayson coughs before responding. "I'd love to help you out, but we have the nets to set up and take down, as well as all the volleyballs to round up and so forth. Just a lot of extra equipment to handle. I'm sure you can understand. I'm sorry, but I do need that extra time. I'll tell you; all that equipment was the whole reason I moved out of the auxiliary gym for this week. I know there's an event going on in there, but since you all don't have much else besides yourselves, you might check out that gym and see about using it for practice. I'm sure that without equipment you can easily get your practices done there."

Kristin sadly says she will investigate and hangs up the phone with a thank-you. She sighs and leans back in her chair. Frustration seems to be a theme today. "Well, not much else to do but go ahead and see what's there," she says to herself.

Kristen gets up from her desk and then walks down the halls and past the classrooms that lead to the auxiliary gym. She gives the customary nod and wave to several teachers and administrators and a serious eye to one of her players who is just making it to class as a bell rings. Not being able to find a place to practice is one thing: having a player not able to come to practice because of detention is another.

At the end of the last hall, Kristin sees several students around the gym doors placing ribbons and making bows. Entering the gym, Kristin finds all the walls covered with decorations. Tables are set up everywhere, and dozens of students are hard at work preparing for something big. One of the students recognizes her and walks over.

"Isn't it turning out great, Coach Brighten?" the girl asks. "It'll take us several days, but this will look pretty good for the Holiday Dance coming up this weekend."

Kristin wearily smiles back and says, "Absolutely, you all are putting a lot of effort into it. I just heard about it and came down to see how beautiful it is."

The girl thanks her and goes back to working on a huge tree placed in the middle of the gym floor. Kristin knows there is no way that this is going to work for practice. She leaves the gym with a few more forced smiles to the hardworking students. Heading back toward her office, she gives one more annoyed sigh. What is she going to do now?

Questions for Consideration

1. Who are the stakeholders in this case?
2. What are some of the internal organizational problems in this scenario?
3. Is there a chain-of-command issue in this scenario?
4. What are some of the things that Kristin could have done to prepare ahead of time?
5. Could the AD have done anything differently so that the outcome might have worked out positively for everyone?

Further Readings

Belzer, J., Pastner, J., & O'Banion, D. (n.d.). Why coaches stumble and how you can help them succeed. *Athletic Director U. (ADU)*. https://athleticdirectoru.com/articles/why-coaches-stumble-and-how-you-can-help-them-succeed/

Hoch, D. (2009, October 2). Contingency plans. *Coach & A.D.* https://coachad.com/articles/contingency-plans/

Hoch, D. (2014, July 23). The three most important AD qualities. *Coach & A.D.* https://coachad.com/articles/the-three-most-important-a-d-qualities/

Hoch, D. (2018, December 13). A.D.ministration: The evolving athletic director position. *Coach & A.D.* https://coachad.com/articles/administration-evolving-high-school-athletic-director-position/

Morioka, K., & Giebel, N. (2002). The first year athletic administrator: Learning to prioritize. *Interscholastic Athletic Administration*, *28*, 26–27.

Myran-Schutte, L. (2020, March 18). Ways athletic/activity directors can show care for coaches/advisors. *National Federation of State High School Associations (NFHS)*. https://nfhs.org/articles/ways-athleticactivity-directors-can-show-care-for-coachesadvisors/

Stevens, G. (2018, August 6). The "Rookie" season: Strategies for managing the first year on the job as a high school athletic administrator. *Coaches Insider*. https://coachesinsider.com/athletic-director/the-rookie-season-strategies-for-managing-the-first-year-niaaa/

Wood, E., Dittmore, S., Stokowski, S., & Li, B. (2019). Division I athletic director trends and perceptions of requisite professional skills. *Journal of Higher Education Athletics & Innovation*, *1*(5), 102–122.

3 Academic Ineligibility

The football program at Hooper High School in Manilopa, Arkansas, is on a roll after winning back-to-back state championships. Over the past two years, the school program sent six players to the National Collegiate Athletic Association's (NCAA's) Division I programs on full scholarships. For head football coach Harry Douglas, everything is falling into place just as he had hoped when he took the job five years ago. He is excited about the upcoming season, as he has a formidable team coming back, including standout star Thomas Runeld. He can't wait to get started.

Thomas Runeld is a five-star running back for the Hooper Hawks and is being recruited by several Division I colleges. As a junior, Thomas ran for 2,300 yards and 28 touchdowns. In addition to his athletic prowess, Thomas is an outstanding citizen and, unlike his two older brothers, has not gotten involved with gangs. Instead, he has his sights set on playing college football, and Coach Douglas is immensely proud of him. In fact, Thomas considers Coach Douglas to be a father figure and always goes to him first for advice.

Thomas visited several universities over the winter break, and his prospects at the next level are excellent. However, when Coach Douglas returns to his office after the winter break, Ms. Apple, the school's academic counselor, has left a letter on his desk. The letter reads:

Coach Douglas,

I am writing this letter to inform you that Thomas Runeld is in serious jeopardy of not being eligible to play football next year. Thomas barely managed to pass English and math first semester, and if he does not pass both second semester, he will be ineligible. I am sure you would like to talk with Thomas yourself, but I think it would be appropriate if all three of us sat down and had a meeting to discuss this situation. There are several options that I feel would help Thomas. I want to see Thomas succeed, as I am sure you do. If you would get back to me after reading this letter, it would be very much appreciated.

Sincerely,
Sue Apple, Academic Counselor

After reading the letter, Coach Douglas immediately goes to Ms. Apple's office to discuss the situation in further detail. Ms. Apple explains what is going on and goes over

DOI: 10.4324/9781003375449-4

what she thinks are the best options available to assist Thomas with his academic progress. She wants to work with him one-on-one and primarily during times that might interfere with his practice. Coach Douglas is stunned by what he hears, mainly because Thomas never had any problems before, especially with his academics. He asks Ms. Apple if he can have some time to think about the situation and get back to her in the morning.

This is not the first time Coach Douglas has been forced to deal with a player not taking academics seriously, but never has he encountered such a situation with this much at stake. He goes home and thinks about how he can help Thomas without going through all the extensive paperwork and drawn-out plans Ms. Apple proposed. He decides that the best course of action is to recruit a tutor to help Thomas with his homework after school. This will allow him to monitor both Thomas and the tutor. Satisfied, he types out his plan for a tutor to work with Thomas. After further thought, he decides not to mention that the tutor he is recommending is a good friend of his.

When Coach Douglas presents his plan to Ms. Apple, she is hesitant at first, but eventually she warms to his idea and agrees to hire the tutor he recommends. Once the arrangements have been made, Coach Douglas calls Thomas into his office to talk to him about the situation and the threat of ineligibility to play football next season.

"But don't worry about it too much, Thomas," he says. "The school has hired a tutor named Jason Alexander to help you in both English and math after school for one hour every day."

"Coach, I'm really sorry about being placed on academic probation. You know that during the season all I care about is football. I really don't know what I'm doing in those two classes, but I'll make sure I show up for tutoring every day. I won't let you down."

"Just go to the tutoring appointments and everything will be fine, Thomas," says Coach Douglas.

When Coach Douglas gets home, he immediately picks up the phone and calls the tutor.

"Jason, I hear you're going to come tutor one of my athletes every day after school for an hour."

"Yes, I am, and I'm very excited about it," Jason replies.

"I need you to do whatever you have to do to help my athlete pass, and I'll make it up to you this summer. Sound good?"

"I understand you, Coach," Jason answers.

Jason is excited about helping a superstar like Thomas. As his tutor, Jason is required to help Thomas after school every day for one hour, the time equally divided between math and English. The next day after school, Coach Douglas introduces Thomas to Jason, shows them where they will be working together in the coach's office, and then leaves for a staff meeting. Jason and Thomas sit down and begin to talk about last year's football season and the official visits Thomas took over the winter break. In fact, Thomas and Jason end up talking almost the whole time they are supposed to be studying.

Finally, Thomas realizes how long they've been talking and says, "I know our tutoring session is about up, but I've got a paper to write for next week and some math problems to finish for tomorrow."

"I'm really sorry for getting off topic," replies Jason. "Tell you what, if you give me the topic and rubric for your paper, I'll see what I can come up with tonight. Also, if you give me your username and password, I can go online and finish your math problems, so you don't have to worry about those tonight either."

Thomas gives Jason the information he needs and goes home thinking this is too good to be true.

The next afternoon, Thomas and Jason meet in the coach's office again. Jason brings Thomas the paper he wrote last night and has him read it to make sure it is what the teacher is looking for. As Thomas begins to read the paper, the smile on his face gets bigger and bigger. Thomas is sure the teacher is going to give him an A on the paper. In fact, it turns out that's exactly what he gets.

At their next meeting, Jason explains to Thomas how the tutoring sessions are going to be run. Thomas is to bring the work to Jason and explain what the teacher expects, and then Jason will do the work for him. As Jason continues to tutor Thomas, Thomas's grades improve dramatically. Ms. Apple writes another letter to Coach Douglas:

Coach Douglas,

I am writing this letter to inform you that Thomas is doing an extraordinary job in the classroom. I think the tutoring is really helping him understand what the teachers are expecting of him. I am pleased with the way Thomas has progressed and would like to thank you for thinking of this tutoring plan. I am sure you are pleased that Thomas is doing so well and will be eligible to play next season. If there is anything I can do, just let me know.

Sincerely,
Sue Apple, Academic Counselor

A few weeks later Thomas's English teacher posts a list of the class grades on the door. Two cheerleaders in the class notice that Thomas's name is at the top of the list with the highest grade in the class. They are surprised after listening all semester to Thomas complaining about his low grades. They go to the teacher and ask her if she might have made a mistake on the grades. She confirms that the grades are indeed accurate and even double-checked them the night before just to make sure.

Later that day, the two cheerleaders see Thomas in the hall and ask him what he did differently on his homework to get the highest grade in the class. Thomas, trying to impress them, tells them that he had a tutor who did his homework for him. The cheerleaders head straight to the principal's office to report what Thomas told them.

"What can I do for you both?" asks the principal.

"Well," one of the girls replies, "we just talked to Thomas Runeld about what he's doing differently in English, because he has the highest grade in the class, and he was failing in the fall."

"Okay. What did Thomas tell you?" the principal asks.

"Thomas told us that the tutor is going to do all his homework for him," says the other girl.

The principal, who is unaware that Thomas is being tutored, replies, "Thank you for letting me know. I'll look into it."

Immediately, the principal contacts Ms. Apple and decides to attend one of Thomas's tutoring sessions to see for himself what is going on. Although he saw nothing untoward occurring at the time, he confronts both Jason and Thomas about the allegations, and they confess to academic cheating. The principal is furious. If word of this incident got out, it would ruin the reputation of the school. The principal calls Coach Douglas, Thomas, Ms. Apple, and Jason into his office for a mandatory meeting, the outcome of which is more than a little uncertain.

Questions for Consideration

1. Who are the stakeholders in this case?
2. Do you think Coach Douglas knew that Jason would take this kind of approach when he asked him to do whatever it took to help Thomas pass?
3. What could Coach Douglas have done differently that would have changed the eventual outcome?
4. What effect will this situation have on Thomas's future personal life and professional career? On Coach Douglas's?
5. What should end up happening to Thomas, Coach Douglas, Ms. Apple, and Jason?
6. To what degree do you think that academic ineligibility is an issue in high school sports?
7. In tutoring athletes, what are some guidelines you would recommend putting in place to ensure that this scenario would never happen?
8. What other safeguards could you put in place to ensure that your athletes remain eligible?

Further Readings

Abrahamian, J. (2020). The forgotten "student" in "student-athlete": Why a new cause of action is needed to remind universities that education comes first. *Arizona State Law Journal, 52*(4), 1303–1336.

Alabama High School Athletic Association. (n.d.). *Athletic directors and coaches association.* http://dnn.ahsaa.com/Coaches/AHSADCA/tabid/2583/Default.aspx

Beasley, E. M. (2014). Students reported for cheating explain what they think would have stopped them. *Ethics & Behavior, 24*(3), 229–252. https://doi.org/10.1080/10508422.2013.845533

Heath, S. (2022, June 2). Augusta men's basketball program committed academic misconduct violations. *NCAA.* www.ncaa.org/news/2022/6/2/media-center-augusta-mens-basketball-program-committed-academic-misconduct-violations.aspx

Holt, B. (2009, June 1). Beverley: Cheating not limited to him. *Arkansas Democrat Gazette.* www.arkansasonline.com/news/2009/jun/01/beverley-cheating-not-limited-him-20090601/

Ithaca City School District. (2022). *ICSD scholar-athlete and family handbook.* https://docs.google.com/document/d/195JLIJdg26EmmauIOAz5AToZ_2s3GRFJsBpduxyFD1o/edit

Kelley, C. P., Soboroff, S. D., Katayama, A. D., Pfeiffer, M., & Lovaglia, M. J. (2018). Institutional reforms and the recoupling of academic and athletic performance in high-profile college sports. *Sport Journal* (NPAG).

Pinak, P. (2022, March 7). Take the "Final Exam" from Georgia basketball's 2003 academic scandal. *FANBUZZ.* https://fanbuzz.com/college-football/sec/georgia/uga-basketball-scandal-final-exam/

Tedx Talks. (2017, May 16). Game day rivalry: Academics vs athletics – Mary Willingham – TEDxUCDavisSF [Video]. *YouTube.* www.youtube.com/watch?v=iTRCqi_ttWc

4 Running Up the Score

Coach Stephanie Larousse has been coaching girls' soccer at Maple Christian Academy in Maple, Oregon, for several years. The school isn't particularly large, but for a private school it is one of the biggest in the region. The soccer team has become better each year, due in no small part to her outstanding coaching. Stephanie feels that this year they have a chance at going undefeated. This has never happened in the school's history, and she is excited that her team might set a milestone to which others might be compared.

Maple Christian is a member of a small division of eight private Christian schools. Each of the schools varies in size, but the schools' teams play each other because of the religious status of the institutions. It is now midseason, and, as hoped, Maple Christian's soccer team is undefeated. There have been one or two tight matches, but for the most part the team cruised through its league fixtures.

Parents and students at Maple Christian love sports, and the school's sporting events are always well attended. The principal at Maple Christian frequently attends sporting events and believes that sports provide students with an opportunity to develop a Christian character that could not be obtained in a traditional classroom setting. Famous quotes supporting this focus are visible throughout the locker rooms.

Stephanie is particularly looking forward to the upcoming game on Friday against Branch Orthodox. Last year, the two games they played against them were a little too close for comfort, 5–4 and 6–4, respectively. Stephanie is still a little disappointed about the close outcome of those games, especially given that Maple Christian is twice as large as Branch Orthodox. However, this is a different year, and her pool of players is exceptional. A good victory on Friday would make a statement to the rest of the division that her team wants the title.

Game day arrives, and Stephanie can tell that her players are ready. The bleachers are filled with parents and fans, and the conditions are perfect for a great game of soccer. After a pregame warm-up, she gathers her players in the locker room.

"Okay, girls, let's spend a little time talking about the game," says Stephanie. "Remember last year and how close those games were. They were closer than they should have been, so I don't want you to take them lightly. You're playing well, and we've got a bunch of people watching today. Make sure you push forward at every opportunity and take every chance you've got. If we beat Branch decisively, it'll show the rest of the schools how much we want the title this year. Make sure you have fun doing it, though!"

DOI: 10.4324/9781003375449-5

The team responds with a cheer and huddles together for the pre-match prayer before the players head out of the locker room, determined to erase the uncomfortable moments of last season and gain an impressive victory. The first half couldn't go any better. In front of an avid home crowd, Stephanie's girls put on a clinic, scoring four goals without conceding any. Forays into Maple Christian territory are very rare, and the score could easily have been higher without the intervention of Branch's goalkeeper, who made some exceptional saves. Although she is delighted with the first half, Stephanie knows that she can't let up. She has seen leads slip before, and if her team could score four in one half, so could Branch's.

In the second half, Maple Christian continues to dominate. With 20 minutes to go, the game is all but over, with the scoreboard now reading 7–0. The home fans love the action and cheer every time the ball nestled into the back of the net. Some are now even shouting for 10 goals. Branch Orthodox is clearly waning, and Branch's coach doesn't have the quality substitutes to replace the obviously exhausted starting 11. The substitutes who do come in are clearly of lesser caliber. There is no mercy rule in this league, so the game will have to continue regardless of the score.

It is at this point that Stephanie faces a quandary that will ultimately change the course of her career forever. She knows that, typically, when a team has a commanding lead, the best players are substituted to allow lesser players to gain experience and essentially run out the clock. However, Stephanie has never been a fan of this policy.

"It's not fair to the substitutes," she thinks to herself, "because they know they're just being used to save the better players. Also, doesn't the Bible say something about fighting the good fight and racing to the very end? How Christian is it not to put 100 percent effort in for the entire match? It's also demeaning to the Branch players if I put in the second string with 20 minutes to go and they know it. It's not giving them much respect. If I did that, I'd almost be telling my players to handicap themselves in the future and that we should settle rather than push on."

In the back of her mind, Stephanie can also hear the fans' desire for a 10–0 win. She remembers what she told her players at the beginning of the game: that they were to give 100 percent the entire match and make a statement to the rest of the teams. Regardless, she decides to keep her team pushing forward and is rewarded with a final 10–0 score.

Both teams exit the field to cheers. The Maple Christian players are gracious in victory, and the Branch Orthodox players are commended for their willingness to give their all to the very end. Stephanie could not have been more delighted with the performance. It is a comprehensive victory against a potentially tricky opponent during which her girls competed with honor and integrity by playing hard to the very end.

There is no way that Stephanie could have foreseen the firestorm of controversy that soon follows their victory. The media jumps on the story, particularly because the clearly uneven result occurred at a Christian school, and many argue that it did not represent true Christian values. Unfortunately for Stephanie, Maple Christian's principal agrees with the media. Citing the need for Christian values of compassion and mercy in his coaches, the principal relieves Stephanie of her duties. The principal also requests a forfeit of the game and withdraws the team from the rest of the season, declaring that its victory did not adhere to the school's "Competition with Honor" code for its athletes.

Questions for Consideration

1. Who are the stakeholders in this case?
2. What would you have done with a substantial lead and 20 minutes to go? Why?
3. Do you think Stephanie should have been fired? Should she have faced any disciplinary action?
4. Do you think Stephanie would have been fired if this situation had occurred in a public school?
5. Do you think it is fair to the players at Maple Christian that they were removed from competition for the rest of the season? Why or why not?
6. How, as a coach, can you balance good sportsmanship with competitive instincts?
7. Do you think junior high and high school sports should have a mercy rule whereby games are ended if a certain score is achieved? Should it be only for certain sports? What about collegiate sports?
8. Do you believe that the competitive nature of sports conflicts with or complements other sports values? Explain your answer and how it may affect your coaching philosophy.

Further Readings

Adam, D. (2020, October 30). Mercy rules not needed in most prep sports. *Herald-Whig*. www.whig.com/archive/article/mercy-rules-not-needed-in-most-prep-sports/article_77d12df2-5b75-56ec-a55d-fb123e66a736.html

Carson, D. (2014, October 24). Peewee football team fined for breaking mercy rule. *Bleacher Report*. https://bleacherreport.com/articles/2243514-pee-wee-football-team-fined-for-breaking-mercy-rule

Hardman, A., & Fox, L. (1996). On sportsmanship and "running up the score": Issues of incompetence and humiliation. *Journal of Philosophy and Sport, 23(1)*, 58–69. https://doi.org/10.1080/00948705.1996.9714531

Harper, B. (2017, December 14). Should the youth sports "Mercy Rule" still exist? *Fatherly*. www.fatherly.com/play/coaches-speak-out-against-mercy-rule-youth-sports

Hensley, L. (2006). Mercy rules adopted by several states. *National Federation of State High School Associations*. https://www.google.com/url?sa=t&rct=j&q=&esrc=s&source=web&cd=&ved=2ahUKEwjl-oDz1J_-AhVSkmoFHYHaAAUQFnoECCcQAQ&url=https%3A%2F%2Fwww.nfhs.org%2Fmedia%2F1019918%2Fhst_topical_index.pdf&usg=AOvVaw0lce85uZItjyv9mhYxoopG

MLB Network. (2022, May 24). Should there be a mercy rule? [Video]. *YouTube*. www.youtube.com/watch?v=VbktrhURHMY

Nelson, J. (2005, April 30). Column: Softball coach snaps the unwritten rules. *The Enquirer-Journal*. https://freedom4um.com/cgi-bin/readart.cgi?ArtNum=4540&Disp=4&Trace=on

Sailors, P. (2010). Mercy killing: Sportsmanship and blowouts. *Journal of the Philosophy of Sport*, *37*(1), 60–68. https://doi.org/10.1080/00948705.2010.9714766

5 Juggling Jobs, Juggling Life

Demanding work is not something Haley Turner has ever shied away from. She always gives every situation she encounters her full focus and effort. She approaches every challenge she faces with a "do or die" attitude. Her approach to doing things was influenced by her dad's philosophy of never quitting and never accepting less than the best.

Coming from successful athletic programs, Haley had the support of some influential coaching mentors. Thus, it comes as little surprise when she lands her first head volleyball coaching job right out of college at Middleton High School in Middleton, Delaware. As a young college graduate, a newlywed, and now a head coach she thinks things can't get much better. Haley knows the program she will soon lead has struggled in the past, but she is confident that with time and hard work she will turn it around.

That first season is long and taxing. Haley feels like she spends all her time in the gym. She goes in before school to do lesson plans for her math classes and stays late after each practice to evaluate her own performance as well as the team's progress. If she makes it home before 8:00, she's early. But she wouldn't have it any other way. Her husband, Josh, is incredibly supportive. He comes to most games and cheers for the team just like a proud parent would. Haley spends most of the first several weeks teaching new fundamental skills and gaining the respect and trust of her new team. Despite all her hard work and time, though, her team manages to win only one game all season. Although she is extremely disappointed, both she and Josh try to remain positive about the work that Haley is doing and about the potential of the program.

After a hard off-season, Haley is ready for her second season as head coach. Josh is still as supportive as ever. He wishes he could spend more time with his wife, but he understands the demanding nature of her profession and admires her commitment to her job. Haley spends just as much time as before preparing for practices, games, and classes. Occasionally, she brings home scouting reports to go over or algebra papers to grade when time runs short. It all seems to be paying off except in the wins/losses column. The team is obviously improving, but it just can't get many wins.

Haley maintains high expectations for herself and her team. Although she still outwardly expresses a positive attitude around her colleagues, her players, and her husband, Josh, she feels a great deal of internal stress. She knows her players work hard; they just don't know how to win. The administration is on board with everything Haley is doing, but she is tired of continually losing and just wants some success for the team and herself. By the end of the season, the team manages to win only four games.

DOI: 10.4324/9781003375449-6

Haley starts feeling sick and fatigued. She is sick to her stomach every day and can barely stay awake to eat dinner every night. She tries to convince Josh she isn't sick.

"I'm just run-down and exhausted. It's been a long season," she says.

"Well, I worry about you. You're too hard on yourself. You'll never accomplish your goals if you're sick all the time. Please take care of yourself," Josh implores.

Finally, Haley breaks down and goes to the doctor. There she learns that she isn't sick—she's pregnant! She and her husband want to have a big family, but they just never expected it to happen so soon. Haley hasn't really made her mark yet in the coaching world, and she isn't too sure about juggling her career and a baby.

During the spring, when Haley gets to the point where she can't conceal her pregnancy any longer, she finally tells her extended family—her athletes. Much to her surprise, they are all ecstatic about having a baby to spoil. Since Haley is due in June, she's relieved that maternity leave won't conflict with the end of the school year or the upcoming season.

When the baby arrives, Haley again feels like her life is perfect. She has a great marriage; she loves her job; and now she has a beautiful baby girl, Elizabeth. When August rolls around, she can't wait for the season to begin and is looking forward to developing her team. She wants her players to begin to see the benefits of all their arduous work from the past two years. Haley knows it will take long hours and late nights to continue moving the program—her program—forward. But she is committed.

The first couple of weeks of practice are okay, but Haley is worn out each day by the time she gets home. Consequently, she doesn't get to spend much quality time in the evenings with Josh and Elizabeth. She feels frustrated about missing time with her new family, but she believes her efforts will pay off eventually. She is confident that her daughter is being raised well, and she's glad that she can be a positive role model for her athletes, some of whom lack good role models at home.

As the season goes into full swing, most nights Haley spends more time away from home. She stays late either to work on game footage and practice plans and to grade papers or because of games. Rarely does she get home early enough to spend any time with Elizabeth. She has always been proud of her work ethic, but she regrets not being there to put her baby to bed.

Haley is frustrated that the season hasn't shaped up the way she had planned. She had felt confident that the team would finally turn the corner and start to win more games. But as the season nears the end, the team has been able to win only six games, and only one was a district game. Haley feels like a failure and struggles to avoid dropping into the abyss of depression. She wants so much for her team to taste the success she knows her players can achieve, but she can't understand what went wrong.

"I don't understand, Josh. How could we make such positive strides at the end of last season and show no progress this season? I feel like we've gone backward! I put in more time this year, even with Elizabeth coming, and we're no better off. What happened?" Haley questions.

"I'm sorry, Haley. I know how frustrated you are. So is Elizabeth. She misses seeing her mommy every night. You are spending more time with the team than before, and the only people it's affecting is us. Elizabeth and I need you just as much as the girls at school! I really do respect your dedication, but have you thought that maybe you should be spending more time at home with your family?" Josh replies.

As Haley prepares for the last game of the season, she wonders if her hard work ever made a difference. She finally finishes her game plan and scouting report. She packs up her briefcase and heads for the door. While she is walking through the school parking lot, her cell phone rings. It's Josh. Haley wonders what he could want; he knows she's heading for home.

"You won't believe what just happened!" he exclaims when she answers. "Elizabeth sat up all by herself! I didn't help her at all! She just pushed herself over and wobbled on up!" Josh explains.

Haley can't believe she missed the first time her baby girl sat up all by herself. And for what? A team that isn't winning and doesn't seem to mind. Was it all worth sacrificing her own family to be with a team of girls to whom she has no biological connection? Her family and her job are supposed to be a perfect combination. How can she ever really balance the two?

Questions for Consideration

1. Who are the stakeholders in this case?
2. What is the major issue in this case? What factors make this a difficult dilemma?
3. Is this situation as much of a factor for male coaches as it is for female coaches? Why or why not?
4. What possible changes could Haley make to remedy this situation without changing jobs/positions?
5. What are some alternative career or job choices that Haley could make that could help fulfill her professional goals while maintaining her personal life?
6. Where might Haley go for help in making such a major decision that will affect her personal and professional lives?
7. What do you imagine will be the final outcome of this situation?

Further Readings

Arkansas Razorbacks. (2013, October 22). The life of a coach's family [Video]. *YouTube*. www.youtube.com/watch?v=p1MTenIoROM

Foston, N. (2004, February). Dual career couple teaches together: The Harpers balance coaching and parenting together. *Ebony*. https://books.google.com/books?id=V9YDAAAAMBAJ&pg=PA102&source=gbs_toc_rv&cad=2#v=onepage&q&f=false

Graham, J. A., & Dixon, M. A. (2014). Coaching fathers in conflict: A review of the tensions surrounding the work-family Interface. *Journal of Sport Management*, *28*(4), 447–456. https://doi.org/10.1123/jsm.2013-0241

Graham, J. A., & Dixon, M. A. (2017). Work-family balance among coach-fathers: A qualitative examination of enrichment, conflict, and role management strategies. *Journal of Sport Medicine*, *31*(3), 288–305. https://doi.org/10.1123/jsm.2016-0117

Graham, J. A., Smith, A. B., Dixon, M. A. (2019). Choosing between work and family: Analyzing the influences of work, family, and personal life among college coaches. *Journal of Issues in Intercollegiate Athletics*, *12*, 427–453. chrome-extension://efaidnbmnnnibpcajpcglclefindmkaj/http://csri-jiia.org/wp-content/uploads/2019/09/RA_2019_20.pdf

Hoffman, K. (2017, May 10). Balancing coaching with family. *Coach & A.D.* https://coachad.com/articles/balancing-coaching-family/

6 Coaching Girls Versus Boys

Dave Campbell was the starting forward for the Creighton Tigers for three years in high school, leading the team in scoring almost every game. He led them to the Nebraska state tournament during his senior year. An athletic scholarship soon followed, and he went on to play college basketball at a Division II school not too far from his hometown. After a solid but unspectacular athletics career at college, it is time to start looking for a job.

Dave reads in the newspaper that Coach Scott Mendez, his old high school coach, is retiring at the end of the current basketball season, after a staggering 42 years of coaching. Dave is sad to hear that Coach Mendez's career is coming to an end. However, he can't help but be excited. In college, he majored in kinesiology, and it would be his dream job to coach his hometown team. Immediately, he begins working on his resume and cover letter for the position, hoping that his excellence at college will influence the search committee to pick him above other well-qualified applicants. He is not to be disappointed; two weeks after applying he is interviewed for the position.

Upon arrival at the school, the athletic director (AD) and the principal greet him in the boardroom. The principal is quick to congratulate Dave on his academic and athletic performances at college and makes no bones about how proud they are to see a student from their school who has done so well.

The interview couldn't have gone any better. However, Dave leaves suspecting there are things that the AD and the principal left unsaid. Although Dave applied for the position of head boys' basketball coach, they had casually mentioned that other coaching assignments might be necessary. However, enamored by the glowing praise they heaped upon him, Dave doesn't think to dig deeper.

A few short days after the interview, the principal calls Dave back to offer him the position of assistant boys' basketball coach and head girls' junior high basketball coach. "What?" Dave thinks to himself. "Girls' basketball?"

The principal explains that they gave the head coaching position for the boys' team to the current assistant coach, who had been there for the past five years. However, they really need someone to fill the coaching position for the girls' team. He could take on that role and fill the assistant coach position for the boys' team that was left open.

Dave is incredulous. "How could they not just hand me the job? Don't they remember what I did for this program?" he thinks to himself. However, he thanks them and promises to give them an answer the following day. After thinking it over that

DOI: 10.4324/9781003375449-7

night, weighing the pros and cons, he decides to accept the offer and hope he isn't making a huge mistake.

Six years later, Dave is working almost exclusively with the girls' junior high basketball team. He found after the first year that there wasn't enough time to work successfully with both teams. Consequently, the school hired another assistant for the boys' team. This allowed him the time to develop a quality girls' program that soon developed winning habits. His girls respond well to his cooperative coaching style and hold him in high esteem. One of his star players exemplifies this respect midway through the season.

"Coach, can I see my stats from last night's game?"

"Sure, Katie, but I already told you, you led the team in scoring, with eight points, and you were huge on the boards, with three offensive and six defensive rebounds."

"I know, Coach, but look at this—I only had two assists and I had three turnovers. That could have cost us the game!" Sometimes the discipline and heart in these girls still surprised him.

Although things are going well for Dave, sometimes he wonders what it would be like coaching boys' basketball team and whether he would be a different person if he had been offered the head coach position of the boys' high school team. He knows deep down that coaching the girls' team removed that egocentric view of life that he had when he first began coaching, and he learned that it is the individual, not the gender, that can teach the value of teamwork and hard work.

At the end of another winning season, Dave gets a phone call from the AD. The boys' team has been performing poorly over the past couple of years and the AD wants him to turn it around. The AD praises him and the girls' program and tells him he thinks now is the time to transition to "something bigger."

This is a life-changing decision for Dave. On the one hand, he doesn't want to abandon his girls, who taught him so many lessons. The reality is that he's really grown to love coaching junior high, developing younger players, and teaching them values and skills they will need for the rest of their lives. To him, his job is more than just basketball.

However, coaching boys' basketball has been a dream for as long as he can remember. It is an opportunity to highlight what he has learned over the past several years. He knows that the stakes will be higher, but so will the attention and salary. Right now, he never makes front-page news in the local paper, not even when his team won state, but it's a good bet he would have if he was coaching the boys' team. It is a tempting offer that gives Dave a lot to think about.

Questions for Consideration

1. Who are the stakeholders in this case?
2. What is the critical issue of this case?
3. The job Dave was initially offered was not what he had been interviewed for. Would you have taken it?
4. What benefits and complications do you see in coaching the opposite gender?
5. What steps could you take to limit or circumvent potential issues that might arise from coaching the opposite gender?

6. What actions or qualities do you think made Dave a successful coach?
7. What is a cooperative coaching style, and how does it differ from other coaching styles?
8. Dave ended up teaching at the junior high level. Is it more important to win at this age or impact your kids?
9. Who could help Dave to reach a decision about taking the job? Whom would you ask for help in a comparable situation?
10. Why do you think so much more emphasis is placed on boys' sports than girls' in junior high and high school?
11. What benefits and complications do you see in coaching the opposite gender?

References and Further Readings

Anonymous. (2008). Coaching—Do female athletes prefer male coaches? The foundation position. *Women's Sports Foundation.org*. www.womenssportsfoundation.org/Content/Articles/Issues/Coaching/C/Coaching%20%20Do%20Female%20Athletes%20Prefer%20Male%20Coaches%20The%20Foundation%20Position.aspx

Blom, L. C., Abrell, L., Wilson, M. J., Lape, J., Halbrook, M., & Judge, L. W. (2011). Working with male athletes: The experiences of U.S. female head coaches. *ICHPER-SD Journal of Research*, *6*(1), 54–61. chrome-extension://efaidnbmnnnibpcajpcglclefindmkaj/https://files.eric.ed.gov/fulltext/EJ936021.pdf

Carcagno, S. (2018). The effect of collegiate head coach's gender on female athlete outcomes [ProQuest LLC]. https://www.proquest.com/openview/e85273e9501df3362e258d24e4d8bdd0/1?pq-origsite=gscholar&cbl=18750&diss=y

Coaching – Do female athletes prefer male coaches? (2011, August 2). *Women's sports foundation*. chrome-extension://efaidnbmnnnibpcajpcglclefindmkaj/www.womenssportsfoundation.org/wp-content/uploads/2016/08/coaching-do-female-athletes-prefer-male-coaches-the-foundation-position.pdf

Custodio, D. (2021, December 24). Do female athletes need female coaches? *Tri Training Harder*. https://tritrainingharder.com/blog/2021/10/blog-template-jdb6k

Frey, M., Czech, D. R., Kent, R. G., & Johnson, M. (2006). An exploration of female athletes' experiences and perceptions of male and female coaches. *Sport Journal*, *9*(4), 10.

LaFountaine, J., & Kamphoff, C. S. (2016). Coaching boys' high school teams: Female coaches' experiences and perceptions. *International Journal of Sports Science & Coaching*, *11*(1), 27–38. https://doi.org/10.1177/1747954115624815

McGillis, R. (2020, August 5). Being a successful male coach of female runners. *Outside*. www.outsideonline.com/health/running/culture-running/people/being-a-successful-male-coach-of-female-runners/

Rima, M., Weishaar, R., & McGladrey, B. (2019). An exploration of female athletes' experiences and perceptions of male and female coaches: Ten years later. *Sport Journal*.

Whitaker, G., & Molstad, S. (1985). Male coach/female coach: A theoretical analysis of the female sport experience. *Journal of Sport & Social Issues*, *9*(2), 14–25. https://doi.org/10.1177/019372358500900202

7 Coach Relationships

Know Your Role

It is the beginning of a new year for the Brightside High School baseball team. Brightside is a public school located in a small town in Pennsylvania with a population of 25,000; most of the residents are Caucasian. The school is extremely competitive both academically and athletically. Last year, the team narrowly lost in the state championship game.

At the field house, Coach Laramie is sitting at his desk thinking about the coming season. At the adjacent desk, Coach Kearney, the pitching coach for the Brightside Grizzlies, is preparing pitching charts and various evaluation sheets for practice. Both coaches are eagerly awaiting the start of the season because they desperately want another shot at the title.

Three weeks and seven games into the season, the two coaches are hunched over their stats in the field house, discussing the strengths and weaknesses of their upcoming opponent. So far, the fierce Grizzlies are undefeated. The team's captain, Bo Bigly, is having a particularly stellar season, batting a .540 with eight runs batted in. The team's star pitcher, Alex Yates, is also having a great start, with a .045 earned run average. A knock on the door interrupts their conversation.

Sung Yuan nervously enters the office, noticing all the trophies from past seasons sitting on the shelves. Pictures of past players who went on to play professionally line the walls.

Coach Laramie watches Sung's jaw drop. "You like what you see?" Coach Laramie asks with a grin.

"Yes!" Sung responds excitedly. "I hear you have a good baseball team?"

Coach Laramie proudly smiles and replies, "We're strong competitors. What's your name, kid?"

"Sung Yuan. My family moved here from China two years ago. Now my father has a job here in Brightside. I play baseball and I pitch. Can I join your team?"

Coach Laramie stands up and shakes his hand. "Well, my name is Coach Laramie, and that's Coach Kearney, the pitching coach, over there. I'll let Coach Kearney evaluate your skills. How about you both go over to the ball field?" Sung nods enthusiastically.

Once Sung and Coach Kearney are at the ball field, they walk over to the bullpen, where they interrupt Chad Perkins, the team's starting catcher, to get his help. Sung introduces himself and begins to warm up with Chad. Coach Kearney stands behind a

DOI: 10.4324/9781003375449-8

chain-link fence holding a radar gun. After a few minutes Sung is ready. He winds up and almost effortlessly slams the ball into Chad's leather mitt. It sounds like a gunshot. Immediately, Coach Kearney's eyes light up as the radar gun reads 92 miles per hour. It is not a fluke. Sung continues to power down fastballs, but he also demonstrates a mean changeup and a wicked curveball.

Later, Coach Kearney fills in Coach Laramie after the demonstration.

"So, how'd our new kid shape up?" asks Coach Laramie.

Coach Kearney grunts noncommittally. "He did all right. I mean, he hit 92 miles per hour on the radar gun."

"What?" gasps Coach Laramie. "This kid hit 92 miles per hour on the radar gun! Dang, Kearney, that's Major League material. We are definitely going to win state this year."

"I know," says Coach Kearney with a huge grin on his face.

The next day, Coach Laramie holds a team meeting before practice. He introduces Sung and tells the team of Sung's extraordinary pitching ability. However, the team had already heard rumors from Chad. Coach Kearney can sense tension from some of the other pitchers. However, this doesn't stop him from audaciously telling the team that Sung will be starting the next game instead of Alex.

After the meeting, Alex is visibly distraught. "How could Coach start this new guy over me?" he thinks to himself. "It's one of the biggest games of the year, and I've worked so hard to get where I am."

Bo, one of Alex's best friends, seeks out Alex in the locker room after the coaches, and most of the players have left.

"Hey, Alex, this is ridiculous. There's no reason for Coach not to start you Saturday. How can he really think this foreigner is better than you? You have worked so hard to get where you are, and for it to be ripped out from underneath you is just not right."

Alex shakes his head in agreement. "Don't you worry about it. I'll get my spot back one way or another!" Alex slams his fist into a locker and leaves in frustration.

Saturday arrives, and Sung is untouchable. However, as Sung hustles off the field at the end of the game, only a few of his teammates shake his hand with enthusiasm. It's obvious that his presence isn't welcome by some of his teammates.

Coach Laramie and Coach Kearney stay after the game to talk about the team's performance.

"Kearney, I can't believe this kid. He did great! I was a little nervous about starting him so soon, but he couldn't have proved himself better."

Coach Kearney looks down at the grass and then back up at Coach Laramie.

"I'm not sure it was the best thing for this team, though. I mean, sure he did great, but the rest of the team did horrible. We only scored two runs."

Coach Laramie disagrees. "Look, Kearney, we played a talented team tonight. We can't expect to win every game by ten or more runs. They had a good pitcher on the hill who threw hard, so give our guys some credit."

Coach Kearney nods his head but remains unconvinced.

Several weekends, and a few close wins later, Coach Laramie and Coach Kearney are in their office preparing for the upcoming week. Bo and five other players walk in.

"What's going on, guys?" Coach Kearney asks.

"Coach, uh, I'm not sure how to put this, but me and the guys don't think it's right that Alex isn't the number one pitcher anymore," says Bo. "We've played with Alex our entire life, and we trust him. We want him to lead us to the state championship, not Sung. Besides, he didn't work for it like Alex did. He wasn't there for all the conditioning that we had to go through. It's not fair!"

"Sung is pitching great," Coach Laramie responds. "He's winning, and no one can touch him. With him on the mound we're guaranteed the state championship."

Chad steps up. "Sure, he's a good pitcher and all, but like Bo said, we just don't trust him. He's not like us, Coach. Not like us at all." Coach Kearney sees that the players are nodding angrily and hears some of them muttering racist remarks.

Coach Laramie can't believe what he is hearing. He tells them that Sung will continue to start if he keeps winning. Unhappy with what they have been told, the boys storm out of the office. It is pretty clear that team unity isn't what it could or should be.

Coach Kearney wants to start Alex for the next big game, but Coach Laramie insists on Sung starting. As soon as the first pitch is thrown, Coach Kearney knows it's going to be ugly. Clearly rattled by his teammates' hostility toward him, Sung pitches poorly and is pulled from the mound in the second inning. For the remainder of the game, he endures angry stares from his teammates. Alex, who replaced Sung in a bid to save the game, fares no better than he did. And it's not just the pitchers who perform poorly. Bo goes without a hit, along with seven other of his teammates. Not surprisingly, the Grizzlies suffer their first loss.

Back in the field house, it's evident to both coaches that the season's drive to the championship hangs in the balance. The team is fractured, and even the coaches are struggling to agree on the best course of action.

"I should've listened to you," says Coach Laramie. "I didn't think they would hit Sung's pitches as hard as they did."

Coach Kearney nods his head but remains silent.

"Kearney, you need to have a talk with those kids. The team's falling apart. If we don't nip it in the bud right now, we won't have the type of season for which we were hoping. They don't like Sung, and it appears they aren't going to play to their full potential when he's on the mound. I know they want Alex to be number one, but Sung is by far the better pitcher, and we'll always have a better shot at winning a game with him on the mound."

"I agree," says Coach Kearney. "But the reality is, the team won't play for Sung like they will for Alex."

"I know! It makes no sense. Why can't they see that Sung will lead them to the title?" Coach Laramie pauses and then says, "Kearney, I want you to go talk to those kids to see if you can get some sense into them."

"Now wait a minute!" Coach Kearney retorts. "Why me? Don't you think it should be the responsibility of the head coach to do something like that?"

"Perhaps, but he's a pitcher and you're the pitching coach. Anyway, you've got a much better relationship with the team. They're more likely to listen to you, aren't they?"

Coach Kearney mulls the situation over in his mind. It was true that Coach Laramie did offend several of the players by insisting on starting Sung when Alex would have been the right pick. However, he was the head coach, after all. Then again, as the head coach he had the right to command his coaching staff. He reluctantly nods to Coach Laramie and heads for the locker room. He has no idea what he is going to say.

Questions for Consideration

1. Who are the stakeholders in this case?
2. Should Sung have been allowed to play that season?
3. What strategies could the coaches have implemented with the team to make Sung feel more welcome and accepted?
4. What steps could the coaches have taken to cut short the exclusion of Sung that was evident in the players' actions and comments?
5. Why was there so much confusion and disagreement between the two coaches and their roles? Who should talk to the team?
6. If you were Coach Kearney, what would you have said to the team?
7. Coach Kearney overheard his players making racist remarks but did nothing to stop them. What strategies can you implement as a coach to (a) reduce the potential for racism and (b) act appropriately if it occurs?

References and Further Readings

Cooper, J. N., Davis, T. J., & Dougherty, S. (2017). Not so black and white: A multi-divisional exploratory analysis of male student-athletes' experiences at National Collegiate Athletic Association (NCAA) Institutions. *Sociology of Sport Journal, 34*(1), 59–78. https://doi.org/10.1123/ssj.2016-0015

Halsey, A. (2020). Integrating new team members. *Brianmac Sports Coach*. www.brianmac.co.uk/articles/article612.htm

Lovejoy, J. (2007, January 14). Where are the Asian players? *The Times*. www.thetimes.co.uk/article/where-are-the-asian-players-r7wc92rxgzv

TedxTalks. (2017, June 13). Race, sports, and telling true stories – Morgan Campbell – TEDx-UTSC [Video]. *YouTube*. www.youtube.com/watch?v=pdvkRBJpRBg

Thames, A. (2022, July 2). Equity in sports has focused on gender, not race: So gaps persist. *The New York Times*. www.nytimes.com/2022/06/30/sports/title-ix-race.html

8 Booster Pressure

As a kid growing up in Missouri, Randy Hendricks developed an intense passion for swimming. He became a successful performer, and after competing on the swim team in high school, he went on to compete in college on a full scholarship. He loves the sport so much that he decides to become a swim coach. As he finishes his last semester of college, he keeps his ears open for a job for the upcoming school year.

Randy graduates in December, but there are very few jobs available midyear, which puts him in a tight spot. So, when a job opens unexpectedly at a high school close to his hometown, he doesn't hesitate in applying. It's a large school with a good swimming program. The swimming coach who is leaving was offered a college job and decided to take it without finishing out the year. The school has a very nice natatorium, and Randy thinks the job will be a perfect fit. He believes this could be a terrific opportunity to get his foot in the door and gain some invaluable experience. At his interview, he finds he really likes the staff and hears good things about the school. He feels comfortable with the situation, and when he's offered the job, he is honored and accepts without hesitation.

As the January semester begins, a new chapter in Randy's life is also beginning. The swim team is in off-season, but most of the team's members are involved in other sports during the spring. This allows Randy time to get to know his future swimmers and spend some time adapting to the new surroundings, staff, and students. When summer arrives and as the swimming season quickly approaches, Randy decides to hold a parent's meeting. He's still new to the school and wants to introduce himself. There is a great turnout, with almost all the swimmers' parents showing up. Randy discusses his coaching methods and how he plans to develop their sons and daughters into quality swimmers and individuals. He has developed a detailed code of conduct for both swimmers and parents that explains his coaching philosophy and the rules and expectations he has for the team. To swim on the team, both the player and his or her parents or guardians must sign a form agreeing to the code of conduct. This is designed to ensure that the school is represented appropriately and that everyone is held accountable for his or her behavior and actions. The parents really like the idea of a code of conduct and are more than willing to sign the agreement form.

At midseason, Randy's team is struggling. As a team, his swimmers have lost more events than they've won, and it is becoming quite evident that most of the swimmers

DOI: 10.4324/9781003375449-9

lack real talent. The team has only two good swimmers, but they are not performing as well as they could. When these two swimmers don't win their respective races, the team's overall score is appalling.

As a whole, the team isn't giving a consistent effort. Brock, one of the more experienced swimmers, is a prime example. Some days, he blasts off the starting block, but on others, he seems to need prodding just to stop goofing off and start his laps. His dad, Harding, happens to be the president of the school board and one of the main boosters for the athletic program and swim team.

Harding begins to show up at practices. At first, Randy thinks he is coming to practice merely to show his support to the team and his son. However, he gradually starts shouting instructions from the bleachers beside the pool to Randy's swimmers. A casual observer would think he was an assistant coach. Randy isn't sure how to deal with the situation. With each passing practice, it worsens. Randy is still unsure what to do. If he asks Harding to calm down or leave, it could seriously jeopardize his coaching position, so he opts to do nothing.

Another week passes, and the swimmers are growing sick and tired of Harding's shouting instructions from the stands. It is particularly bad because Harding's shouts echo around the natatorium, making it almost impossible for Randy to coach. A couple of swimmers approach Brock and ask him to talk to his dad, but he just smiles, shrugs his shoulders, and says it has nothing to do with him. Randy, still unsure exactly what he should do, tells the team that he will handle it. However, when nothing is done, the frustrated swimmers complain to their parents.

Once the parents become involved, the situation quickly grows out of hand. The swimmers ask to have a meeting with their parents and Randy but without Brock and his dad present. With the parents' insistence, Randy reluctantly agrees. During the meeting, the parents ask Randy why one parent is allowed so much apparent authority. They also tell him they think it's ridiculous that they all signed a code of conduct, but it wasn't being enforced. Randy is accused of being a suck-up to a powerful booster.

Randy tries to appease his swimmers and their parents. He tells them that something will be done, but he has no idea what to do. It is obvious that any further inaction could permanently ruin any relationship he still has with both his swimmers and their parents. He is so frustrated! This type of thing wasn't covered in his college classes. If the problem involved any other parent, things might not be so difficult. But when his job partly rests on the good graces of Harding, he knows he must tread lightly. Also, Harding's contributions make up a large part of the funding for the team. Without his support, the team could be in jeopardy.

Although Randy leaves the meeting promising the parents to resolve the issue, some of them are unconvinced. Without his knowledge, they approach both the athletic director and the school board and request a meeting. Randy is summoned to the meeting not knowing what to expect other than more fire and brimstone. He thinks to himself, "Do things like this *really* happen to a first-year coach?" He is beginning to wonder whether he is cut out for the job.

Questions for Consideration

1. Who are the stakeholders in this case?
2. Would you give a code of conduct to your athletes and their parents? If so, what would it contain? If not, why?
3. Do you think a player whose parents are important or powerful to the athletic program gets better or worse treatment than a player whose parents are not?
4. How would you have handled Brock's dad when he came to practice? Would you let him stay or tell him that he needed to stay out of the natatorium?
5. Do you think you would handle the situation differently in your first year of coaching versus when you have become more established?
6. What way(s) might Randy have involved Harding in the swimming program that might have circumvented the problems that arose?
7. Where could Randy turn for help?

Further Readings

Boys of Baseball – National Travel Team Code of Conduct Agreement. (2009, October 30). *Boys of baseball national travel team*. www.boysofbaseball.com/conduct.html

Driver, B., & Wharton, C. (2004). *The baffled parents' guide to coaching youth hockey*. McGraw-Hill.

Eitzen, D., Sage, G. H., & Beal, B. (2018). *Sociology of North American sport* (11th ed.). Oxford University Press.

Grace, B. (2019, May 28). Helping the first year head coach avoid costly mistakes – developing a plan for year one. *Coaches Insider*. https://coachesinsider.com/athletic-director/helping-the-first-year-head-coach-avoid-costly-mistakes-developing-a-plan-for-year-one/

Pritchard, J. (2021, February 17). How to avoid coach burnout. *Stack*. www.stack.com/a/how-to-avoid-coach-burnout/

Smith, L. (2021, February 25). 4 tips for first time coaches. *Stack*. www.stack.com/a/4-tips-for-first-time-coaches/

Weng, G. (2017, August 2). How to deal with difficult parents as a coach. *SISU*. https://blog.sisuguard.com/how-to-deal-with-difficult-parents-as-a-coach

9 Athlete Injuries

It is the middle of October and Coach John Kilmer is anticipating the upcoming ice hockey season. Preseason practices are planned, and he is expecting another great year. Coach Kilmer is entering his 24th year as a coach and his 18th year at Panama High School. Panama is a small Minnesota community, and the people there love their hockey.

Prior to Coach Kilmer's arrival at Panama, the hockey program had struggled and was infamous for one of the longest losing streaks in the state. When he arrived as an assistant, the program was going through a transition phase. New head coaches had come and gone almost on a yearly basis. During his early days at the school, Coach Kilmer was required to teach science and work on the coaching staff of several teams including hockey. After three years, he was awarded the head coaching position. It was quite a challenge considering the 6–14 record the team had posted the previous year. In the team's history, it had never made the playoffs.

In Coach Kilmer's first season, it was apparent that things were definitely different. Coach Kilmer is an old-school, hard-nosed coach who believes in developing and implementing toughness in his players. His practices were hard, and he wanted his players to be disciplined. They would practice for hours. They were not allowed to take off their helmets, and only occasional water breaks were allowed. He also believes that his teams should have a lot of contact during practice and would regularly run full-contact hitting drills. During that first season, Coach Kilmer's Panama team lost several players to injuries, but the team made a noticeable improvement, going 10–12, just shy of the playoffs. The following year the team had a breakthrough season, going 17–5, eventually losing in the semifinal round of the playoffs. The community of Panama went crazy, and Coach Kilmer was an instant star.

Over the next 15 years, Coach Kilmer's team made the playoffs every year, one year even recording a perfect season. Since that memorable undefeated season six years ago, the Panama Tigers made the playoffs every year but never won a playoff game. People began to question Coach Kilmer's coaching style, suggesting that it wasn't as effective as it once was. The players hated his drill sergeant coaching style and feared him. Some players admitted to playing injured because of their fear of Coach Kilmer. Stories circulated about players running until they passed out and Coach Kilmer ignoring the severity of an injury. Over the years, Coach Kilmer had become obsessed with his win-loss record and the number of conference championships he had won.

DOI: 10.4324/9781003375449-10

Coach Kilmer ran full-contact practices where everyone including the goalies participated in hard-hitting drills. One of his players, goalie Jake Parker, suffered a hard hit from a teammate during practice in his junior year. Jake's head and the back of his helmet hit the ice with such impact that he saw stars. He quickly got back up but was very dizzy. Nevertheless, he somehow skated back to where the drill was continuing. He felt funny but didn't want to say anything to Coach Kilmer because he was scared that he might lose his starting spot.

Jake carpooled with Bill Davis, a forward, and that night he complained of having a headache and said he really couldn't remember what happened in practice.

"Should I tell the trainer about what happened on Monday?" he asked Bill.

"I wouldn't do that if I were you," Bill replied. "Do you remember what happened to Steve Grondholm?" Steve had suffered a concussion and told the trainer. He was forced to miss three weeks of the season. Coach Kilmer thought Steve was weak and benched him for the remainder of the season.

Because Panama is such a small community, it didn't have a full-time trainer on staff; a trainer from a larger neighboring town would come to practice and check on the players once a week. When the trainer came to practice the following Monday to check on any injuries sustained the prior week, Jake stayed quiet. It was an unspoken rule that Coach Kilmer did not want anyone going to the trainer unless it was an obvious visible injury like a broken bone.

Jake eventually recovered and finished his junior season successfully. He hoped that the same issues would not arise during his senior season.

Hopes are high for Coach Kilmer's 18th year of coaching and Jake's senior year as all-state goalie. The Tigers are projected as preseason locks for the playoffs and contenders for the state championship. Anything less than a title shot would be a failure to Kilmer and the Panama community.

The first week of practice the players go through a brutal conditioning regimen. Jake can't believe how hard Coach Kilmer is pushing them this year. Practice this year is harder than it was his first three years of hockey, and he never imagined that that could be possible. Even more surprising is that established starters and seniors are being beaten down as much as the rookies. Like everyone else, Jake groans in silence and takes the punishment.

With conditioning well underway, the players are looking forward to the first week of full-padded practices. Coach Kilmer's practices have become legendary, and all the players are preparing themselves for all the high-speed collisions they are about to experience.

Coach Kilmer matches up Jake with Bill, the starting forward, in a drill that Coach Kilmer calls "blood alley." This drill consists of the two players standing 10 yards apart and then skating full speed toward each other with the objective of knocking down the opponent. Jake and Bill line up facing each other. They know not to go easy on each other because Coach Kilmer will go ballistic on them if they don't go all out. The first collision is a stalemate. Coach Kilmer rushes up to Jake and gets in his face.

"Is that all you've got, Parker?!" he screams, spittle practically covering Jake's visor. "I thought you were the leader of this team."

This angers Jake, so he forgets that it's his best friend opposite him. The second collision puts Bill on his back. This time Kilmer screams at Bill, who is lying on the ground dazed. The third and final collision is so hard that Jake and Bill both hit the ground and stumble to get up. Coach Kilmer helps Jake up.

"That kind of heart and effort is going to take us to the state championship," Coach Kilmer says.

The rest of the day Jake feels similar to the way he did during his junior year. He has a headache and is dizzy, but he tells no one about it.

The season continues, and the Panama Tigers start a worrying 9–10. Bill and Jake are both having great seasons, and the Tigers' playoff chances would have been all but over had it not been for their ability to carry the team. In their 20th game against Ridge Port, Bill suffers a season-ending knee injury. At that point, Jake knows that he has to put the team on his shoulders and carry the load if they are going to make it to the playoffs as expected. In the next two games, Jake has his best performances of the year. It seems that Coach Kilmer is actually satisfied with his senior goalie.

With an 11–10 record and only three games remaining in the season, everything is on the line in the Tigers' next home game against league leaders Harrisburg. A win here would put them in the playoffs. Before the game, Coach Kilmer gives a speech about how they are warriors and how they should leave everything they have on the ice.

"The only way you should be coming off the ice is if you're on a stretcher!" he shouts at them before the game. "There's no room for sissies tonight!"

Late in the second period, Harrisburg is on a power play. After the Harrisburg players pass the puck around to pull out the shorthanded Panama team, they find a gap. Their star forward powers toward the goal and takes a shot. Jake manages to deflect the puck past his goalpost, but the forward can't stop his momentum and crashes into him. Arms flailing, Jake stumbles, and there is a sickening thud as his head slams onto the ice.

Jake lies unconscious for close to a minute. He awakes with Coach Kilmer leaning over him and the Emergency Medical Services (EMS) crew beside him. The crew helps him up and takes him to the sideline. During the second-period break, Coach Kilmer reassures Jake that his opponent has only rung his bell and he'll be fine for the third period.

Jake knows that something is extremely wrong and that it's more than just having his bell rung. He has trouble seeing and can't remember much prior to the hit. All he can remember is the speech that Coach Kilmer gave about being gladiators and not leaving the game unless on a stretcher. He plays the third period, but Panama eventually loses 4–2.

After the game, Jake vomits and complains to his parents of a brutal headache. His parents take him to the hospital, where he is diagnosed with a severe concussion. Jake finally confesses to the doctor and his family that he has probably experienced three concussions over the past two years. The doctor explains to him the severity of concussions and that he won't be able to play for at least a minimum of the next three weeks.

Jake knows there are only two weeks left in the season. If they don't win one of those two remaining games, they won't make the playoffs. Coach Kilmer's playoff streak will be over. The following week, Jake sits out the whole game and Panama loses 5–4. The final game of the regular season, an away fixture, is approaching, and Jake sits out the entire week of practice. On the way to the final game that Friday, Coach Kilmer asks Jake how he's feeling. After two weeks of rest Jake does feel better, but he is afraid of taking another hard hit. Coach Kilmer asks him to play and reassures him that everything will be fine. He tells Jake that he'll take him out of the game as soon as they get the lead. Jake is unsure but decides to play, disobeying the orders of both his doctor and his parents.

Shortly after the first period, Jake takes himself out of the game and goes to the sidelines. He is experiencing dizziness and double vision. Coach Kilmer and the rest of his staff are confused because Jake never got hit during play. However, when he begins to vomit, he is rushed to the hospital. The doctors explain that Jake has a brain edema, extreme swelling of the brain. He is unconscious for several days.

Months after the season, Jake still can't remember what happened. Although he can finish his senior year of high school, he never plays hockey again.

Questions for Consideration

1. Who are the stakeholders in this case?
2. What was the first mistake that Coach Kilmer and Jake each made?
3. What could Coach Kilmer and Jake each have done to avoid getting into this situation?
4. How was the situation affected by the lack of a full-time trainer on the staff?
5. What do you think should happen to Coach Kilmer?
6. Discuss the term "concussion" and its symptoms. How do you think coaches and players perceive concussions?
7. Should coaches and student athletes be mandated to take classes on concussions?
8. What are schools' and coaches' legal implications regarding concussions? What were the policies/procedures regarding concussions at your high school?

References and Further Readings

Battista, J. (2022, October 2). Changes coming to NFL concussion protocol a needed step for player safety. *NFL*. www.nfl.com/news/changes-coming-to-nfl-concussion-protocol-a-needed-step-for-player-safety

Burker, M., & Alexander P. (2022, October 1). Consultant who cleared Dolphins' Tagovailoa to play after head blow is fired. *NBC News*. www.nbcnews.com/news/us-news/consultant-cleared-dolphins-tagovailoa-play-head-blow-fired-rcna50327

Centers for Disease Control and Prevention. (2019). Heads up to school sports: Coaches. *Heads Up*. www.cdc.gov/headsup/highschoolsports/coach.html.

Daugherty, J., Waltzman, D., Popat, S., Horn Groenendaal, A., Cherney, M., & Knudson, A. (2022). Challenges and opportunities in diagnosing and managing mild traumatic brain injury in rural settings. *Rural and Remote Health*, *22*(2), 7241. https://doi.org/10.22605/RRH7241

Guskiewicz, K., Weaver, N., Padua, D., & Garrett, W. (2000). Epidemiology of concussion in collegiate and high school football players. *American Journal of Sports Medicine*, *28*(5), 643–650. https://doi.org/10.1177/03635465000280050401

Haarbauer-Krupa, J. K., Register-Mihalik, J. K., Nedimyer, A. K., Chandran, A., Kay, M. C., Gildner, P., & Kerr, Z. Y. (2021). Factors associated with concussion symptom knowledge and attitudes towards concussion care-seeking among parents of children aged 5–10 years. *Journal of Safety Research*, *78*, 203–209. https://doi.org/10.1016/j.jsr.2021.05.003

Lipp, K. (2021, October 1). School district sued over 2019 football game injury. *New Times*. www.newportnewstimes.com/news/school-district-sued-over-2019-football-game-injury/article_95df7572-224c-11ec-8640-c70e51ab92c2.html

Miller, G. F., Sarmiento, K., Haarbauer, K. J., & Everett Jones, S. (2022). The association between school district-based policies related to concussions and concussions among high school students. *Journal of School Health*, *92*(2), 140–147. https://doi.org/10.1111/josh.13113

Waltzman, D., Sarmiento, K., Devine, O., Zhang, X., De Padilla, L., Kresnow, M., Borradaile, K., Hurwitz, A., Jones, D., Goyal, R., & Breiding, M. J. (2021). Head impact exposures among youth tackle and flag American football athletes. *Sports Health: A Multidisciplinary Approach*, *13*(5), 454–462. https://doi.org/10.1177/1941738121992324

10 Crippling Success

Coach William Leonard is in his 17th season as the head football coach at Oak Bower High School in North Point, Indiana. He began his career at Oak Bower as a student intern while completing his education degree and gradually moved up the ranks. Oak Bower has about 200 students in grades 9 through 12, and the football team has an average of 30 kids dress out each year. Coach Leonard is well liked in the community, and even though the team averages a .500 season every year, the small town is content with the job he is doing. His team made it into the first and second rounds of the AA state playoffs a few times in the past ten years, but the team isn't considered a power program by any measure.

The head athletic trainer is Eric Waynes, who teaches at the nearby liberal arts college. He and Coach Leonard are good friends, and Eric has "helped out" at the high school with the football team on Thursday and Friday nights for years. Both men get along well and have similar philosophies. As Eric gained experience as a trainer, he spent less and less time researching and reading the latest literature in areas such as athletic injury management and rehabilitation. He relied more on his gut instinct and past experiences to make decisions instead of using a more technical, academic approach for making injury decisions. Very seldom does a player miss a game due to injury. Eric believes he can wrap, brace, or tape any injury well enough for the injured player to continue to participate. Coach Leonard likes this about him and is even sometimes amazed at what he can do. However, Eric is preparing to retire from his position at the college and will also be leaving his volunteer role at Oak Bower. Coach Leonard is going to miss having Eric's help, especially since it frees up Coach Leonard and his staff, giving them time to complete other duties.

Fortunately for Coach Leonard and Oak Bower High School, a new state-funded initiative has passed that is going to fund full-time athletic trainers at high schools. The key to the new initiative is that the schools are required to hire new athletic trainers with less than five years of experience in an attempt to stimulate the job market for athletic trainers in the state. Michael Sims recently completed both his undergraduate- and graduate-level studies in athletic training and is hired to take over for Eric at Oak Bower. His master's thesis, "Revising Return-to-Play Criteria: An Evidence-Based Model," focused on the importance of athletes' meeting certain objective measurements before he deemed they could safely return to sport. This model eliminates use

DOI: 10.4324/9781003375449-11

of the "tough it up, you can be hurt tomorrow" mentality that has predominated the school for more than a decade. He is excited to finally have a full-time position where he can really use his research to help athletes.

Within the first month of Michael's tenure at Oak Bower, he sidelines six key players with injuries. In the very first game of the season, a senior starting offensive lineman sprains his wrist and is in obvious pain. Instead of taping the wrist and allowing the player to continue, Michael tells the player and Coach Leonard that he can't continue to play.

"Sorry, Coach. We need to wait until Monday, just in case it might be broken," says Michael.

"He's just soft. There's nothing wrong with him," Coach Leonard says. "You're just making it worse."

"It's just not a chance I'm willing to take," responds Michael. "He says he's hurt, so he's hurt."

While this argument is taking place, Oak Bower's defensive line collapses, and its quarterback is sacked for a 12-yard loss. Coach Leonard is infuriated.

On Monday, the offensive lineman in question has his wrist x-rayed. It's negative for a break, and he's back in practice Tuesday.

The second and third games of the season are no better. Michael benches a safety with a stinger and a linebacker with a knee sprain. This cripples the team's defensive element, and although the team remains competitive throughout the game, Oak Bower loses by a touchdown late in the fourth quarter.

All season there is a back-and-forth battle between Coach Leonard and Michael. Michael sits a player out, and Coach Leonard neither understands nor agrees with the decision.

"I just don't get it," says Coach Leonard. "You seem to bench anyone with any kind of injury. You do understand that I need enough players to actually play, don't you?"

The sarcasm in Coach Leonard's voice isn't lost on Michael.

"Look, Coach. I know you don't agree with a lot of my decisions, but I have to put the player first. I've got plenty of statistical data to validate my decisions."

"Well, that's just great. But when Eric was here, he never would have benched a player. No one ever missed a game when he was around."

"Well, I'm not Eric," Michael quickly replies, "and I have to do what I know is right. I can't just ignore it when a player is at risk. I don't know what kind of relationship you had with Eric and what he was willing to ignore, but I just can't. My responsibility is the health and well-being of these athletes, not whether you have enough players to put on the field. Maybe if you examined your coaching methods, you could reduce the number of players getting injured."

Coach Leonard, too offended to even respond, storms away.

The relationship between Coach Leonard and Michael continues to deteriorate as players continue to be sidelined. A team of 30 healthy players is whittled down to about 24 dressing out. Coach Leonard doesn't have enough players to provide depth to his squad and is having to play a lot of his team on both sides of the ball. At his wit's end, he goes to see Athletic Director Allison Jameson to vent.

"I just don't know how you expect me to win ball games when my best players are missing practice and games. Michael keeps benching all my players because of so-called 'injuries,'" says Coach Leonard, his fingers mimicking quotation marks.

Athletic Director Jameson responds, "I understand your frustration, Coach Leonard, but the school district has my hands tied. With this new directive there's little I can do about it. Michael is empowered to make all the injury decisions. Apparently, it's supposed to protect us from liability. There've been some litigation issues in other states, and we don't want to be put in a situation where a player's parents sue over something like that."

"This is just absurd! I know winning isn't everything in this school, but there's no way an athletic trainer—a newbie at that—determines our win-loss record."

"I know this is tough, and it's going to take time working things out with Michael. But this is what it is, and maybe you both got off on the wrong foot. Why don't you try talking to Michael again and see if you can both work something out? If things get worse, then maybe we can all meet to find a resolution."

"I guess I've got nothing left to lose at this point," says Coach Leonard. "I'll give it a shot, but I'm not holding my breath."

Frustrated as ever, Coach Leonard goes back to the field house and finds Michael.

"Look, Michael, I think we may have had a bad start. I appreciate that you're trying to protect the players, but are you sure all these kids are really as bad as you say they are? I've never seen so much missed playing time."

"Well, Coach," says Michael, "I'm sure some of them can probably still play, but do you really want to take any chances? Based on my examinations, I'm not too comfortable letting them on the field."

"Next week is our final game of the season, and everyone wants to see our team finish well. But for now, I'll hold off on bringing anyone back, because I think we have enough players to compete," replies Coach Leonard.

"Okay, Coach. I think you made the right choice."

Although it appears that Coach Leonard and Michael have made a good start at repairing their relationship, it is tenuous at best, and it all comes unraveled during the final full-contact practice before Friday's finale. The starting star tailback for the team pulls up during a drill and grabs his hamstring. When Michael examines him on the sideline, he's concerned about his ability to play. He approaches Coach Leonard.

"Coach, if he can go full speed without limping and has good strength, I'm comfortable with letting him go, but that's a game-day decision. If he can't do all the drills I ask, I have to hold him out."

"This is ridiculous!" Coach Leonard exclaims. "I need him to win. He told me he's fine and it was just a tweak."

"Sorry, Coach. Winning doesn't matter to me. My job is to make decisions based on what I think is best for the player." He tells Coach Leonard that he will probably need to find a replacement for this week's game.

Coach Leonard is again at his wit's end. With his tailback out, he sure isn't going to win, and it looks like his players will once again be forced to play more than one position. He thinks to himself, "Why can't Michael just do the job he's supposed to and patch up his players?" He is beginning to wonder who is really running the team.

Questions for Consideration

1. Who are the stakeholders in this case?
2. Who do you think has the most to lose by the decisions being made? Who has the most to gain? Why?
3. Who or what could be potentially held liable for the decisions being made to hold players out of competition?
4. Should coaches have any say on whether or not an athlete is allowed to participate following an injury? Should the player? Should the parents?
5. In the absence of an athletic trainer, could a coach/school be at fault and held liable for allowing a player to continue participating following an injury?
6. Do athletic trainers increase or decrease a school's liability? What about the coaches?
7. What can be done to improve the working relationship between Coach Leonard and the athletic trainer?
8. Should coaches receive more education on the impact of sports injuries?
9. As a coach, would you be willing to do whatever it took to ensure a win, no matter the health cost of an athlete?

References and Further Readings

Hutsick, M. (2016, October 21). Coach conflict. *Training & Conditioning*. https://training-conditioning.com/article/coach-conflict/

Pike Lacy, A. M., Bowman, T. G., & Mazerolle Singe, S. (2020). Challenges faced by collegiate athletic trainers, part I: Organizational conflict and clinical decision making. *Journal of Athletic Training (Allen Press)*, *55*(3), 303–311. https://doi.org/10.4085/1062-6050-84-19

Pike Lacy, A. M., Eason, C. M., Stearns, R. L., & Casa, D. J. (2021). Secondary school administrators' knowledge and perceptions of the athletic training profession, part I: Specific considerations for athletic directors. *Journal of Athletic Training (Allen Press)*, *56*(9), 1018–1028. https://doi.org/10.4085/54-20

Pike Lacy, A. M., Eason, C. M., Stearns, R. L., & Casa, D. J. (2021). Secondary school administrators' knowledge and perceptions of the athletic training profession, part II: Specific considerations for principals. *Journal of Athletic Training (Allen Press)*, *56*(9), 1029–1036. https://doi.org/10.4085/55-20

Wolverton, B. (2013, September 2). Coach makes the call: Athletic trainers who butt heads with coaches over concussion treatment take career hits. *The Chronicle of Higher Education*. www.chronicle.com/article/coach-makes-the-call/

Zettlemoyer, A. (2014, November 7). Coaches and certified athletic trainers: An important relationship. *National Federation of State High School Associations (NFHS)*. www.nfhs.org/articles/coaches-and-certified-athletic-trainers-an-important-relationship/

11 The Importance of Policies and Procedures

Jack Sampson finally feels that all his hard work has paid off: he has just been named a physical education teacher and head eighth-grade boys' basketball coach for Mingle Middle School in Cambridge, Florida. Being a basketball coach is something that Jack has always wanted to do, but it has taken a long time to become a reality. After Jack finished high school, he was pressured into working on the family farm instead of pursuing an education in the teaching field. However, after 14 years he decided to go to college and fulfill his lifelong dream of becoming a basketball coach.

Jack spent four years working on his undergraduate degree in kinesiology. His internship coordinator assigned him to Ms. Justice, a well-respected physical education teacher at Mingle Middle School. This particular middle school is one of two in a town that doesn't have an athletics program. It's a disappointment, but he's still looking forward to learning under Ms. Justice.

Ms. Justice is immediately impressed with Jack's strong work ethic. She quickly realizes that he is serious about his career change and up to the challenge, and as a consequence, she starts giving Jack more responsibilities. In just a few short weeks Jack is planning and teaching almost every lesson by himself. He loves teaching at the school and, toward the end of his internship, is shocked to be offered the opportunity to become the first boys' basketball coach at Mingle Middle School. Jack jumps at the chance to be the inaugural coach.

Over his first summer as coach, Jack puts together practice plans to make sure that he's ready to start the new school year and begin working with the team immediately. He already has an idea of the kids who will be on his team because he taught them in physical education class during his internship. The first day of school arrives, and the students who want to be on the basketball team are ready and eager to start practicing. Because of the small number of students who want to play, there is no need to have a tryout.

Practice over the first couple of weeks goes great. Jack is pleased that his players are working extremely hard, and he can see progression in his team's overall fitness and skill development with each passing week. However, coaching middle school students does present some challenges and learning experiences.

Dennis Wilson, one of Jack's students, is regarded as the best athlete in school. Even at the elementary school level he excelled at sports. Throughout his intern year, Jack taught Dennis and understands his potential. Unfortunately, Dennis also

DOI: 10.4324/9781003375449-12

has the reputation of being a troublemaker, with lots of problems in the classroom and outside of school. Dennis is only in the eighth grade, but he's already been in trouble with the police for minor infractions. Jack was warned about Dennis but has never had a problem with him personally. Dennis shows up, dressed out, and is always ready to participate during physical education classes. In Jack's class, he always stays on task and even helps other students who can't grasp certain skills. To Jack, Dennis is a model student, and from what Jack understands from other teachers, Dennis turned himself around over the summer and is doing well in his other classes too.

One day during practice about two weeks before the first game, Dennis approaches Jack.

"Coach, I know it's close to the start of the season, but I'd really like to join the basketball team."

Jack doesn't know what to make of this. He knows that if he allows Dennis to play, his team will be much better, but, at the same time, Dennis missed the entire off-season, and it wouldn't be fair to the team.

"Dennis, why are you trying to join so late? The team has been working hard for over four months now!"

Dennis looks down at his feet and says, "Coach, I had a lot of trouble last year with my behavior. I've worked hard this year to change, and I feel I'm ready to take on a new challenge. I've known all year that I wanted to play, but my parents wanted to make sure that my behavior and grades were going to be better this year."

It's a sensible explanation, and Dennis sounds genuine, which makes it a tough decision for Jack. Many questions are going through his head. "What would other teachers think?" he wonders to himself. "Should I talk with the principal about this? What would the other players want to do? Would Dennis stay eligible? What's the right thing to do?"

Jack has always been one to believe in second chances—after all, he was given a second chance at a career—and it is inevitably his decision to make. Jack weighs the pros and cons, while Dennis stands waiting for an answer.

"Dennis, as long as you get a physical before next week you can start practicing with us on Monday," says Jack.

"Does that mean I'm on the team?" Dennis excitedly responds.

"Yes, Dennis, that means you're part of the team. See you Monday."

Jack feels confident about his decision all weekend and is excited about seeing Dennis at practice the following Monday. Dennis shows up with a signed physical in hand and ready to practice. It is quickly obvious that Dennis is much better than anyone else on the team. The team seems to embrace his presence, and all the players are excited about their first game that Friday.

The team has a great week of practice leading up to the big game. Dennis is there every day on time and continues to shine throughout practice. Jack goes home at the end of the week ecstatic about how his team is looking and how well the team included Dennis. He's a little surprised that he hasn't received any complaints from players or parents about Dennis being allowed to join the team late. In fact, it's just the opposite.

The players comment on how happy they are to have Dennis on the team and how important he will be to their success throughout the season.

The Thursday before the Mingle Middle School's inaugural game, Dennis approaches Jack after practice and tells him he needs a ride home.

"Coach, my mom has to work late tonight, and my dad is out of town, so would you mind giving me a ride home today?"

Jack is caught off guard. He wants to take Dennis home but knows it would be a mistake. He discussed just this type of scenario with Ms. Justice during his intern year and was instructed never to give a student a ride, no matter what. He knows that the best thing to do is to find Dennis another ride home. He calls over Aaron, the starting point guard, and asks him if his mom can drop off Dennis on their way home.

"No problem, Coach. My mom'd be happy to!" Aaron replies.

Jack feels that he's done the right thing by having another player's parent drop off Dennis at his house. The two boys run off to Aaron's mother's car, and Jack watches as Aaron explains the situation to his mother. Aaron's mother smiles and waves at Jack as if to say, "No problem," and they drive away.

Mingle Middle School starts its season with a victory the next day. Dennis is phenomenal and seems to inspire his teammates to play better than they thought they could. Even one or two onlooking teachers are a little surprised at the effort that Dennis puts forth. Jack can't help but smile smugly at their disbelieving expressions.

The next week's practices go as planned, and the team is clearly beginning to bond. Dennis exceeds the school's expectations and continues to work diligently both in class and in practice. However, after Thursday's practice, as parents are picking up their sons, Dennis once again approaches Jack.

"Hey, Coach."

"Good practice today, Dennis. What's up?"

"Well, my mom's working late again, and my dad's still out of town. I talked to my mom this morning, and she said Aaron's mom could take me home again. I asked Aaron if that was okay, and he told me that they have an appointment to go to. So, I don't have a ride home, Coach. Can you take me?"

There is no easy way out this time.

Questions for Consideration

1. Who are the stakeholders in this case?
2. What are the major issues in this case? Are there any legal issues?
3. What could Jack have done to help prevent the situation of Dennis needing a ride home?
4. What should Jack do now that he's in this dilemma of Dennis needing a ride home?
5. As a coach, should you allow an athlete's so-called track record to influence your opinion of him, or should you give him a clean slate?
6. Even though all the players "appeared" happy to have Dennis on the team, who might not be happy about the situation?
7. Did Jack make the right decision to let Dennis on the team? Why or why not?

References and Further Readings

Cotterill, T. J. (2017, March 18). Wash. Wrestling coach says he was fired for giving kids rides home. *The News Tribune*. www.kiro7.com/news/local/lincoln-wrestling-coach-says-he-was-fired-for-giving-kids-rides-home-lincoln-high-school-wrestling/503909810/

Murphy, C. (2022, October 26). State high court: Coach's supervisory role during athlete's warm-up injury governed by 'simple negligence standard'. *ALM|Law.com*. www.law.com/njlawjournal/2022/10/26/state-high-court-coachs-supervisory-role-during-athletes-warm-up-injury-governed-by-simple-negligence-standard/?slreturn=20221001123034

Roberts, G. (2014, July 18). A special relationship – A coach's duty in sports law. *CoachesInsider.com*. https://coachesinsider.com/track-x-country/a-special-relationship-a-coachs-duty-in-sports-law-article/

Siddons, S. (2009, June 3). Should volunteer coaches have liability insurance? *HowStuffWorks.com*. https://money.howstuffworks.com/economics/volunteer/opportunities/volunteer-income-tax-assistance.htm

The Academy. (2022). *Athletic handbook for parents and athletes*. chrome-extension://efaidnbmnnnibpcajpcglclefindmkaj/https://resources.finalsite.net/images/v1655752360/theacademyk12org/w9v4qwdyh8lww7vjirm8/AthleticHandbook2022-2023.pdf

12 Parents and Principals

Jessica Sharpe has been at Greenwood High School in Greenwood, Arizona, for three years as an assistant softball and basketball coach and as a social studies teacher. In her short tenure, she has won a state championship and made another playoff appearance. There is a definite advantage to coaching in a small town like Greenwood: everyone knows who the coaches are, and when successful, the community treat them like royalty.

Although she enjoys her job, Jessica has larger aspirations and wants to be a head coach at a 5A school. She really wants the opportunity to prove herself. Thus, when a position for head coach of softball at 5A Northside High School in Frankfort opens up, she jumps at the opportunity to apply for the position. The school has just built a new field and has excellent facilities. It's everything she has hoped for and more.

Jessica's interview goes well, and a few days later she gets a call.

"Hi, Jessica. This is Asa, the athletic director of Frankfort Public School District."

"Hi, Asa. How's it going?"

"Well, I have what I hope is exciting news for you. I am calling to ask you to join the coaching team at Northside High School as head softball coach. You'll also be expected to teach some general-studies classes. What do you think about that?"

"That's great news! Thank you very much. I'm looking forward to this opportunity."

"Great! Well, come by the administration office next week, and we'll get everything finalized. I'm looking forward to working with you, Coach Sharpe. See you soon!"

Jessica can hardly believe it. She quickly finds her husband, Irwin, to give him the news. He is excited for her and about what her new job will mean for their family. The best part of the whole situation is that they won't have to move. It's only about a 30-minute drive from their house to the high school in Frankfort. He will be able to keep his job as a science teacher at Greenwood Middle School, and their children won't have to be uprooted to a new school system. Their lives will more than likely stay the way they are.

Jessica has been dreaming about an opportunity like this for as long as she can remember. She graduated from the University of Central Tennessee with a master's degree in kinesiology and had a coaching endorsement. She was also a graduate assistant for the softball program there and gained invaluable experience.

Jessica begins her tenure at Northside High School by having practice after school every day. She focuses on teaching fundamentals, running basic plays, and conditioning

DOI: 10.4324/9781003375449-13

her team for the season's start. Things are going extremely well. Her players are noticing her coaching and improving their conditioning every day. They demonstrate good team chemistry and sound fundamentals. However, she is missing a couple of players who are currently playing on the volleyball team. She knows that these players will be behind at the beginning of the season but figures that they will catch up fast because they are natural athletes.

Volleyball season finally ends, and three more players join the softball team. One of them, Heather Cook, is more athletic than most, but she doesn't have the throwing and catching skills to justify making her a starter. However, she is a good hitter and is effective entering the game as a pinch hitter. Using this strategy, Jessica wins her first game as head coach.

The following day, Heather's mother comes to watch practice but leaves without a word. She does exactly the same thing the next day. Jessica thinks this is a little unusual but figures she's probably just taking an interest in her daughter's softball team.

The next couple of games are close, but Jessica's team loses one game in overtime and one in the final inning. Consequently, the team's morale is low. Jessica is hoping that her players will learn from their mistakes and rebound.

One day after practice Ms. Cook comes up to Jessica.

"Hello, Coach. I'm Heather's mom. Can I talk to you for a minute?"

"Sure, come into my office. What do you need to talk about?"

"Well, I've got some concerns about the team, and I'd like to talk about my daughter. She's a great athlete, and she should be starting. Pinch hitting shouldn't be her role."

"I see. Heather is a talented athlete, but she's still behind some of the others because of volleyball season and still needs practice time throwing and catching before I'm willing to let her start. Besides, I like bringing her in off the bench because I think she brings a boost to the team. She's a great hitter."

"I understand, but I think Heather's better than some of the starters. Something needs to be done about this."

"Well, I appreciate your bringing this to my attention; however, it's ultimately my decision, and for now I want her coming in to pinch. There's always the chance that I'll change my mind, but for the time being I think it's better for the team to keep things the way they are."

The next game, the team loses another close one. Heather once again contributes a single coming in to pinch-hit but then has mixed results on the field. Her throwing is too hard and produces a couple of errors. Jessica tells her to calm down, but it's like Jessica's mind is elsewhere.

After the game Jessica asks to see Heather in her office.

"S'up, Coach?"

"Come in and have a seat. Do you know why I asked you to come see me?"

"Not really."

"Well, although you did well hitting, you continually overthrew first base. They scored a run from one of them. What were you thinking? Those kinds of mistakes really cost us!"

"Sorry, Coach, but I was told to throw harder no matter what you said to do, or I'd get in trouble."

"In trouble? With whom? What are you talking about?"

"My mom. She said that I needed to show you my arm strength and that I should be starting."

"I see. Well, I'm the coach, and you should be listening to me, because when you don't, it hurts the team."

Later that night, without Jessica's knowledge, several of the parents get together to talk about the softball team. Ms. Cook is trying to convince the rest of the parents to sign a petition to get rid of Jessica and tells them she will present it to the school board if they sign it. After some debate, three other parents agree to sign the petition. Ms. Cook knows it won't be enough to get rid of Jessica; she just wants to put pressure on her to make Heather a starter.

The next day at school, Jessica is called into the principal's office.

"Good morning, Coach Sharpe."

"Good morning, Mr. Benson. What can I do for you?"

"Well, I had a conversation last night with a member of the school board about Heather Cook, a player on your team. The board member wanted to know why Heather isn't getting to play as a starter."

Coach Sharpe can't believe what she's hearing. This is a coach's decision, not a decision to be questioned by a school board member or the principal of the school.

"Well, Jessica isn't ready to be a starter because of volleyball season, and although she's a good hitter, she doesn't have the throwing and catching skills necessary to be a starter. I've explained this to her mother. Last night, in fact, Heather cost us a run by overthrowing first base."

"Jessica, I understand where you're coming from. However, I'm getting pressure from the school board because you've started the season 1–4, not to mention, Jessica's mother has gotten some of the other parents to sign a petition to replace you as the head coach."

"Are you telling me to give Heather more playing time, Mr. Benson?"

"Of course not! However, I'm suggesting that it'd be better for all involved if that were to happen. It would keep her mother off your back and might help you win a few more games. I talked to Ms. Cook, and if Heather is made a starter and given more playing time, she will back off. Just take some time, and think about it."

Coach Sharpe leaves Mr. Benson's office in disbelief. She thinks to herself, "What am I going to do? Should I stick to my guns and do what I know I should do as a head coach, or should I give in and start Heather in the next game?" This coaching position was supposed to be her big opportunity, but now she faces this dilemma.

Questions for Consideration

1. Who are the stakeholders in this case?
2. What is the critical issue in this case?
3. What might Coach Sharpe have done wrong in this situation? What, if anything, should she have done differently?
4. What would you have expected from a parent, an athletic director, a school board member, and a principal in this situation?
5. What should Coach Sharpe do to help remedy this situation?

6. Based on the current school and athletic environment, where do you think Coach Sharpe will be in three years' time?
7. The administration didn't really emphasize the importance of Coach Sharpe's teaching responsibilities and focused primarily on her job as a coach. Do you think this is a common occurrence? Why or why not?
8. Do you think coaches in high school should also have to teach? Why or why not?

References and Further Readings

Holden, S. L., Forester, B. E., Keshock, C. M., & Pugh, S. F. (2015). How to effectively manage coach, parent, and player relationships. *Sport Journal, 1*. https://doi.org/10.17682/sportjournal/2015.025

Horne, E., Woolf, J., & Green, C. (2022). Relationship dynamics between parents and coaches: Are they failing young athletes? *Managing Sport & Leisure, 27*(3), 224–240. https://doi.org/10.1080/23750472.2020.1779114

Robinson, M. J. (2010). *Sports club management* (1st ed.). Human Kinetics.

Sabedra, D. (2017, May 31). High school coaching conundrum: Is it too easy for parents to get you fired? *East Bay Times*. www.eastbaytimes.com/2017/05/31/high-school-coaching-do-parents-have-too-much-power/

Skiver, K. (2018, June 14). High school coach wins $50,000 settlement in lawsuit against parents who got him fired. *CBS Sports*. www.cbssports.com/general/news/high-school-coach-wins-50000-settlement-in-lawsuit-against-parents-who-got-him-fired/

Skolnikoff, J., & Engvall, R. (2013). *Young athletes, couch potatoes, and helicopter parents: The productivity of play*. Rowman & Littlefield Publishers.

Witt, P. A., & Dangi, T. B. (2018). Helping parents be better youth sport coaches and spectators. *Journal of Park & Recreation Administration, 36*(3), 200–208. https://doi.org/10.18666/JPRA-2018-V36-I3-8619

13 Winning Versus Player Development

As the final whistle blows, Alex smiles; turns to his assistant coach, Mike; and shakes his hand. It is the end of a long yet successful boys' middle school soccer season. Alex had only recently been assigned the team, as a coaching activity for him to do, in the off-season of his regular high school baseball coaching gig. Although it's only middle school, the soccer coaching job was an important one and something Alex took very seriously. It also allowed Alex to earn a little extra money before the baseball season really gets going. Its adjoining district feeder high school is something of an enigma in boys' soccer. A couple of California titles and several players receiving college scholarships had put Springtown High School on the national map with respect to soccer.

"Hey, Mike," Alex says. "You and the wife meeting us at Pepper's for dinner?"

"You bet," Mike replies. "See ya there."

At dinner Alex and Mike reminisce over the ups and downs of the season. It was a season that started out with a thud, with losses in the first two games and ties in the next two against weak opponents. Alex knows this was partly his fault because he had moved some players around to find out how they might perform at different positions. This seemed like an appropriate thing to do because some of the kids had limited playing experience and several had gotten much bigger and faster over the last year. Besides, he was told by Mitch, the athletic director, that the real purpose of this eighth-grade soccer team was to find guys who would be ready to step up and play the following season on the successful varsity high school team. It was all about player development. Also, there were no playoffs or tournaments for middle school athletics and, as a consequence, not too much was at stake.

Alex's experimentation with player positions seemed to have really paid off. He found that several kids had discovered new positions that were much better suited to their specific skills. After those first four games, the season really turned around. Springtown Junior High won four of its next six games and tied against the two best teams in the league. The kids also had a great time, with several of them asking if Alex and Mike could work with the high school team next year. Alex felt that he had really prepped these guys to be effective at the high school varsity level.

"Can you believe how good Hector and Paul started playing when they moved to forward?" Alex asks Mike.

"Yeah, and who would have ever thought that high-energy kid Aidan would wind up being so talented as a goalkeeper!" Mike replies.

DOI: 10.4324/9781003375449-14

"Well, that's credit to you," Alex says. "Your hunch really paid off with that kid."

"Here's to a great year, Coach," Mike says, holding up his glass.

"Thanks, Mike," Alex responds as he clinks glasses with everyone at the table.

Later that night, as Alex checks his email one last time before going to bed, there is a new message in his inbox. It's from Mitch. It's a reminder about the annual end-of-the-year awards banquet the school has for the athletes. It's always a pretty good time, with faculty and parents giving homage to the hard work their kids and coaches have done during the fall sports season. Most of the email contains pretty standard stuff: start times for the banquet, awards to be given, food to be served, and so on. But there is a small caveat at the end that gives Alex pause. The line simply states, "Coaches Alex and Mike, please stay after the banquet for a quick get-together and talk."

Alex tells his wife, Charlotte, about the email. "I don't know what to think about it," he says.

"They probably just want to give you additional thanks for the job you did," Charlotte replies. "After all, you did really help them out by taking the soccer position for them at the last second."

Charlotte is right about Alex helping the school get out of a bind. The previous middle school coach left suddenly to take a high school coaching job in another state. This left the school scrambling to find a coach at the last second. Administrators called Alex a real team player and a "godsend" for agreeing to pick up the extra coaching responsibilities so late in the year.

"Do you really think that's what this is about?" Alex asks. "I see Mitch in the halls at school almost every day, and he never mentioned that anything was wrong."

"Of course I do. You know how much those kids love you. And you just know their parents feel the same way."

Alex heaves a sigh of relief. "You're right, honey," he says. "I'm probably just overthinking it."

Alex spends the next day at work excitedly awaiting the awards banquet and the subsequent meeting. He feels like a little kid waiting for Christmas morning not knowing what exactly he's getting but knowing it's going to be great.

That night the awards banquet goes off without a hitch. All the student athletes and parents alike seem to have a great time. As the banquet is winding down, Charlotte kisses Alex and tells him she'll meet him back at the house after his meeting is over.

"Enjoy your moment, honey. You really deserve it," she says.

He smiles back at her. "Thanks. See ya at home."

After the room empties of most of the guests and athletes, Mitch asks Alex and Mike to come up together to the front of the room and sit with him. Both Mike and Alex grin a little as they prepare for the praise they are about to receive and sit down on either side of Mitch.

"Okay, everyone, let's take a seat and get the meeting started," Mitch announces to the group.

Mitch begins reading from a prepared page of notes. "Let me start by saying that we all really appreciate the service that these two men have done for our school. We were in a bind, and they stepped up and helped us out. With that said, though, some of the parents and administrators have concerns about some of these gentlemen's coaching practices and the subsequent results of those practices this past season."

Alex and Mike stare at each other absolutely stunned by what they have just heard. At first, they both sit silently.

Then Alex speaks up. "I don't understand, Mitch."

"You'll have your chance to speak, Alex," Mitch replies. "Let's give everyone who came here a chance to talk first; then you'll have an opportunity to respond to their concerns."

The first to voice his opinion is Aidan's father. "Why is my son, one of the fastest kids in the county, playing as a goalkeeper? He should be on the front line scoring goals, not in the goal watching the game like a spectator."

Next to speak are Paul's and then Hector's parents. Paul's parents argue that Paul is better suited on defense and shouldn't be wasting his time on the front line because by doing so he has little hope of getting that college scholarship he wants so badly. Hector's parents argue a different point. They feel that the offense is too conservative and that Hector is not able to showcase his talents. A large contingency of parents is also very upset about the overall record of the team.

"If we had left things the way they were when the season started, we wouldn't have those two bad losses and all those ties," one parent retorts.

"Why would you change things around and screw up our record?" another one chimes in.

As the complaints continue, Alex sits there dumbfounded, waiting for his turn to speak. He has no idea what to say when his chance to defend himself arrives. Replaying the season over in his head, he reflects on a few comments by parents that, at the time, seemed completely innocuous. Comments like "A loss is better than a tie" and "at least he's enjoying being on the team" now take on a different meaning. What had come across as parents' support might have actually been a building frustration. Even more surprising is the complete turnaround of his athletic director. What about those statements Mitch fed him about "player development" and "getting the kids ready for varsity" before he agreed to coach the team? Alex feels completely blindsided. This night has certainly not ended the way he thought it would.

Questions for Consideration

1. Who are the stakeholders in this case?
2. What should or could Alex have done to avoid the miscommunication and subsequent negative experience that he and his assistant were forced to endure?
3. Do you think that Alex is at fault? Who else in this scenario might be at fault? Why?
4. If you were Alex, what would you do next and why?
5. How much emphasis should be placed on winning versus player skill development? How might it be situation specific?
6. Many parents are going to provide you with their input. What strategy or strategies can you implement to ensure that communication between parents and coaches is effective and mutually beneficial?

References and Further Readings

Dorsch, T. E., Wright, E., Eckardt, V. C., Elliott, S., Thrower, S. N., & Knight, C. J. (2021). A history of parent involvement in organized youth sport: A scoping review. *Sport, Exercise, and Performance Psychology, 10*(4), 536–557. https://doi.org/10.1037/spy0000266

Harwood, C. G., & Knight, C. J. (2016). Parenting in sport. *Sport, Exercise, and Performance Psychology, 5*(2), 84–88. https://doi.org/10.1037/spy0000063

Lephogole, P. (2022, April 11). Parental involvement must feed sport development. *Sunday Standard.* www.sundaystandard.info/parental-involvement-must-feed-in-sport-development/

Settembre, J. (2022, September 23). Hey, helicopter parents – Your bad sportsmanship is killing kids' love of the game: Experts. *New York Post.* https://nypost.com/2022/09/23/helicopter-parenting-is-ruining-youth-sports-and-harming-kids/

Villano, M. (2022, September 6). How parents can keep youth sports fun for kids. *CNN.* www.cnn.com/2022/09/06/health/youth-sports-fun-wellness/index.html

14 The Unsupportive Parent

Christy Robinson is about to be a ninth grader at Washington Jr. High. She just moved to Laughlin, Nevada, over the summer and is ready to take on the challenges that lie ahead of her at her new school. Christy has always been a very good athlete and is looking forward to competing as a gymnast for the Washington Wildcats. She practiced throughout the summer and worked out regularly at a local gym. She dreams of one day competing in college. She understands that in order to achieve her dream, she is going to have to work very hard and devote the majority of her time to gymnastics. She is a rather good student, and in her elementary and middle school days, she was always able to make at least Bs, even without studying.

Christy was transferred to her new school because of her father's job in the military. Michael Robinson is an extremely strict father who expects a lot out of his daughter. He doesn't necessarily care for sports, but he's somewhat supportive of Christy's gymnastics. Michael places higher emphasis on getting an education, being respectful, and doing what is right. Christy hasn't seen her father much over the past few years due to several deployments overseas and is glad he is back.

The first week of school, Christy tries to get her bearings. Finding her classes in an unfamiliar setting is a challenge in itself. She begins to meet other students, but it's hard to fit in not only because she's a freshman but also because she's a member of an ethnic minority. Washington Jr. High is a primarily Caucasian school without much diversity, and its students are of a high socioeconomic status. Christy's family is middle class, but her father is African American, and her mother is Caucasian. She resembles her father more than her mother and is a lean and toned 5 feet 6 inches. She is a noticeable addition to Washington's hallways. Gradually, she settles in and feels comfortable at her new school. She can't wait to start competing for the Wildcats.

Christy met Coach Becky Anderson before the school year started. She is the head gymnastics coach for the female Wildcats, but she has also been coaching swimming at the junior high. Gymnastics is always put on the back burner at Washington until the fall sports are over, so there are no coaches to run the squads until the fall season is over. This is the case for all the schools throughout the conference in which Washington competes. Christy is enrolled in athletics for seventh period; however, as a gymnast, she goes to study hall for that hour until the competitive season begins.

The first semester is going well for Christy. Her classmates are all nice to her, and she is making several new friends. She met two other girls in study hall, Vicky and

DOI: 10.4324/9781003375449-15

Shannon, who are also on the gym squad, and they quickly became friends. They found out that Christy moved into the neighborhood where they live, and they all spend time together after school and on weekends. Christy has walked into what she believes to be the perfect fit for her ninth-grade year.

October arrives, and although the fall sports program is still in full swing, the gymnastics season is quickly approaching. At this point, Coach Anderson meets with the girls who are hoping to join the team. They discuss what is expected of them the coming season. One of Coach Anderson's rules is that if you don't come to practice, you don't compete. Before every season, she always has a team rules sheet that all the girls take home to their parents. She has each player and the players' parents sign the sheet so that if anyone breaks a rule during the season, she has in writing what the consequences will be. She talks to the team members about the importance of following the rules and how they will be enforced. She has also created a code of conduct that is prominently displayed in both her office and the gym.

Christy spends most of her time in the gym practicing gymnastics hoping to be a starter when season time comes. However, because she's spending so much time on gymnastics, she's not spending very much time on her studies. This is not uncommon for her, but this year is a little different. She's in ninth grade now, and the academic standards are higher at her new school. Even though Washington isn't actually part of the high school campus, ninth grade is still considered high school as far as academics are concerned. The curriculum is more complex and requires more time to study and prepare. As a result, Christy's grades aren't as high as usual: she has two Cs, three Bs, and one A. When her father finds out about the Cs, he gets very upset. He gives Christy a stern talk about how academics need to be a higher priority than gymnastics and makes Christy come directly home after school to study.

The fall sports season finally ends, and gymnastics and the other spring sports quickly become the topic of conversation around school. Christy is extremely excited to start practice and show her new coach what she's capable of. When the Wildcats start practice, Coach Anderson immediately knows that Christy is going to make a significant impact on the team. Without question she is the best gymnast on the team and will help turn last year's average team into a conference contender.

The first meet is a spectacular start. Christy is the overall high scorer and is already starting to take leadership of the team. Her teammates like her and don't mind that a new kid has come into the spotlight. They win the meet, and Christy wins all around. Everything is going great, and it looks like the Washington Wildcats are on their way to a winning season. Coach Anderson loves the way things are going and is delighted to have such a star.

The following week, while the team is practicing for its conference meet, Christy's father walks into the gym. He immediately heads over to Coach Anderson and waits for her to finish talking to one of her gymnasts.

"Coach, Christy is going to have to leave practice early today," Mr. Robinson says.

"Is everything all right?" Coach Anderson asks.

"Yes, we just have something we need to take care of at home."

"Okay. We need her back as soon as possible, though. Christy is a huge part of this squad."

"She'll be back whenever we get things straightened out at home."

Coach Anderson is left speechless in the middle of her own practice. She isn't really sure what to say to Mr. Robinson, Christy, or any of the other squad members. She continues on with practice without her star athlete but keeps wondering what is going on with Christy and her father. "Is everything going to be all right? Am I going to have Christy at practice tomorrow?" she asks herself. They have another important meet in two days, and her best gymnast has just been pulled out of practice by her father.

The next day at school, Coach Anderson goes to Christy's first-period English class and asks her teacher for permission to talk to Christy out in the hall.

"Is everything okay, Christy? What was yesterday all about?" Coach Anderson asks.

"Well, Coach, my dad isn't going to let me practice again today. He's making me come home right after school," Christy answers.

"What's the deal? Are you in trouble? Is there anything I can do to help? I really need you on this squad, Christy."

"My dad's not happy with my grades, for one thing. You saw my mid-quarter report, Coach. My grades aren't that bad, but my dad has very high expectations of me when it comes to my grades."

"So that's it? It's just your grades? We can get help with your grades if that's the problem."

"Well, with all the time I've been spending practicing, I haven't been getting most of my chores done either. My dad is pretty strict, and he thinks that because I'm spending all of my time with gymnastics, I don't understand what's really important. I dunno."

"Let's see if we can get something worked out. I want to help you, Christy, so I'll give your dad a call today and see if there's anything I can do. You're a very good gymnast, and I think you have a future in gymnastics. We don't need to let something as simple as chores keep you from participating. Get back to class, and work hard to get those grades up."

"Thanks, Coach. I will."

Coach Anderson walks down to her office and begins looking for the sheet that contains the phone numbers of all her players' parents. She finds Michael Robinson's number and dials it. The phone rings three times and then a deep voice answers, "Hello."

"Hi, Mr. Robinson. This is Christy's gymnastics coach, Becky Anderson," Coach Anderson says.

"Hello, Coach Anderson. What can I do for you?" Mr. Robinson responds.

"I was just calling to check in with you on Christy's situation. I spoke with her this morning, and she said you aren't going to let her practice again today."

"That's right. Christy needs to get her priorities straight, and I think a little time off from gymnastics might help her do that."

"Christy, as I'm sure you already know, is a very talented gymnast, Mr. Robinson. We really need her on this team to be a—"

"Coach Anderson," he interrupts, "with all due respect, gymnastics is not something that I'm interested in my daughter excelling at. Ever since she started gymnastics at your school she's been slacking in the classroom, not spending any time at home with her family, not getting simple household responsibilities done, or, quite frankly, anything that she should be doing. I understand that you want her to help make your gymnastics squad better, but in reality, I don't really care. There are more important things, and in my house that's the way it's going to be."

"Mr. Robinson, I—"

"Thanks, Coach Anderson, but this conversation is over."

Mr. Robinson hangs up without letting Coach Anderson say anything else. She is very confused. She isn't sure if she has offended Mr. Robinson or not. It wasn't her intention, but this is a no-nonsense man with whom she is dealing. Furthermore, she can't understand why Mr. Robinson can't see the potential that Christy has and why he wouldn't want to see it develop into something more. She is very frustrated.

That afternoon at practice, Christy is nowhere to be found. Coach Anderson doesn't really expect to see her but is hoping that through some miracle she might show up. A couple of the gymnasts approach Coach Anderson to ask what's going on with Christy.

"Is she going to be able to compete, Coach?" one of the gymnasts asks.

"Girls, I'm not sure as of right now what's going on," Coach Anderson replies. "We have to focus on the next meet for now. We're going to continue on with what we have and adjust to the situation. Now let's get to work!" She doesn't want to let her team see how worried she is, so she does her best to hide it. Practice goes on without Christy as they prepare for their next meet.

The next day at practice, Christy still isn't there. Coach Anderson spoke with Christy at lunch and was informed that she wouldn't be at practice again, so her absence really isn't a surprise. She wants to call Mr. Robinson again but is afraid it will just make the situation worse. She stares at her phone trying to think of something to say to him but just can't pick it up and call. She assumes she isn't going to have Christy for the meet the next day since she hasn't shown up for practice.

The day of the meet Coach Anderson hasn't seen or talked to Christy. She has already made a contingency plan since it looks like her best gymnast isn't going to be at the meet. When the seventh period comes and all of the gymnasts are out on the mats getting loosened up, she notices Christy out laughing and joking with the rest of the girls.

"Christy?" Coach Anderson calls out. "Come over here for a second."

"Yeah, Coach, what's up?" Christy says.

"Are you going to be here for the meet tonight?"

"Yeah, Coach."

"So, is everything cleared up with your dad?"

"Yeah, Coach, everything's cool."

"Okay, get out there and get warmed up."

Christy runs off and begins warming up with her teammates. Coach Anderson is relieved in a way, but the team had agreed with the rule that if you don't come to practice, you don't get to play. She decides not to say anything about it and start Christy anyway. "The other girls won't say anything," she thinks to herself. "They want to win, and they like Christy. They know we're a much better squad with her. Anyway, it isn't her fault she couldn't practice."

That night, Christy leads the team to a second victory. Afterward, Coach Anderson gives her post-meet talk in the locker room, telling the girls how proud she is of their improvement from last year and how she hopes that they will continue to work hard and get better throughout the season. No one mentions Christy missing practice, and it looks as if she's going to have her star back. But that all changes very quickly. As Coach Anderson makes sure everyone has cleared the gym and starts to lock it up, she hears someone open the back door. When she peeks around the corner to see who it is, she sees Mr. Robinson.

"Hey! Mr. Robinson!" Coach Anderson says excitedly. "Christy sure did vault gre—"

"Coach Anderson," he interrupts, "I don't know who you think you are, but Christy is my daughter, and when I tell her to do something, I expect her to do it, and I don't care what her gymnastics coach thinks."

"What are you talking about?" Coach Anderson asks, very confused. "Christy said that everything was straightened out at home."

"I told her this morning that she was not supposed to compete tonight, but apparently her gymnastics coach talked her into sticking around for the meet. I do not appreciate it. It is not your place to interfere with the way I want to handle my daughter. Christy will not be a part of your team anymore, and thanks to you, I may never allow her to compete again because you broke your own rule," Mr. Robinson proclaims and then slams the door behind him, leaving Coach Anderson frustrated, frightened, and completely confused.

She waits several minutes to make sure that Mr. Robinson has had time to leave the parking lot before she walks to her car. Once she sees that the coast is clear, she heads home with all sorts of thoughts racing through her head. She replays the entire incident from the talk with Christy to the run-in with her father over and over in her mind. She can't figure out where she missed something, but obviously there had to be something that she just wasn't seeing. She goes to bed that night not knowing what to expect on Monday morning.

Questions for Consideration

1. Who are the stakeholders in this case?
2. What are the critical issues in this case?
3. Do you agree with Coach Anderson's decision to let Christy compete in the first meet? Why or why not?
4. At what point do you think Coach Anderson should have contacted Christy's father? Or should she even have tried to contact him?
5. How do you feel about the way Coach Anderson spoke with Christy's father over the phone?
6. What do you think Coach Anderson could have done differently to handle the situation of Christy missing practice?
7. Is there anything you should do about players with grades that are below average, or do you believe that as long as a player is eligible it doesn't matter?
8. What do you think Coach Anderson's next step should be in handling the situation with Christy's father?
9. What do you think of codes of conduct created by coaches? What do you think should or should not be included?

References and Further Readings

Cross, J. L., & Fouke, B. W. (2019). Redefining the scholar-athlete. *Frontiers in Sports and Active Living, 1*, 10. https://doi.org/10.3389/fspor.2019.00010

Farnsworth, M. L., & O'Neal, C. W. (2021). Military stressors, parent-adolescent relationship quality, and adolescent adjustment. *Journal of Child & Family Studies, 30*(11), 2718–2731. https://doi.org/10.1007/s10826-021-02106-y

Fowler, B. (2021, November 10). Mother accused of fighting coach at Dawkins Middle School. *WSPA.com*. www.wspa.com/news/local-news/mother-charged-after-fighting-coach-at-dawkins-middle-school/

Janssen, J. (2013, November 6). Involving your athletes in team discipline. *Coach & A.D.* https://coachad.com/articles/involving-your-athletes-in-team-discipline/

Lopez, L. (2022). Factors affecting enrollment in the military youth sports program at Naval Station Rota, Spain [ProQuest Information & Learning]. *Dissertation Abstracts International: Section B: The Sciences and Engineering, 83*(11–B).

Wretman, C. J. (2017). School sports participation and academic achievement in middle and high school. *Journal of the Society for Social Work and Research, 8*(3), 399–420. https://doi.org/10.1086/693117

Yankowski, P. (2022, October 3). Parent assaulted Norwalk youth football coach during game, officials say. *The Hour*. www.thehour.com/news/article/Norwalk-youth-football-coach-injured-parent-17483302.php

15 Stretching the Rules

Coach Carl Malone is nearing the end of his third year at St. Pete High School in Petersburg, Texas. He enjoys his job as a physical education teacher and head football coach and considers himself lucky to be the head coach at such a prestigious high school, especially so early in his coaching career.

St. Pete is a typical football town where the football players and coaches are widely recognized. On a typical Friday night, the entire town closes down to attend the night's big game, leaving a ghostly quiet downtown. The school has a rich football tradition, having won six of the last ten state championships prior to Malone's arrival.

Coach Malone inherited an undefeated state championship team and had to fill the shoes of the local coaching legend, Coach Gerald Wilson, who coached at the school for 25 years. Wilson won 8 state championships and made 16 consecutive playoff appearances in his tenure. The school administration was publicly questioned for hiring outside the district when it sought out Coach Malone from a neighboring town. Although he was already successful at 4A, many felt he couldn't live up to the pressures of 7A football. However, Coach Malone has demonstrated that he has the integrity and leadership necessary to be a successful coach, a point he emphasized in his interview.

Coach Malone's first year is a rough one considering the previous year's unbeaten season. Many regarded the team as the best in state history. It's a tough legacy for him to live up to. In his first season, the team finishes with an 8–5 record, makes the playoffs, but loses in the first round. Despite the early playoff exit, his job remains secure. Coach Malone is still upset with the team's showing and vows to do better the next year.

That following summer, Coach Malone reevaluates his coaching philosophy and system. At his previous school he used a passing offense that utilized a lot of gadget plays. At St. Pete he wants to carry on the tradition set forth by Coach Wilson but knows he will have to blend styles and have the program take on a new identity. Adjustments will have to be made if he wants to retain his dream job as the head coach at the most successful school in the state.

The coaching staff is busy that summer attending coaching clinics, where they get to meet with fellow coaches in the area. At one of the meetings, Coach Malone is able to meet and talk with Coach Brad Johnson, an up-and-coming head coach at the junior high level in the neighboring town of Charleston.

"Brad, why aren't you at the high school level? You're a proven winner, so why haven't they moved you up yet?" Coach Malone asks him.

DOI: 10.4324/9781003375449-16

"Well, it's kind of complicated." Brad replies. "Someone once had the audacity to accuse me of cheating. Nothing ever came of it, but it's been hard for me to move up because my reputation has taken a hit."

"Well, I'd take you on my staff any day. I'm looking for winners, so if something comes up, can I give you a call?"

"I wouldn't say no to the offer if you did. I've been wanting to move up for some time, and it would get my foot in the door. Keep me posted."

The dog days of summer arrive, and another season of high school football beckons. Coach Malone has retained his entire staff from the previous year and feels good about entering his second year at the school. Using the knowledge acquired from the past season and summer clinics, they decided to implement a more sophisticated offense without fully abandoning the hard-nosed mentality that was the previous regime's forte. Practices seem to fly by, and before they know it the first game arrives.

Coach Malone knows the first game will be a big one because St. Pete is pitted against the previous year's runner-up, Kringle High. "Put up or shut up time for the St. Pete Saints," reads one of the local papers. Another states, "If they stumble out of the blocks, look for Coach Malone to be replaced at season's end." The game has the feeling of a playoff game even though the August night air warms the stadium. Coach Malone is nervous but eager to see the new offense come to life on the field.

The game goes better than Coach Malone could have hoped. His Saints, using their new offense, blow out Kringle 36–10. In fact, the next five games see St. Pete beat all its opponents, averaging a staggering 32 points per game. With a 6–0 record, Coach Malone is feeling fairly good about the direction the season is heading.

Game seven, however, is a different matter altogether, for St. Pete faces Charleston, its fiercest rival. Although the Saints jumps to an early 14-point lead, the team crumbles in the fourth quarter and eventually loses 28–17. "This is unacceptable," Coach Malone thinks to himself. "We have to find ways to win the big games." He knows that the two teams will probably meet again later in the year and the outcome will have to be different.

As if predestined, both Coach Malone's Saints and their rivals Charleston make it to the championship game.

The game begins in dramatic fashion with St. Pete's quarterback the recipient of a cheap shot. Coach Malone recalls their earlier meeting and is reminded of how dirty the Charleston players had been. He hopes that this play doesn't set the tone for another nasty game.

The game remains close the entire evening, and with only seconds left on the clock, Charleston has the lead, 31–24. St. Pete has the ball at the opponent's 30-yard line, but the quarterback throws an interception sealing their fate. Bitterly disappointed, Coach Malone can't help but think of what might have happened if his quarterback hadn't been hurt.

Over the next few weeks, Coach Malone reflects on how the season ended. Although he can see the improvement his team made, he knows that Charleston's dirty play potentially cost him the championship. One week before spring practice, Coach Malone is informed that he's going to have to replace one of his coaches at the end of the school year. His offensive coordinator is retiring. Coach Malone doesn't hesitate to offer the job to Coach Johnson, the coach he met the previous summer. He is eager to work with such an accomplished young coach who has just completed an undefeated season at Charleston Junior High.

Coach Malone calls Coach Johnson into his office to discuss the upcoming season. Coach Johnson vows to do everything in his power to make sure that the team wins the championship. Coach Malone is impressed with Coach Johnson's determination and willingness to go beyond what is expected.

Spring practice begins the following week, and the players start with light workouts in shorts and shoulder pads. The state mandates that practice is to last two hours and that teams are allowed full-contact drills only during the second week of spring practice. During the first two days, Coach Malone follows the schedule he implemented last spring. However, on the third day, Coach Johnson approaches him with the idea of extending the practice time and starting practice in pads early.

"This is how we're going to get better," says Coach Johnson. "We've got to get a head start on the competition."

"That's illegal and we can't do it," Coach Malone responds.

"It's not like anyone will know. We'll just say we were unaware of the rules if we do get caught."

Coach Malone thinks maybe this is why Charleston has a much better team, and he eventually gives in. The team moves inside to avoid prying eyes, and full-contact drills are conducted, and practices are extended an hour. Coach Malone knows that he could get in trouble but figures the sanctions would be minimal even if they do get caught.

Coach Johnson continues to push the boundaries. During a phone call between the two coaches, Coach Johnson tells Coach Malone that they have to take some risks in order to guarantee success.

"I know you were worried about making the decision to start full contact early. I was like that once too, but everyone else is bending the rules and so should we if we're going to beat them," Coach Johnson says.

"What are you suggesting?" asks Coach Malone cautiously.

"How do you think I only lost four games in four years? At times you have to bend the rules if you want to win. I thought you brought me here so we could win championships."

"Of course I want to win!" Coach Malone exclaims. "But we must be careful. I don't want my career in the gutter."

"Trust me on this, and we'll be champs before you know it."

The phone call ends, and both coaches begin working on the game plan for next week's practice.

Spring practice ends without a hitch, and there is a noticeable improvement in the team's offense through the summer. Coach Malone is eager to get the season started and erase any memory of last year's defeat in the state championship. He feels that he is building a legacy of his own at St. Pete because he is coming off a state championship appearance. However, he knows he will have to win the state championship to truly get the critics off his back.

The first five games are blowouts, with St. Pete averaging 44 points per game. The coaching staff seems to work well together and has all the players buying into the new offensive system. St. Pete is now the number-two team in the state, trailing Charleston. The stage is set for an epic showdown between the two teams.

The following week is going to be hectic, and there is a definite "big game" atmosphere in the air. Coach Malone feels that he has to win against Charleston; the Saints have suffered two losses in a row against Charleston, and a third would be demoralizing to his team. He also knows in the back of his mind that Charleston sometimes plays dirty and thinks there must be some way of leveling the playing field.

Coach Malone conducts his usual Sunday afternoon staff meeting to discuss the game plan for Charleston. Coach Johnson stands up and tells the staff that he has a play that might catch the Charleston defense off guard at the end of the game; however, he won't tell anyone what it is.

All week the team practices hard to slow down Charleston's high-scoring offense. Coach Malone remembers that some of the opposition's players have played dirty and can't help but think the coaches are advocating this type of behavior. After all, in each of the three previous meetings with Charleston, one of his players had been injured from some form of questionable hit.

Friday night arrives, and it's obvious that both the St. Pete players and the coaches want this one bad. The game begins, and St. Pete receives the ball. On the tenth play of the game, St. Pete's quarterback drops back to pass but is struck in the knee by an opposing player. Although it's flagged for a late hit, Coach Malone is infuriated that his players are once again getting taken out by cheap hits.

As the clock winds down in the fourth quarter, the score is tied at 14. Coach Malone knows he doesn't want to go into overtime and tells Coach Johnson he wants to go for broke. Coach Johnson smiles at him and tells him he has just the play in mind.

With 30 seconds remaining, a time-out is called to set up the play. Coach Johnson says the play has never been practiced before because it's simple to run. He calls in his offense closely so that no one else can hear. Four receivers are to run to the wide side of the field where St. Pete has its bench. Coach Johnson tells the receiver closest to the sideline that when the ball is snapped, he is to run off the field and onto the sideline. He explains that this will throw off the defender and that he will probably follow the receiver out of bounds. He also instructs another player on the bench to count to six and step out farther up the field. The play is designed to provide a distraction and have one player run off the field and another run back on and slip behind the defense for a wide-open touchdown catch. It is an illegal play, but they haven't yet been caught bending the rules, so there is no reason to think this won't work.

The ball is snapped, and the play is run. Coaches, players, and fans of both sides hold their collective breath. The players do exactly as instructed, and the "receiver" who stepped back onto the field is behind the defense and wide open. The quarterback turns and fires the ball deep. Touchdown! There are no flags on the play, and the touchdown stands. They have finally beaten Charleston!

One day passes, and nothing is made of the play. After the game was over, Coach Johnson had told Coach Malone what he did. Coach Malone's fury had been tempered by the knowledge that they had won and nothing had been said. However, on Sunday, Coach Malone receives a call from the athletic director requesting an immediate meeting. Upon arrival, the athletic director replays the play on tape and asks Coach Malone to explain it. Trying to formulate a response, Coach Malone can't help but wonder what might have happened if he had never met Coach Johnson.

Questions for Consideration

1. Who are the stakeholders in this case?
2. What punishment do you feel Coach Malone and Coach Johnson should receive? Should anyone else affiliated with the team or the school be punished?
3. Should the players be punished?
4. What warning signs did Coach Johnson give? Do you think Coach Malone was aware of what Coach Johnson had planned?
5. Whom could the student-athletes have turned to if they felt they had been asked to cheat?
6. Do you think Coach Malone gave Coach Johnson too much authority?
7. How would you define the role of an assistant coach?
8. Do you think it would make a difference if governing bodies of sports required all coaches to attend ethics training?

References and Further Readings

Cheating in Youth Sports and the Psychology Behind It. (n.d.). *National sports ID*. www.nationalsportsid.com/cheating-in-youth-sports-and-the-psychology-behind-it/

Chen, Y., Buggy, C., & Kelly, S. (2019). Winning at all costs: A review of risk-taking behaviour and sporting injury from an occupational safety and health perspective. *Sports Medicine—Open*, *5*(1), 15. https://doi.org/10.1186/s40798-019-0189-9

Fenoglio, R., & Taylor, W. (2014). From winning-at-all-costs to give us back our game: Perspective transformation in youth sport coaches. *Physical Education and Sport Pedagogy*, *19*(2), 191–204.

Hurst, P., Kavussanu, M., Swain, J., & Ring, C. (2022). The role of moral identity and regret on cheating in sport. *International Journal of Sport and Exercise Psychology*, *21*(2), 230–248. https://doi.org/10.1080/1612197X.2022.2057567

Stephenson, C. (2022, March 12). Will Wade fired by LSU after NCAA accuses him of 5 major violations, unethical conduct. *AL.com*. www.al.com/sports/2022/03/will-wade-out-as-basketball-coach-at-lsu.html

Sumner, D. E. (2013). Cheating in sports. *Saturday Evening Post*, *285*(6), 56–58.

16 Age and Competition

It is a hot August afternoon when Joan Williams picks up her nine-year-old daughter, Shelby, from her first day of school outside Rowley School for the Deaf. Joan is nervous about hearing how the day went, but Shelby greets her with a smile, a hug, and a kiss on the cheek. Shelby can't wait to tell her mom about all the things they did in school that day, especially on the field during hockey practice. After listening to her giving all the details, Joan feels relieved that her daughter experienced a good first day of school. Shelby's father Doug is also delighted at her first day's experience.

The Williams family moved to southern Virginia before Shelby entered fourth grade. They did so in order to allow Shelby to attend Rowley School for the Deaf, where she would be surrounded by other deaf students her age as well as nuns experienced in working with children who are deaf or have hearing impairments.

Each student at Rowley School for the Deaf is encouraged to participate in an extracurricular activity of his or her choice for his or her seventh-hour class. This activity period takes the place of the physical education class that would typically be part of the curriculum in a traditional elementary school. Shelby and her parents think field hockey will be a good sport to learn, so she is enrolled. It seems they have made the right choice.

The year progresses smoothly, and Shelby is playing field hockey as well as or better than the sixth-grade girls. By the end of the first semester, Sister Helena, Shelby's coach, moves Shelby to play with the sixth-grade girls because of her obvious natural talent for the sport. Field hockey quickly becomes one of Shelby's favorite things to talk about, and she is soon recognized as a great student–athlete at the school. Shelby has a smile on her face every day when her mom greets her outside the school after practice. Joan and Doug have met with the nuns several times throughout the year and have heard nothing but positive comments about Shelby's performance in the classroom and at field hockey practice. They are both ecstatic to know her daughter is making an impact at the school as well as having wonderful teachers to give her the education and physical exercise she needs to succeed.

As her first day in fifth grade begins, Shelby is excited to see her old classmates and, of course, her field hockey coach, Sister Helena. A week of classes passes by uneventfully before practices can begin. When the seventh hour finally arrives, Shelby throws down her pink backpack in the locker room and quickly changes for field hockey practice. She slips on her jersey, shorts, shin pads, and cleats and runs to the field and

DOI: 10.4324/9781003375449-17

begins to stretch, awaiting Sister Helena to begin the day's practice. Shelby knows that this year will be fun since she is going to compete in her first game with the older teammates.

With her hand, Sister Helena signals the team to run two laps around the field. Shelby jumps up from her sitting stretch and runs straight to the front of the group to run her laps. Sister Helena watches Shelby run and knows she is going to be the star of the team once again. With Shelby's combined running speed and her flawless technique with the hockey stick, they will have a chance at their first state championship appearance in more than a decade.

Each day Shelby improves, and she loves the one-on-one attention she receives from Sister Helena after their practices. Sister Helena is sometimes gruff, but Shelby knows field hockey is particularly important to her, and she's just trying to get the best out of her players. The day before Shelby's first game, Sister Helena sits down next to Shelby and signs to her.

"Get some sleep tonight; tomorrow is your first big game. If you play like you did today in practice, I'm pretty sure you're going to score! Do you want to score a goal tomorrow?"

Shelby without hesitation nods with a big smile on her face and wriggles in her seat with excitement and anticipation about the next day's game.

"Okay, good. I need you to be ready tomorrow, Shelby. We're expecting a lot from you."

The next day, school goes by quickly. Shelby and her teammates get dressed and are excited to play their first game against the team from a rival deaf school that traveled from Georgia. A big green light glowing in the stadium-lit field represents the "go" buzzer to begin the game. Shelby automatically gets into position to receive the ball from her teammates. She dribbles the ball closer to the goal, where the rival school's goalie stares Shelby in the eyes. However, she shows no sign of being intimidated by the older player. Instead, in one smooth movement, she swings her stick and strikes the ball right past the goalie, scoring her first goal. Shelby throws her arms in the air and looks to the crowd to see her mom and dad on their feet clapping. Sister Helena also signs excitedly, "Yes! Great job, Shelby!"

The team is extremely excited. The score stays at 1–0 until halftime, but a minute into the second half, the opposition ties the game at 1–1. Sister Helena is fuming on the sidelines. Shelby knows she needs to score another goal to help her team win. Play continues, and the ball is hit toward Shelby; she looks over to Sister Helena for directions and receives the signal to run. Shelby runs full speed and begins dribbling the ball toward the opponent's goal. However, she doesn't look up and runs into an opposing player twice her size. She collapses to the ground and grips her right knee, screaming at the top of her lungs. Sister Helena runs to Shelby and signals her to get up. Slowly Shelby pushes herself up and limps to the sideline, where she sits on the bench for the remainder of the game.

The opposition scores another goal with only minutes left in the game, effectively winning it. Sister Helena signs to the girls to go into the locker room for the postgame talk. The girls slowly walk into the locker room, still breathing hard as sweat continues to drip from their faces.

"Girls, what happened out there?" Sister Helena signs to the team. "I thought we were ready to play hard."

Sister Helena looks at Shelby and signs, "Shelby, how could you not see that person in front of you? If you hadn't gotten hurt and instead had been a big girl and stayed in the game, we would've had a shot at the win. We've only just started the season, and we're losers." She then adds, "Monday before school I want you to come see me on the field."

With a sigh, Sister Helena looks away and signs to her other players, "You are all dismissed; I'm done talking to you."

The girls look around the room at each other and then slowly get up and walk out the door to the field, where their parents are waiting.

Monday arrives, and Shelby is dropped off at school 30 minutes before her first class starts, as Sister Helena requested. She walks into Sister Helena's office, and she signals Shelby to sit down.

"I expected more from you Shelby," signs Sister Helena. "I thought you wanted to make it to the state championships. As a Rowley School athlete, you have to get up from being pushed down and continue to play hard. So, you realize how important it is that I want you to run laps this morning and every morning before school. That should teach you to put in a little more effort when we play." With that, Sister Helena makes Shelby run laps fully dressed in her uniform before the start of classes. Her knee still hurts, but she tries not to let it show. With only a few minutes before the start of classes, Shelby is now limping and very sweaty. Sister Helena ends the "practice" and lets Shelby go. She reminds Shelby that the extra practice is for her own good and isn't to tell anyone else about it. Sister Helena then asks Shelby if there is anything she needs to say about letting her team down in the game the previous Friday night.

Shelby puts her hands in front of her and looks down at the turf before signing, "I'm sorry. I'll do better next time."

Shelby doesn't know what she's done wrong but has a feeling it's not going to be the last time she'll be doing extra practice.

Later that day, after practice, Joan is at the school leaning on her car waiting to pick up her daughter. However, Joan senses something different about Shelby. Although she's very excited to see her mother, she doesn't have the twinkle in her eyes that she usually does. Joan signs to Shelby to ask her if anything is wrong, but Shelby just shakes her head no. The look on her face concerns Joan.

The next morning, Joan goes inside the school to speak to Sister Helena to find out why Shelby is being required to come in early and to see if anything of consequence happened the day before to make Shelby upset. Sister Helena assures Joan that Shelby will be fine; she tells her that Shelby didn't have her best practice yesterday and that Shelby is upset with herself. She explains that she wants Shelby to come in early so that she can teach Shelby some of the tactics that the older athletes on the team already know.

Over the next several weeks, Shelby continues to work hard on her homework and field hockey but isn't her energetic self on the field during practices. The early morning runs are exhausting, and her knee is still sore. Joan and Doug can't understand why she is struggling so much in practice when she has such a great coach to help her succeed. They wonder whether they are putting too much pressure on her at such an early age.

Shelby's grades get progressively worse, and she hasn't scored another goal. Still, Sister Helena assures Joan and Doug that the dedication to field hockey will help Shelby not only with her falling grades in school but also with the challenges of life.

The second quarter of school begins with Shelby failing to show enthusiasm about going back to school even after a week away from her friends and teachers. One of the other nuns signs to Shelby asking her whether she is ready for practice. Shelby doesn't respond. Instead, as she looks at the nun a tear rolls down her little face. The nun, knowing something is wrong, decides to ask Sister Helena. Sister Helena thanks her for her concern and tells her she will take care of it.

The next morning, at "practice," Sister Helena is furious. Shelby can see the dark clouds passing over Sister Helena's face and knows she is in for it.

"I don't know who you've been talking to, Shelby, but you shouldn't be whining," Sister Helena signs aggressively. "I can't believe you're complaining when I'm only trying to help you. Do you think I enjoy coming out here before classes to work with you? Don't you want to be the best player you can be?"

Shelby is terrified and can only nod her head.

"Maybe I'm being too easy on you," Sister Helena continues. "Maybe some shuttle runs will teach you to appreciate what I'm doing for you."

Although Shelby gives it everything she has, as she returns to the start line on her second sprint, she feels and hears tearing in her knee. The pain is blinding, and she collapses to the turf unconscious.

When Shelby regains consciousness at the hospital, she finally tearfully tells her parents what has been going on. The doctors tell her parents that her knee will never be the same. Field hockey, which had once been the highlight of her day, has become her own personal nightmare.

Questions for Consideration

1. Who are the stakeholders in this case?
2. Who or what action could have helped to prevent such a situation?
3. Do you think children should be placed in competitive sports at such an early age? Why or why not?
4. Do you think this is the first time that Sister Helena has used such punishments to "educate"?
5. What action might you take as an athletic director of a school when a situation like this occurs?
6. Are coaching standards different in public versus private schools?
7. Coaches can have enormous influence over athletes, particularly those who are young. Do you think coaches should be more closely monitored?
8. Were your opinions influenced by the private, religious school setting?
9. Do you think Shelby should have been placed on a team with athletes her own age?
10. As a coach, you notice a drastic difference in one of your athlete's demeanor over a period of time. The student denies that anything is wrong, but you know something is going on. Should you do anything about it? If so, what would you do and to whom would you speak? Can you justify why you would take this course of action?

References and Further Readings

Amaro, S. (2021, December 20). Setting practice limits to promote wellness in high school sports. *National Federation of State High School Associations (NFHS).* https://nfhs.org/articles/setting-practice-limits-to-promote-wellness-in-high-school-sports/

American Academy of Orthopaedic Surgeons. (2022, June). A guide to safety for young athletes. *OrthoInfo.* https://orthoinfo.aaos.org/en/staying-healthy/a-guide-to-safety-for-young-athletes/

Barney, D., Pleban, F. T., Fullmer, M., Griffiths, R., Higginson, K., & Whaley, D. (2016). Appropriate or inappropriate practice: Exercise as punishment in physical education class. *Physical Educator, 73*(1), 59–73. https://doi.org/10.18666/TPE-2016-V73-I1-5952

Grasdalsmoen, M., Clarsen, B., & Sivertsen, B. (2022). Mental health in elite student athletes: Exploring the link between training volume and mental health problems in Norwegian college and university students. *Frontiers in Sports and Active Living, 4*, 817757. https://doi.org/10.3389/fspor.2022.817757

Horst, E. (2021, December 27). Pushing through the pain. *Scot Scoop.* https://scotscoop.com/pushing-through-the-pain/

Rosenthal, M., Pagnano-Richardson, K., & Burak, L. (2010). Alternatives to using exercise as punishment. *Journal of Physical Education, Recreation & Dance (JOPERD), 81*(5), 44–48.

17 Eating Disorders

Watch What You Say

Coach Michael Brown's second year as the head volleyball coach for the Riverview High Ravens is off to a great start. It's a sunny August in Connecticut and two-a-days have begun. The team is returning all its starters from the previous year, and he is hoping to go one better than state runner-up this year. Michael has four all-state players returning, and practices are going great. He thinks to himself, "Life can't get any better. If everything goes as it should, my team and I will be getting our state championship rings in about three months."

Out of all the returning all-state players, sophomore Sylvia Cortez is by far the most promising. As a freshman last year, she was voted by the coaches in the conference as an all-state selection. Michael knows that Sylvia could be a great college player one day, but there is something holding her back. Sylvia is well over 6 feet tall, but she's about 50 pounds overweight. Sylvia is a dominating force in the middle, averaging more than 15 kills per match, but Michael has always thought she could be even better if she were at her peak fitness level and lost some weight. He has no idea how to broach this subject with Sylvia, as he doesn't want to hurt her feelings.

One day after practice, Sylvia's mom approaches Michael.

After some small talk about the season she says, "Sylvia's always asking me how she could improve. I know she's a bit overweight, but she doesn't listen to me these days. I think that if you approached her privately after practice one day and explained to her that it would greatly improve her game if she dropped some weight, it might help her to get serious about it. I know she'd take it a lot better from you than me, since you're her coach."

Michael thinks hard about what Ms. Cortez has just asked. Even with her mom's blessing, he's more than a little apprehensive about bringing this up with Sylvia. He tells Ms. Cortez how he feels, but Ms. Cortez is insistent that this conversation needs to happen between Michael and Sylvia and tells him she will support him completely.

Michael decides he will talk to Sylvia about her weight issue but not before producing a good way to approach her so that he won't hurt her self-confidence. A few days after his conversation with Ms. Cortez, and after considering his options, Michael pulls Sylvia over to the side one day after practice and carefully broaches the subject.

"Sylvia," Michael says with a caring tone, "your mom and I had a little talk about you a few days ago. We were discussing many things about your game and in what ways you could improve on your outstanding freshman year. We also talked about how you

DOI: 10.4324/9781003375449-18

could improve your game so that colleges would seriously start taking a look at you for a scholarship. We both agreed that you are an awesome player already but that you could take your game to the next level if you got a little more disciplined with your eating and exercising habits. I am not saying that you are obese or terribly overweight, but we both think you would feel a whole lot better, and your game would improve by leaps and bounds, if you could lose a little bit of weight."

Sylvia doesn't know how to respond to what Michael has just said. "He thinks I'm a nasty, obese whale who is never going to get better until I drop a hundred pounds," she thinks to herself. She is incredibly embarrassed and hurt by what he has said but decides not to share those feelings with her coach. She just looks at him, with anger filling her up inside, and forces a smile.

"Thank you for caring so much about me, Coach," she replies. "If this is what you think I should do, then I'll work very hard and try to lose some weight. I know you have my best interests in mind, so I promise you I'll do better."

Sylvia can't sleep that night. She keeps replaying the conversation over and over again. Did he not know how hard it is to be a larger girl in a society that places so much emphasis on being thin? Did he not know that she knows she is big but is really trying to work on it and doesn't need him to remind her of it? Sylvia has never told her mom or anyone else that people have always talked about how big she is and that it really bothers her.

Sylvia decides that night that enough is enough. She is tired of everyone looking at her and talking about how much she weighs and how big she is. She is tired of other coaches always calling her "the big girl." It's bad enough that all the other coaches talk about her, but now her own coach and her own mother think she's fat.

"From now on, I'm just not going to eat at all," she says to herself. This is a rash statement, and she knows she's being overdramatic, but she is so fed up with the situation that she doesn't care.

Sylvia knows she isn't really going to stop eating completely, but she decides she's going to "take a break" from eating for a few days, just to get a jump start on her new diet, whatever that is going to be. Coach asked her to lose weight, but he never advised her how to go about it.

The first two days of Sylvia's "break from eating" are really challenging, but she has always been stubborn and had made up her mind that she wasn't going to give in. She doesn't stop eating completely; she drinks a Diet Coke and eats a few saltine crackers each day for lunch and dinner. She thinks this will suffice for these first couple of days. As the next two days go by, she can't believe how much easier it's getting to not eat regular meals. Sometimes it gets a little tempting, but she just drinks her Diet Coke, and her hunger goes away. Any time her hunger gets really bad, she tells herself, "If I'm ever going to get to Michael and my mom's standards, then I'd better just get over these hunger pains."

By the next week, Sylvia hasn't really eaten anything of substance in six days. She is ecstatic to find that she has lost 6 pounds and can't wait to get to practice to tell Coach. "I'm not that fat whale everyone thinks I am," she says to herself. She isn't going to stop this new diet of Diet Cokes and saltines until she is skinny and beautiful.

Sylvia arrives at practice 30 minutes early and is ready to get started. She immediately finds Michael.

"Coach, I've already lost 10 pounds! This whole diet thing is going great, and I'm going to be so good by the end of the year."

Michael pauses with a slight frown on his face. "That's a lot of weight to lose in one week." Not wanting to disappoint her, he adds, "But I've always heard that when you start a diet, you lose a lot of weight the first two weeks and then the weight loss levels off. Make sure you're taking care of yourself. I'm proud of you. It's tough to sacrifice certain foods, but remember, in the end it's only going to help you out. Keep up the good work!"

For the rest of that week, Sylvia continues with her meager diet and notices that it's getting easier to not think about food. She starts to believe she can go on living her life on Diet Cokes and crackers. She does feel tired a lot but figures it's just a passing phase.

Sylvia becomes good at lying to anyone who wonders about what diet she is on. She tells people she's eating three small meals a day and just cutting back on fatty foods. Every night at dinner her mother makes her a healthy dinner before she leaves for her night shift, and Sylvia takes it upstairs and flushes it down the toilet. She always tells her mother how delicious her meals were, and her mother never catches on.

The next week school officially begins, and Sylvia is excited to start the new year looking skinnier than ever. She hasn't been this thin in years but knows she has a long way to go to get as skinny as she wants to be. She can't believe how many people notice her weight loss. So many girls who have never really been that friendly with her pass by her in the halls and tell her how skinny she looks. She says to herself, "People are finally noticing me for something more than my huge size. This whole diet thing is really working. Maybe Coach really *was* trying to help me."

Michael begins to notice that Sylvia is acting differently. She's not as animated as she normally is, and she really isn't playing as well as he had expected. She is lethargic and seems abnormally weak. He figures that she has just had a long week since it's the first week back at school, but he pulls her aside at the end of practice just to check.

"Sylvia, I've noticed that you aren't playing the same way you normally do. Is everything okay?" he asks. "You've obviously taken seriously what I talked about with you earlier this month, and you look great. I'm just worried that you're not getting enough nutrition for your body to keep up with our workouts. Are you trying to make sure that you get a lot of protein, vitamins, and minerals in your diet?"

"Yeah, Coach," Sylvia responds. "It's just been a long week, but I'm really trying to take care of my body."

During the next week of practices, Michael notices that Sylvia's game is getting progressively worse and that she's still rapidly losing weight. He starts getting concerned that she isn't telling the whole truth about her "wonderful" diet. He doesn't know what to do. He feels he was really pressured into talking to Sylvia about her weight in the first place, and maybe that caused something negative to happen.

Michael decides to call Sylvia's mom to relay his concerns about Sylvia.

"Mrs. Cortez, this is Coach Brown."

"Hello, Coach. What can I do for you?" asks Ms. Cortez.

"I'm calling to let you know that I'm a little concerned about Sylvia. If you haven't noticed, she's losing weight pretty rapidly and seems really weak and slow as of late. Have you noticed any changes in her behavior, other than that she's on a low-fat diet?"

"Coach," Ms. Cortez responds, "Sylvia just took your advice to heart and has been very disciplined on her diet. I make sure she's getting good meals for dinner, so she's fine. She just has to adjust to her new body, and her metabolism is still adjusting to her diet changes. Just make sure you keep on telling her to keep up the good work and encourage her to pick up the pace at practice."

Michael feels better about Sylvia after his talk with her mother. He doesn't think much more about Sylvia over the weekend. When he gets to school on Monday, he heads to his office to plan his practice for the day. About 30 minutes later the principal, Dr. Rimmer, knocks on his door. He has a very concerned look on his face.

"Coach," Dr. Rimmer says, "I have some bad news for you. This weekend, Sylvia Cortez collapsed at her house. She was rushed to the hospital, and after some testing, they realized that Sylvia is extremely malnourished. Child Services was about to take her mother into custody for child abuse, but Sylvia confessed that it has been more than three weeks since she has eaten anything more than a few saltines and three or four Diet Cokes a day. She's been diagnosed with anorexia nervosa, and she'll be out of school for the rest of the semester. Her family now must try to find her help with her eating disorder. I know that she's your best player, but you're going to have to try to compete without her now. I don't know what caused this, but maybe you could check in with her later to see how she is."

Michael is shocked. "What have I done?" he thinks. "I know exactly what caused this eating disorder. If I had followed my gut feeling, I would never have talked to her about her weight. Now I've got my star player out for the rest of the semester, and she'll never be the same. I wish I could have known about what was going on in her life outside of school hours. I just don't know what I'm going to do."

Questions for Consideration

1. Who are the stakeholders in this case?
2. What are the underlying issues in this case?
3. What role did Ms. Cortez play in Sylvia's eating disorder? Did anyone else play a role? How?
4. What could Michael have done differently when he discussed the weight issue with Sylvia and afterward to prevent something like this from happening?
5. What other ways could Michael have handled discussing Sylvia's weight issue with her?
6. Should Michael be held accountable for the drastic actions that Sylvia took and the resulting consequences?
7. What advice would you give Michael on what to do now that Sylvia's condition is out in the open?
8. What are anorexia nervosa and bulimia nervosa? Which sports are most likely to contribute to an athlete's developing these disorders?
9. What other eating/body image disorders might exist within athletics? How can these be combated?

References and Further Readings

Baghurst, T., & Lirgg, C. (2009). Characteristics of muscle dysmorphia in male football, weight training, and competitive natural and non-natural bodybuilding samples. *Body Image, 6*(3), 221–227. https://doi.org/10.1016/j.bodyim.2009.03.002

Bothwell, S. (2021, December 20). What athletes are most likely to have an eating disorder. *Eating Disorder Hope.* www.eatingdisorderhope.com/blog/what-athletes-are-most-likely-to-have-an-eating-disorder

Chapa, D. A. N., Johnson, S. N., Richson, B. N., Bjorlie, K., Won, Y. Q., Nelson, S. V., Ayres, J., Jun, D., Forbush, K. T., Christensen, K. A., & Perko, V. L. (2022). Eating-disorder psychopathology in female athletes and non-athletes: A meta-analysis. *International Journal of Eating Disorders, 55*(7), 861–885. https://doi.org/10.1002/eat.23748

Harrel, T. L. (2022). Female athletes' perceptions of coach responsibility when managing female athletes with an eating disorder: A systematic literature review [ProQuest Information & Learning]. *Dissertation Abstracts International: Section B: The Sciences and Engineering, 83*(2–B).

Neglia, A. (2021). Nutrition, eating disorders, and behavior in athletes. *Psychiatric Clinics of North America, 44*(3), 431–441. https://doi.org/10.1016/j.psc.2021.04.009

Stiles, B. (n.d.). Eating disorders in athletics: Pressure from parents, coaches, and appearance expectations play role. *Moms Team.* www.momsteam.com/nutrition/eating-disorders-in-athletics-external-pressures-and-societal-expectations-play-large-role

Steinbach, P. (2022, April 28). UF soccer coach leaving amid eating habits controversy. *Athletic-Business.* www.athleticbusiness.com/operations/personnel/article/15291417/uf-soccer-coach-leaving-amid-eating-habits-controversy#:~:text=The%20University%20of%20Florida%20fired,eating%20habits%20and%20body%20compositions.

Walter, N., Heinen, T., & Elbe, A. M. (2022). Factors associated with disordered eating and eating disorder symptoms in adolescent elite athletes. *Sports Psychiatry: Journal of Sports and Exercise Psychiatry, 1*(2), 47–56. https://doi.org/10.1024/2674-0052/a000012

18 Coach–Athlete Relationships

Sarah Johnson is ecstatic about the prospect of getting hired her first year out of college and is ready to take on the world. Although graduating with her master's in English should ensure a steady job, her true passion in life is cheerleading. She was a member of a cheerleading squad throughout high school and college. Cheerleading is in her blood, and she really wants the opportunity to be around the sport for years to come as a coach.

Shortly before graduation, Sarah receives a phone call about an application she submitted for a job teaching freshman and sophomore English at Gilbert High School. She is asked to come in for an interview. The school is small and located in a district just outside of Sarah's hometown in Wisconsin. It's a perfect setup. Her family would be nearby, and she still considers the area her home.

The interview goes great, and at the end Mr. Bell, the principal, asks if Sarah has any questions regarding the position. She wonders whether it would be wise to ask about a cheerleading coaching spot but decides to wait to make sure she gets the job first.

Sarah's phone rings two days later. It's Mr. Bell calling to offer her the position.

Sarah doesn't hesitate to give him an answer. "Yes, I accept. Thank you, Mr. Bell!" She is so excited that it almost slips her mind to mention the cheerleading coaching spot. She blurts out, "Mr. Bell, I'd like to take this opportunity to express my interest in any cheerleading coach opening that may become available, at any level."

He pauses and then replies, "Oh, okay. There are no positions open at this time that I'm aware of, but I'll keep your name in mind for the future."

"I would appreciate that. Thank you again!" Sarah replies.

About two weeks before the first day of school, Sarah has settled in the area and is preparing for her classes. One day while she's in her classroom hanging up posters, Mr. Bell walks in.

She smiles and says, "Hello, Mr. Bell!"

"Hi, Sarah," he responds. "I've got some news for you." He pauses as they sit down. "Sarah, the cheerleading coach has found out she's pregnant, and she's not planning to return after the birth of her new baby. I know this is your first year as a teacher, and you're still getting settled into your new life here, but I wanted to offer the spot to you first before—"

Sarah cuts off Mr. Bell. "*Yes!* I would love to take the position! Thank you so much!" He chuckles and congratulates her on her new title.

DOI: 10.4324/9781003375449-19

Sarah begins planning that night; she has so many things to get ready for the girls, so much planning to do with the camps, the uniforms, and dances. She quickly becomes consumed with her new appointed position; her role as an English teacher takes a back burner to her new cheerleading coach duties. Her mother stops by one evening to help Sarah with the unpacking. Her mom is a little surprised by the cheerleading magazines scattered everywhere and the printouts of cheers and chants and the spreadsheets of her budget that are taped all over the living room walls. Herself a former teacher, she reminds Sarah that she was hired to teach English and that the cheerleading coaching position should come second to that. Sarah nods her head but is thinking of the new uniforms she has ordered.

The school year begins before Sarah knows it. She is soon overwhelmed with everything that her new career is throwing her way. Her days are long and tiresome. She wakes up at 5:45 A.M. to ensure enough time to work out and shower before having to be at school at 7:30. She teaches English classes for five periods. During her planning period, she prepares for cheer practice and then holds practice with the girls until 5:00. After the school day is over, Sarah heads home to make dinner, tries to fight off her closing eyelids long enough to make her lesson plans for her classes the next day, and then goes to bed exhausted.

Game days are a different story. Sarah fits in her planning for English whenever she can; sometimes it never even happens, and she just wings her class. She and her team meet at the football stadium to practice before the game or to hop on the bus for the trip. Those nights are the toughest, and the following mornings are even worse.

Sarah was very close with her cheerleading coach in high school, Ms. Goodman. She was a role model and good friend to Sarah and many of the cheer girls. Ms. Goodman seemed to have a supernatural ability to balance her time among teaching, cheer responsibilities, family time, and being there for the girls. Many of the relationships she established with her cheer girls resembled those between a mother and a daughter. They not only respected her but also trusted her. It is exactly the type of relationship that Sarah wants to share with her squad members.

Sarah knows very little about the previous cheerleading coach, but she was successful, even if a little outdated. A change in style is necessary, but it isn't well received by everyone; there are mixed reactions from the girls, the parents, and the community. However, once Sarah establishes all the rules and begins to implement her style of coaching, the murmurings lessen. The girls love the new dances and uniforms, and everyone notices the nontraditional route Sarah is taking. The squad becomes very close, and the girls' dedication is obvious. The practices are longer, and more is expected out of the girls this year, but the results pay off. Over time, the squad begins to look better than it has in years. Everywhere Sarah goes in the small town she is congratulated. The girls begin to trust Sarah, and the bond between them grows. She consistently stresses the importance of the squad being close and reassures the girls that they can come to her anytime with anything.

A handful of the parents become concerned about the time that is required for an extracurricular activity. They are worried that cheerleading is going to take away from the girls' schoolwork. Sarah addresses this issue through emails and phone calls but never holds a face-to-face meeting to discuss the issue.

Sarah gave all the girls a handout at the beginning of the year that outlined the team's rules and expectations. She included all her contact information including her cell phone number so that the girls could contact her if they were going to be late or absent. As the relationship between her and the girls has grown, however, some of the girls have called her on a regular basis just to talk. There have even been several occasions when some of the girls have shown up at her house just to hang out and watch a movie. This has become another concern with some of the girls' parents. They think it is unhealthy to be good friends with a teacher or coach. However, Sarah considers herself more of a mother figure than a friend.

Most of the girls are doing great balancing all of their responsibilities. However, halfway into football season, Sarah becomes concerned about one of the girls. Michelle is a senior and captain of the squad. All the girls look up to her because she's a great role model. She is always early to practice, stays late to help clean up, and offers help to any of the girls who are struggling.

Michelle recently went through a bad breakup with Rylie, a football player she had dated for three years. It is rumored that Michelle is drinking heavily. She has begun to show up to practice late if she shows up at all. The days she arrives on time, she always has some reason to leave early, or she claims to be sick. Sarah is worried about her behavior and the effect it is having on the squad. She calls Michelle and asks her to come in early to practice one day so that they can talk.

Sarah is in her classroom when Michelle shows up at the door and knocks, "Hey, Miss Johnson."

"Michelle. Hi! Come in." Michelle walks over to the desk and sits down. It's obvious she hasn't been getting much sleep, as there are black circles under her eyes and her hair is messy.

"How are you?" asks Sarah. "I've been really concerned about you the last couple of weeks. You've been showing up late to practice, leaving early, and just not acting like yourself lately." She decides to wait to see what Michelle says before addressing the drinking issue.

"I've just got a lot on my mind. I don't know what to do without Rylie. We were together for so long, and now that we aren't I feel backward. I don't come to practice late on purpose; I just don't care about anything like I used to."

Sarah hesitates, then replies, "I know this is hard and we all want to be there for you, so you don't have to go through this alone. I just know what you're capable of and I hate to see you waste any more of your time or potential on this boy."

"Okay, I'm going to do better. I promise," Michelle says.

"Michelle, there's one other thing I want to talk to you about." Sarah knows she has to bring up the rumors about her drinking, but it makes her uncomfortable. "I've been hearing some talk about some drinking." Sarah knows Michelle's parents; they have been incredibly involved in the cheer program this year. She is certain they would be furious if they had any idea that Michelle had been involved with alcohol.

Michelle's eyes get noticeably big, and she looks scared. "Ms. Johnson, you *can't* tell my parents. They'll kill me. *Please!* I'm sorry. I'm gonna change, and things will go back to normal. I promise. Please, you can't say a word. My parents would make me quit the squad. My life would be over!"

Sarah is a little shocked at Michelle's reaction. She glances over at the clock and realizes they are late to practice. "Okay, I'm taking your word on this," she replies. "I know you're better than that, and I don't want to hear any more talk about drinking. You know you can always come to me for anything, but if I hear about this again, I'll have to have a meeting with your parents, and there'll be some sort of punishment." Sarah isn't sure if that's the correct response, but it will have to do for now until she has more time to think about the conversation.

Later that night, Sarah thinks back to the conversation and wonders if she handled everything the right way. She felt better after the talk but is worried that maybe she should have talked with Michelle's parents. She just doesn't want to hurt the relationship she has established with all the girls. She knows they trust her, and she doesn't want to break that trust. Besides, she already gave Michelle her word; she can't go back on that.

For the remainder of football season, everything seems to go back to normal. Michelle comes to practice on time, she gives 100 percent, and she seems to be on the right track.

The first playoff game rolls around. Gilbert is playing Bay Side, the neighboring town and biggest rival. The entire week is dedicated to Friday's game. Each day is a different spirit theme, and the excitement is unbelievable. The girls had worked on a halftime routine for weeks, and they are a little nervous because the whole town is expected to be at the game.

At halftime Gilbert is up by 7, and the crowd goes crazy as the girls take the field. Their routine is flawless, and the bleachers roar with applause as the girls finish. For the remainder of the game, Sarah is bombarded with compliments and praise.

Even though Sarah is invited out by some of the coaches after the game, she just wants to go home and crash. Later that night, Sarah's dreams are interrupted by the melody of her cell phone. She scrambles to find it in her purse. She is stunned when she sees her clock: it's 3:45 A.M. The caller is Hannah, another of Sarah's senior cheer girls. She answers the phone, but it's very hard to hear her over the music and people in the background. "Hannah! *Hello!* Can you hear me?" Sarah asks.

"Ms. Johnson! Hey, Ms. Johnson!" Hannah yells. It's pretty obvious that Hannah is at a party and intoxicated.

"Hannah, what's going on? Is everything okay?" Sarah asks, somewhat irritated.

"It's Michelle. We're at this party, and . . . and she didn't mean to drink this much. She . . . she's really sick. You have to come get her. I can't call my parents, and we can't call her parents. You are the only one I knew to call. I'm sorry." Sarah has a sick feeling in her stomach.

"Hannah, can you give me directions to where you're at?"

Hannah gives the directions, and Sarah drives to the party as quickly as she can. There are cars scattered around, and the place is a mess. Music is blaring, beer cans cover the ground and the porch, and people are passed out in the front yard. She is appalled. Hannah rushes through the front door to greet Sarah with a hug that resembles a football tackle. Hannah is extremely drunk, and Sarah can smell the liquor on her.

"I'm soooo happy you're here. Michelle is this way," Hannah slurs.

"I am so disappointed in you girls," Sarah replies calmly but seething with anger. Hannah leads Sarah through the crowded hallways, where she spots many more of her girls with drinks in their hands, stumbling around. Sarah is stopped several times by her girls and football players.

When one of the football players, Adam, sees Sarah, he quickly gives his cell phone to his friend. "Take my picture with Miss Johnson." He hurries over and flings his arms around Sarah's neck.

Snap. "Got it," his friend boasts.

Sarah is outraged at this point but has bigger issues to deal with. Adam and several of the other partygoers follow Hannah and Sarah to the back bathroom. Michelle is passed out on the floor with her hand clasped to the toilet seat.

"Oh my gosh, awesome." Adam chuckles. He quickly begins to snap as many photos with his phone as he can before Sarah demands that he leave the bathroom. He reluctantly obliges.

After several failed attempts to get Michelle to her feet, Sarah instructs one of the boys to pick her up and help carry her to the car. As soon as Sarah turns around, she sees another flash.

"Adam! Not one more picture," Sarah scolds.

They continue outside, and once she gets Michelle into the car, she instructs Hannah to stay with her. She walks back inside to the party and announces, "Party's over." She unplugs the music and adds, "There will be consequences on Monday. No one is to leave here unless you have a sober driver. Everyone else find a spot on the floor." She goes back out to her car, gets in, and drives away.

The drive home is silent; Sarah has no idea what to say or how to handle this situation. "They don't teach you how to deal with these issues in college," she thinks to herself. When they get to her house, Sarah instructs Hannah to go sleep in the spare bedroom while she stays awake with Michelle. After feeding Michelle almost an entire loaf of bread and eight glasses of water, she finally allows her to go to sleep.

Despite her exhaustion, Sarah lies in bed for the longest time wondering how she is going to deal with this. She is worried about where her relationship with the girls has gotten her and what type of problems it's going to cause the squad. Finally, she falls into a restless sleep.

The next morning when Sarah crawls out of bed, the girls are both awake. "Are you two okay?" she asks.

Michelle responds first. She quietly says, "I'm so sorry—"

Sarah cuts her off. "I don't want to talk with either of you about this right now. I'm driving you each to your house, and we'll talk about this after I figure out what to do with you. All I have to say is that I expected better out of you both."

After taking them both home, she heads back to her house to sleep. As soon as she lies down her phone rings. This time it's her home phone. She rolls over and answers with pure exhaustion and disgust.

"Hello?"

"Sarah, it's Mr. Bell."

"Hi, Mr. Bell. How are you?" Sarah answers thinking he must be calling to congratulate her on the outstanding performance from the night before.

"I've been better, Sarah. I'm afraid we have a bit of an issue. Can you come down to the police station immediately?"

Sarah sits straight up in bed. "Police station! Why, what's happened? Is everything okay? Is it one of my girls?"

"Well, Sarah, I'm down here with the athletic director and some very concerned parents. I got a call early this morning about a party last night. Some of our students were brought into custody, and some inappropriate pictures have been found."

Sarah can hear the disappointment in Mr. Bell's voice. She almost drops the phone. She feels sick to her stomach as she remembers the photos that were shot of her at the party. This doesn't look good. She tells Mr. Bell, "I'll be right there."

Questions for Consideration

1. Who are the stakeholders in this case?
2. Did you find it out of the ordinary that Sarah wanted to be so close with her squad members and not her students in class?
3. What are some things Sarah could have tried to implement with her squad in order to build an appropriate rapport with her athletes?
4. Did you foresee the end result? At what point did you realize something was going to happen to Sarah or one of the girls? Could it have been prevented?
5. Do you think Sarah should have called a meeting with Michelle's parents when she first started seeing the change in her behavior?
6. As a coach, if one of your athletes was experiencing a situation similar to what Michelle experienced, whom would you go to first for assistance? Why?
7. Do you think it is appropriate to give out your cell phone number to your athletes? Why or why not?
8. Did Sarah act appropriately by going to the party? What would you have done?

References and Further Readings

Bringer, J. D., Brackenridge, C. H., & Johnston, L. H. (2002). Defining appropriateness in coach-athlete sexual relationships: The voice of coaches. *Journal of sexual aggression*, *8*(2), 83–98. https://doi.org/10.1080/13552600208413341

Drewe, S. B. (2002). The coach-athlete relationship: How close is too close? *Journal of the Philosophy of Sport*, *29*(2), 174. https://doi.org/10.1080/00948705.2002.9714633

Holt, S. (2013, November 18). Coaches as "friends": Females vs. males – Knowing the boundaries. *Youth Development Through Recreation and Sport*. https://youthdevelopmentthrurecreation.wordpress.com/2013/11/18/coaches-as-friends-females-vs-males-knowing-the-boundaries/

Jowett, S., & Carpenter, P. (2015). The concept of rules in the coach-athlete relationship. *Sports Coaching Review*, *4*(1). https://doi.org/10.1080/21640629.2015.1106145

O'Riordan, S. (2021). *Introduction to coaching psychology*. Routledge.

Walsh, K. (2021, November 16). Adult coach-athlete relationships: The complexities and potential risks. *Ann Craft Trust*. www.anncrafttrust.org/adult-coach-athlete-relationships-the-complexities-and-potential-risks-saferculturesafersport/

19 The Importance of Athlete Equality

In Daphneville, Alabama, the unspoken mantra for high school athletics is "Win at all costs." Daphneville High School has put together one of the state's winningest programs in Alabama high school football history, under the watchful eye of 20-year veteran head coach Bill Taylor. With a cavalcade of conference and state title banners decorating the gym, the Devils are primed to make another convincing run for the state playoffs and are said by some to be the favorites to win it all again.

This year will be different, though, because Coach Taylor resigned at the end of the previous season. After winning his seventh state title, he decided to "hang up the cleats" and go out on top. The athletic director and school board took into careful consideration the school's powerful reputation as the standard for excellence in high school football, and an in-depth search was done to find the "next coaching legend" to fill the void. The search team was looking for someone with experience and drive, as well as a disciplinarian who had the same tough style as Coach Taylor.

The hard work finally paid off, and in early February it is announced that new head coach Bo Phillips will be the new field general for Daphneville High School. Bo Phillips was a stalwart quarterback at Spartan State and later served as a graduate assistant for the Southeast Alabama coaching staff. He quickly built an impressive resume. Shortly after his stint in college ball, he moved into the high school realm, where he cut his teeth as the offensive coordinator at Alabama powerhouse Heritage High School. He made a stop at Danner High, winning a state championship in the process, before landing at Daphneville. He is a man with grit and determination.

Coach Phillips wastes no time in whipping his boys into shape through a grueling off-season regimen that's not dissimilar to a boot camp. He has a fairly harsh tongue, which he believes helps to motivate his players. A few of the players decide that they want no more and end up quitting the team. Coach Phillips looks at this as getting rid of weak links and pays it no mind.

Spring football brings about some nice surprises in quarterback Taylor Barnes. The junior-to-be acquired some valuable experience from the previous season when his predecessor was injured for two games. Tailback Drew Jones also shows a lot of promise coming out of spring ball. Unsurprisingly, the town is buzzing about the young talents' potential.

Two-a-days result in a few more kids dropping from the team. Coach Phillips had a knack for getting rid of weakness on his teams in the past. One player whom Coach Phillips sees as a weak link is senior Andre Bauer.

DOI: 10.4324/9781003375449-20

Andre loves football, and it shows. He is always cheering during team drills and conditioning sessions and seems to be the heart of the team. The only problem is that Andre has a mild mental disability. He can practice and compete with the team physically but shows his weakness when it comes to understanding the mental aspects of the game. Coach Phillips doesn't seem to care about Andre's condition and jabs at him from time to time throughout practices. "It's a simple drill, Andre! Are you too stupid to figure it out? I didn't know they allowed idiots to play football!" This is one of many examples of the mistreatment that Andre is forced to endure.

Fall camp follows a similar pattern to that of spring training, and gradually the players are whipped into a unit ready to play under the bright lights of the autumn Friday evenings. The team has weathered the storm of Coach Phillips's first two-a-days and is ready for a bit of downtime. However, the first day of gameday practice comes sooner than any of the players would have cared for. The whistle blows for the start of practice, and immediately the barrage of Coach Phillips's words hits like an artillery strike. "You all move slower'n cow crap! I see what the weekend did for you buncha Nancies!" This catches the players' attention in a less than desirable way.

After practice Taylor and Drew talk about Coach Phillips and the way practice went.

"Hey, Drew, do you think Coach Phillips is just breaking us in still?" asks Taylor.

"I don't know, man," answers Drew. "He was totally getting after us today!"

"Oh, well, he doesn't seem to have much of a problem with me, so whatever," Taylor responds casually.

After a dominating season opener against Metro Christian Prep, the following weeks show why so many have tagged the Devils as favorites to repeat for state. With big nonconference wins coming over North Florida Academy and St. Louis Prep, the Devils are picking up steam as they head into conference play.

Locals aren't the only ones to notice the quick success of the Devils. A few recruitment letters are starting to come in for Taylor and Drew regarding their success early in the season. Coach Phillips has had a small hand in getting his players noticed.

The players are performing at a high level, as was expected by the community; however, Coach Phillips never seems to notice. He still doesn't let up on his bellowing and abusive treatment of his players.

Conference play finally commences, and while the first three games are important, the conference games are serious. The Devils will have their hands full that Friday with Tannersville coming to town.

After practice Taylor and Drew are going to go hang out for supper at Taylor's house. As they drive home, they discuss their lack of approval for Coach Phillips.

"Do you think Coach Phillips hates us?" asks Taylor.

"I dunno," Drew replies. "He sure is being hateful toward us! I mean, I know this is the first conference game 'n' all, but come on! Give us a break! All we do is win!"

"Yeah, I know," replies Taylor. "It just seems like he doesn't care about us at all."

As the season progresses, the wins keep piling up for Daphneville. The Devils are undefeated and playoff bound. The players also seem to have gotten used to Coach Phillips's style, and with the praise that everyone else is showering on them, they lessen their complaining.

With two games remaining of the regular season, the Devils are in the hunt for the number one seed. However, it begins to dawn on some of the players that they are guaranteed only a few more games, and for most of them, this might be the only football they ever play again. The seniors take this to heart and want to make the most of their final campaign. On Monday after practice, a few of the upper-class students approach Coach Phillips to ask if Andre can get some playing time on Friday against the Crossdale Cougars.

"Hey, Coach Phillips," one of the players says. "We've been thinking about there being only a couple of games left in the season, and, well, we really want to see Andre play. He's been here since day one working his tail off, and it would be great to see him rewarded with some p.t."

"Are you boys serious?" asks Coach Phillips. "You really want him to play?"

"Yeah, Coach. We really wanna see him get a chance to get on the field and play a little," replies another player.

"Do you realize that we have maybe the two toughest games we'll play all year still on our schedule? You want a loser like him to potentially ruin your championship?"

"Yeah, Coach, we understand. It's just that we really want to be out there on the field with him, especially on senior night," replies a third player.

"Well, I don't know. We'll see. Maybe we'll get the kid some mop-up duty or something. But only if it's possible."

"That would be awesome, Coach!" a fourth player exclaims.

"Now don't you boys go filling his head and get his hopes up. We still have two games to play, and your heads need to be screwed on straight as ever."

That Friday brings more than the Devils wanted. They are playing away at Crossdale, and it seems as though they have bitten off more than they can chew. Daphneville is down 21 to 7 at the half, with the one score coming off a Taylor touchdown pass. Coach Phillips is so mad he could spit fire! He addresses the team at the halftime with a volcanic eruption of anger.

"What the—what do you call that?! You call that football?! Are you done?! Seniors! Do you just want to throw away a perfect season?! I'm embarrassed to call you my players!" With that, the coaches retreat to their offices to try to salvage what's left of their game plan.

The second half ends much like the first, with the Devils having no answer for the Cougars. Coach Phillips throws every name in the book at his players, even at Andre, who has yet to play but is still shouting encouragement from the bench.

"Just shut up, Andre! I'm so tired of you yelling in my ear. Go grab some bench someplace where I can't hear you and where you belong!"

Daphneville takes its lumps and heads back home to recover from the loss. As soon as they arrive at the school, Coach Phillips asks to see Taylor and Drew in his office.

"Boys, that game was just awful. I know both of you played hard, and I appreciate it. As you know, we've got Lee Academy this next week, and we have to win in order to get the number one seed."

The boys look confused, not sure what the coach is trying to say.

"I think the leadership of the team is in trouble."

"What do you mean?" replies Taylor.

"Well, I've had several seniors and captains come to me and ask if I would give Andre some playing time during the last couple of games. Honestly, I think they have their focus on something that just doesn't matter right now. I don't have time to be concerned with Andre getting on the field, especially after a loss like tonight!"

"What does this have to do with us, Coach?" asks Drew.

"I don't want Andre on this team anymore! He's a distraction that's causing the senior leadership to fall apart. I've put up with him until now 'cause he's dumb and all, but I think it would be in your best interests to take care of this matter. You know that the way this season goes will affect how heavily y'all are recruited."

"Really, Coach?" says Taylor.

"Definitely!" replies Coach Phillips. "You don't want to let the rest of the season tank and show everyone that we couldn't finish, do you?"

"No way, Coach!" Taylor exclaims.

"Good! Then I'm holding you two responsible for making sure that Andre doesn't want to be here anymore. Remember, boys, we must win at all costs!"

That weekend Taylor and Drew discuss what the coach asked of them.

"Do you think Coach wants us to hurt Andre?" asks Taylor.

"Not sure," replies Drew.

"I can see why Coach is upset with the seniors, but why us?"

"I dunno. This is just messed up."

Taylor is deeply troubled by what Coach Phillips asked of him and Drew. He feels that if he talks to his dad, he'll just play it off as no big deal. He also doesn't want to stir up any problems with anyone on the team especially this late in the season and with playoffs coming the following week.

"What should I do?" thinks Taylor. "If I get Coach Phillips in trouble, then what'll happen to the rest of the season? My recruitment could suffer if we don't finish well."

That Monday during lunch, Taylor goes to the school counselor to talk about his sticky situation.

"Ms. Graves, what should I do? I feel like I'm in a no-win situation!"

Ms. Graves assures him not to worry about the situation any longer and that she will deal with it. True to her word, she speaks with the athletic director, Walt Johns. As Coach Phillips is sitting down for dinner that evening, he receives a call.

"Coach Phillips, this is Walt Johns. I think we need to talk."

"Okay. What about?"

"It seems as though there's a situation regarding a couple of your players. They say you asked them to take care of a 'team problem' with respect to Andre Bauer. I need you to come down to the school immediately."

Coach Phillips knows exactly what is going on. He is about to determine how serious Daphneville High School and the town are about winning championships. "Surely they'll put rings before a nonplaying moron, won't they?" he thinks to himself.

Questions for Consideration

1. Who are the stakeholders in this case?
2. In your opinion, was Coach Phillips justified in tagging Andre as the root of the seniors' distraction? Do you think he could have been a distraction?
3. How could Coach Phillips have handled the situation with the seniors differently?
4. How would you define emotional abuse?

5. As a coach, what strategies could you implement in order to avoid becoming emotionally abusive with your players?
6. How would you recognize when you need to push a player to perform harder or better and when you have gone too far?
7. Have you ever witnessed or experienced emotional abuse during your athletic career?

References and Further Readings

Associated Press. (2005, July 15). Coach accused of keeping disabled boy off field. *ESPN*. www.espn.ph/espn/news/story?id=2109016

Blair, F. (2012, March 2). Saints players and coaches involved in scheme to hurt players should face jail. *Bleacher Report*. https://bleacherreport.com/articles/1089174-saints-players-and-coaches-involved-in-scheme-to-hurt-players-should-face-jail

Johnson, C. (2022, May 18). Fort Bend County high school athlete doesn't let his disability slow him down. *Click2Houston.com*. www.click2houston.com/sports/2022/05/18/fort-bend-county-high-school-athlete-doesnt-let-his-disability-slow-him-down/

Samuels, D. (2015, October 15). A HS coach has been accused of devising a plan and sending his players out to hurt an opponent. *Football Scoop*. https://footballscoop.com/news/a-hs-coach-has-been-accused-of-devising-a-plan-and-sending-his-players-out-to-hurt-an-opponent

Stanley, C., & Baghurst, T. (2022). *Reach every athlete: A guide to coaching athletes with hidden disabilities and conditions*. Routledge.

Vargas, T. M., Flores, M. M., Beyer, R., & Weaver, S. M. (2019). Parents' perceptions of coaching behaviors toward their child with a hidden disability in recreational youth sports. *Physical Educator*, *76*(3), 661–675.

Weiss, M. P. (2011). Supporting student athletes with disabilities: A case study. *Journal of Postsecondary Education and Disability*, *24*(2), 161–163.

20 Accusations

It Takes Just One

Life is fairly good for Jamie Bennett, high school biology teacher and head women's basketball coach at Polk High School in Polk, Michigan. It hasn't always been, but a strong work ethic and a willingness to try new things have produced results that are hard to ignore. Now, midway through the basketball season, the team is pushing strongly toward the playoffs. Jamie even suspects that they have an outside shot of winning state this year.

Coaching basketball is something Jamie always dreamed of doing. It wasn't easy trying to get a teaching degree in biology while volunteering as a basketball coach at a local school. However, Jamie never backs down from a challenge. There was certainly no shame in graduating with a 3.0 GPA considering how much time and effort had been put into basketball. At least Polk High School didn't think so when it hired Jamie.

When first offered the job, Jamie wasn't too sure about moving from the Northwest to Texas, but two things stuck out at the interview that were hard to ignore. First, this was the dream job opening that combined teaching biology and coaching a basketball team. Second, Polk is a small town simply crazy about sports, and the athletic director was extremely enthusiastic about a young, energetic coach coming to the school. The choice in the end had been relatively simple.

Although this is still just the first year, success has come quickly to Jamie. Classes are going well, and the athletic director, Paul Mitchell, has only good things to say. "Yeah," Jamie thinks, looking around the office at some of the more recent newspaper clippings, "things are going pretty good, but the season isn't over yet."

Managing a team and coaching a group of young high school girls have been difficult at times. There are the pressures of academics, dealing with in-team squabbles, relationship issues, and making sure the team gives 100 percent all of the time.

Leisha, one of the more talented players on the roster, has been a real issue lately. She is highly popular, which sometimes leads to non-basketball-related issues. Jamie sometimes feels that Leisha isn't putting forth her best effort. Sometimes she comes to practice late or doesn't even show up. In fact, because of her lack of effort and poor practice attendance, Jamie was forced to bench Leisha for the previous game in the hopes that it might initiate a positive change. Instead, Leisha was furious and sulked and scowled the entire game. At first Jamie felt justified in the decision, especially when they downed their local rivals, Monroe High, without Leisha

DOI: 10.4324/9781003375449-21

on the floor. But Leisha's obvious anger caused Jamie to think, "Maybe there's a better way to handle this. After all, I'm a new coach, and this may not be the best course of action for this situation. I don't want to exclude her from the team and make her feel alienated. She's one of my best players, and if she quit, I'd really be short of quality players."

Jamie thinks that Chris Lin, the boys' head basketball coach, might be able to offer some advice. Chris has been at Polk for two decades, and he might know how best to deal with this situation. Unfortunately, the boys' team practices at a different time, so Jamie and Chris rarely see each other except for scheduled coaching meetings. The teams often practice alone because the sports facility is located away from the main portion of the school. This isn't ideal, but there is no other choice. Jamie mentally puts away a note to talk to Chris about Leisha the next time they cross paths.

When practice begins the next day, Jamie does a quick headcount and is disappointed but not surprised to see that Leisha isn't in attendance. Pushing aside any thoughts of Leisha for the time being, Jamie runs the girls through their drills for the day. They are attentive and work hard and seem pretty excited by their most recent performance.

Once practice has ended and the gym is quiet, Jamie goes back to the office to run over some plays for their next game against St. Pierre High. However, a knock on the door quickly interrupts any prior plans. It's Leisha.

"Leisha. Hi! Come on in. We missed you today at practice," Jamie says.

"Hi," Leisha replies and then slowly walks in shutting the door behind her. Jamie feels a little awkward about the door being closed but dismisses her concern as no one is around anyway. Leisha walks over and sits in a chair opposite Jamie. She hasn't dressed out for practice, and Jamie is concerned about the suggestive clothing that Leisha has typically been wearing more frequently. Something is going on in Leisha's life.

"How are you?" Jamie begins. "Is everything all right? When I didn't see you at practice I wondered if something had happened."

"I'm fine, Coach. I've just been a little down lately, and when I didn't get to play the other night, I just wondered what the point was. I *really* wanna play, and even if I'm not the best player on the team I figured I'd always at least get some game time."

"I see," Jamie replies.

"It's just . . . I dunno. I figure if I'm going to be sitting on the bench, then why should I bother practicing and everything? I mean, I may as well quit and chill with my friends or something." Leisha raises her hands up and gestures in the air. "But I wanna play 'cause I love the game." She then slumps forward in a defeated fashion.

"All right. Well, let me explain where I'm coming from and then perhaps we can discuss how we can fix things, okay?" Jamie says. Leisha nods halfheartedly. "When I see you, Leisha, I see what a talented person you are. You're very gifted and have a natural athletic ability. You're one of the most talented players on the team, so it's hard for me and the team to see you not putting forth 100 percent effort. It's not fair to the rest of the team to let you play when you're not playing by the rules by coming late to practice and so on. Do you understand?" Leisha nods her head again, this time a little more positively. "I know you're capable, Leisha, but I can't put you into a game until

I know you're fully committed. I need you to show me how much you want to be on the team." Jamie sits back and waits for her response.

"Okay, Coach. I think I understand now," Leisha says. Resting her elbows on her knees she leans toward Jamie and asks, "Is there *anything else* I can do that might get me play time sooner?"

Jamie is confused by Leisha's question but replies, "No, I don't think so, Leisha, but just prove to me and the team that you're serious about playing."

"Okay. Thanks for seeing me, and I'll see you tomorrow at practice."

"On time," Jamie jokingly responds, to which Leisha laughs, gets up, opens the door, and heads out.

"I'm glad that's over," Jamie thinks. "That was a little strange, but I bet Leisha is going to be on track from here on out. I really think I got through to her. I can't wait until tomorrow's practice with the entire team this time. We're going to crush St. Pierre."

It has been a long day, so after finishing up at the office, Jamie heads home, grades some papers, has a nice supper, and goes to bed early. However, it isn't the alarm clock that wakes up Jamie early the next morning but a call.

"Hello?" Jamie says somewhat groggily.

"Hi, Jamie. This is Paul Mitchell."

"Hi, Paul. What's up?"

"Uh, this is a little difficult for me, Jamie, but I need you to come down to my office immediately."

Jamie is wide awake now. "Okay, this sounds serious. Can't you at least tell me what's going on? Why did you wake me up? I'll be down there in an hour anyway. Can't it wait?"

"Jamie, I've got a police officer here who wants to talk to you about a sexual allegation that's been made against you."

Jamie immediately feels sick and almost drops the phone as it all dawns on him: the after-practice meeting alone, the shut door, the suggestive clothing and body language, the "anything else." He wonders how he ever could have been so stupid!

Questions for Consideration

1. Who are the stakeholders in this case?
2. Who is at fault in this situation?
3. What was the first major mistake that Jamie made?
4. What should Jamie have done (consider logistics and behavior) to avoid getting into this situation?
5. Did you find anything in Jamie's dialogue with Leisha that could have been misconstrued?
6. Did your opinions change when you discovered that Jamie is male? Should they change?
7. What are the similarities and differences between a male coaching females and a female coaching males?
8. What do you suspect will be the outcome in this scenario?

References and Further Readings

Haensley-Clancy, M. (2022, February 8). Nobody believed those teenagers. *The Washington Post*. www.washingtonpost.com/sports/2022/02/08/rory-dames-eclipse-select-misconduct-allegations/

Mennen, J. (2020, September 12). Establishing and maintaining professional boundaries. *Coaches Guild*. www.coachesguild.net/articles/junior-sports/establishing-and-maintaining-professional-boundaries/

Parkinson, J. (2019). *Infractions: Rule violations, unethical conduct, and enforcement in the NCAA*. University of Nebraska Press.

Pépin-Gagné, J., & Parent, S. (2016). Coaching, touching, and false allegations of sexual abuse in Canada. *Journal of Sport & Social Issues*, *40*(2), 162–172. https://doi.org/10.1177/0193723515615176

Robbins, P. (2021, May 10). Coach – Protect yourself! *Culture in Sports*. https://cultureinsports.com/coach-protect-yourself/

Sanderson, J., & Weathers, M. R. (2020). Snapchat and child sexual abuse in sport: Protecting child athletes in the social media age. *Sport Management Review*, *23*(1), 81–94. https://doi.org/10.1016/j.smr.2019.04.006

United States Department of Justice. (2022). *Arizona couple indicted for attempting to extort Georgia Tech*. www.justice.gov/usao-ndga/pr/arizona-couple-indicted-attempting-extort-georgia-tech

USA Volleyball. (2022, November 1). *USA volleyball code of conduct*. chrome-extension://efaidnbmnnnibpcajpcglclefindmkaj/https://usavolleyball.org/wp-content/uploads/2020/12/2023-Code-of-Conduct.pdf

Wrestle Like a Girl. (n.d.). Protecting athletes & coaches. *Coaching Girl Wrestlers: Best Practices*. https://wrestlelikeagirl.org/protecting-athletes-and-coaches

21 In Loco Parentis

Before Coach Mike Smith dozes off, he begins daydreaming about what the upcoming baseball season might mean for him. Will it be another undefeated season and his third state championship? The thought makes Coach Smith smile because he knows this season looks promising. The Grover High School Grizzles are coming off a trip to the state playoffs and have quite a few returning starters. Both Coach Smith and his assistant coach, Jim Waters, are eagerly waiting for the baseball season to kick into full gear.

Coach Smith is in his late 40s and has been teaching physical education and coaching baseball at Grover High, Illinois, for the past 20 years. He is well known in the community for his coaching ability and accomplishments. "Well-spoken," "intelligent," and "compassionate" are all words that people use to describe Coach Smith. He takes the time to make personal relationships with his players. As a coach, he is strict on the practice field, and he always holds his players to extremely high standards when it comes to playing baseball. But off the field, Coach Smith sometimes lets things slide. He knows that boys will be boys.

Coach Waters is in his late 20s and has been coaching at Grover High School for only the past three years. He is young and energetic, and being a baseball coach is something he always wanted to do. He serves as the junior varsity coach and assists Coach Smith with the varsity team. His coaching philosophy is more laid-back than Coach Smith's, and they seem to balance each other out.

As a head coach, Coach Smith's ultimate goal is to win a state championship. He has his heart set on winning state this year because he has such a talented team. He knows without a doubt that his team is full of all-star baseball players. He has thought to himself on numerous occasions, "If I can't win a state championship with this team, I'll never win another." Players Jessy Jones and Matt Robertson especially stand out as stars and frequently carry the team.

Jessy is a senior. "Hardworking" and "dedicated" are words that pop into Coach Smith's mind when thinking about Jessy. He has a true passion for baseball, and although not as talented as many, through hard work he has eventually earned the starting position as second baseman. Coach Smith admires Jessy for his commitment to the team.

Matt's ride to the varsity team wasn't as difficult. Coach Smith had been watching Matt play baseball since junior high and knew that he would make the varsity team his first year in high school. Coach Smith is somewhat concerned that the older players

DOI: 10.4324/9781003375449-22

will give Matt a hard time for being younger but also knows that the team will respect him for being such a skilled athlete and an asset to the team. He is right; the varsity players accept Matt. He's one of the lucky ones.

With the season just around the corner, off-season is finally winding down. "Not too many problems this year, thankfully," Coach Smith thinks to himself. He is glad that he hasn't had to deal with many upset parents or ridiculous player complaints so far. Quite frankly, he thinks petty dramas are a waste of his valuable time and believes they need to be worked out by the players and parents, not him. On occasion, he has had to send the players to talk to Coach Waters, who, depending on his mood, either listened or said, "Go work it out"—usually the latter. After a while, his players stopped coming to him.

A few days before the Grizzles' first game, Coach Waters notices that two of the junior varsity players are acting distantly toward him. This raises a red flag because these are two guys with whom he has bonded. "What could be going on?" he thinks to himself. "Are there problems at home? Did they get in an argument with each other? Are they having trouble with academics? Are they nervous about the game?" He decides to talk to them both after practice. But Coach Waters's conversation with the two players ends without much insight. He gets the typical "everything's fine" and "nothing" from them both.

As in most sports, the varsity players feel as though they are more important than the junior varsity. They constantly mess around with the junior varsity players by teasing and undermining them. Bob Freeman and Hank Mason are both members of the junior varsity team and seem to be getting harassed the most by the varsity players. Both Bob and Hank are undersized and fairly quiet, making them easy targets. Bob absolutely loves baseball and tunes out the comments as much as possible. His main focus is improving his game.

Hank, however, has a harder time ignoring the older guys because he doesn't understand why he's being targeted. He thinks to himself, "I know the varsity team wants to mock and ridicule us as junior varsity players, but why single out me? What makes me different from everyone else on the team?" Hank honestly believes that being part of a team will help him get to know new people and have a bond with guys who have similar interests. However, as it turns out, the two teams are definitely not united but, in fact, much divided.

Both Bob and Hank think this is a phase the varsity players will go through for a few weeks and then drop it. The young players understand that because the seniors are finally at the top, they want to get some revenge for how they were treated coming through the ranks. But the teasing and tormenting don't let up. "Don't they remember what it was like?" Bob thinks to himself. "Why would they want to put others through the same torture they had to endure?" Bob, Hank, and some of the other junior varsity never ask such questions aloud; they are too embarrassed and think it could possibly lead to even more humiliation than they are already receiving on a daily basis. Also, the season is starting. They think that surely once the season begins, the varsity players' focus will shift from pranks to playing time and winning baseball games.

The season finally starts and playing ball and winning games quickly become the focus for the whole team. The players are busy keeping up with their schoolwork, as well as playing baseball both at home and away. The coaches are pleased with the team's 4–0 start. "The season looks promising already," Coach Smith thinks to himself. "Nothing is going to stand in the way of the title this year." After each win, Coach Smith can see the excitement and relief in his players' eyes. They feel the pressure too, especially the seniors. However, after each win, the pressure is off for a little while, and the boys mess around with one another by cracking jokes, telling stories, and generally goofing off.

As the team travels home from its fifth consecutive victory, some of the boys are a little rowdier than normal. The two coaches sit at the front of the dark bus discussing their next game, while most of the players are either sleeping or texting their friends. However, several players are huddled near the back of the bus. Bob and Hank have been wrestled to the floor and are being spat upon, kicked, and taunted. Coach Waters notices the commotion and points it out to Coach Smith. "Ah, boys will be boys," Coach Smith says with a tired shrug. Both Bob and Hank are terrified and unable to understand why the abuse continues when the coaches are present.

A few weeks pass before Bob finally breaks down, humiliated and afraid, and tells his parents about the incident. Bob's mother finally realizes why over the past couple of weeks Bob begged her not to make him go to baseball practice or games. She had been upset and angry with him at times, because he always loved baseball and they had sacrificed a lot to see him succeed. His parents immediately contact the school administration.

Mr. and Ms. Freeman meet with the school administration to discuss what happened to their son. Struggling to keep it together because the coaches are also present, Mr. Freeman begins from the beginning. He explains how his son and others have been hazed by the varsity players since the off-season. He also says that Hank has agreed to come forward as the second assault victim.

"This is a progression of hazing acts," Mr. Freeman states. "The varsity players have been testing their limits, because up until now, no punishments have been given. They have not been reprimanded for one act of hazing." Mr. Freeman looks directly at the coaches and asks, "How can you explain this? Why weren't you looking out for the best interests of your players? Couldn't you see the warning signs?"

Both coaches are at a loss for words. Coach Waters can't help but think back to the day both Bob and Hank were acting so strangely. Now he knew; they were being hazed but were too scared to tell him. He thinks back to the times when Bob and Hank came to talk, and he sent them away and told them to work it out. He feels like a failure as a coach and as a person. Everyone present realizes the seriousness of the situation and knows that the authorities need to be contacted immediately.

With the coaches, administration, parents, players, and police involved, the situation has become much more public and real. Punishments for the violent acts on the bus and the verbal abuse that occurred before this incident have to be enforced. The perpetrators face assault and battery charges. Coach Smith and Coach Waters are immediately suspended from their position at Grover High School and face possible charges of criminal negligence. The perfect season, the lives of several players and parents, the careers of two successful coaches, and the reputation of a school have been left in tatters.

Questions for Consideration

1. Who are the stakeholders in this case?
2. How would you define hazing? Can you give some examples?
3. If a coach knowingly violates a school policy, what should be the consequences?
4. Is there anything that the coaches could or should have done to prevent the hazing?
5. Should the coaches and administrators have handled the hazing situation differently?
6. Was one of the coaches obligated to come forth and handle the situation? Which one?
7. Was the coaches' punishment deserved?
8. What are the statistics on hazing occurring in high school? Do you think hazing is more prevalent in certain sports than in others?
9. Is any form of hazing acceptable or appropriate?

References and Further Readings

Associated Press. (2021, November 13). UC Davis says baseball team hazed students with alcohol. *SI*. www.si.com/college/2021/11/13/uc-davis-says-baseball-team-hazed-students-with-alcohol

Carter, R. (2022, April 4). Oklahoma schools ignoring long-term staff abuse of students. *OCPA*. www.ocpathink.org/post/oklahoma-schools-ignoring-long-term-staff-abuse-of-students

Diamond, A. B., Callahan, S. T., Chain, K. F., & Solomon, G. S. (2016). Qualitative review of hazing in collegiate and school sports: Consequences from a lack of culture, knowledge and responsiveness. *British Journal of Sports Medicine, 50*(3), 149–153. https://doi.org/10.1136/bjsports-2015-095603

ISU suspends hockey club over hazing. (2022, June 28). *Times-republican*. www.timesrepublican.com/sports/local-sports/2022/06/isu-suspends-hockey-club-over-hazing/

Jeckell, A. S., Copenhaver, E. A., & Diamond, A. B. (2018). The spectrum of hazing and peer sexual abuse in sports: A current perspective. *Sports Health: A Multidisciplinary Approach, 10*(6), 558–564. https://doi.org/10.1177/1941738118797322

MacIntosh, E. (2018). Creating an anti-hazing value system: Changing the culture of sport and Entertainment. *Sport & Entertainment Review, 4*(1), 14–19.

Niehoff, K. (2022, September 7). NFHS: Steps must be taken to end acts of hazing in high school sports. *HighSchoolOT.com*. www.highschoolot.com/nfhs-steps-must-be-taken-to-end-acts-of-hazing-in-high-school-sports/20452880/#:~:text=By%20definition%2C%20hazing%20is%20any,school%20sports%20or%20performing%20arts.

StopHazing. (n.d.). States with anti-hazing laws. *StopHazing Consulting*. https://stophazing.org/policy/state-laws/

USA Gymnastics. (2021, November 1). *USA Gymnastics Safe Sport policy*. www.usagym.org/pages/education/safesport/

Waldron, J. J. (2015). Predictors of mild hazing, severe hazing, and positive initiation rituals in sport. *International Journal of Sports Science & Coaching, 10*(6), 1089–1101. https://doi.org/10.1260/1747-9541.10.6.1089

Watson, M. (2022, August 25). A Pennsylvania high school cancels its football season over hazing reports, while 2 other schools grapple with allegations. *CNN*. www.cnn.com/2022/08/25/us/pennsylvania-high-schools-football-hazing-allegations/index.html

22 Cash Is King

Coach Mike Lennon was completing his fourth season at Greenville High School in North Palm Beach, Florida. It had taken a few years to integrate his coaching philosophy and develop a team culture he approved of, but slowly but surely, he was beginning to see it take shape in his players and team. The previous coach had not focused on the "team," and consequently, players sought individual statistics and accomplishments. If they looked good, everything was fine. And, while Mike's first few seasons did not provide statistics to be proud of, he stuck to his plan knowing that success would soon follow. And it did. As his team bonded together, positive results began to follow.

The team that season was the kind that you see in movies and television shows. The players had that special kind of bond with one another that started in the locker room and translated onto the field. There were only ever minor altercations, and they were quickly resolved. Not only did this new team culture help the team bond, but it also helped shape players into confident leaders. The most prominent leader was junior quarterback Jerry Donalds. Jerry had been at Greenville since his freshman year and had been a significant influencer in transforming the program's culture. A natural leader, the entire team looked up to Jerry and admired his ability to play the game and lead a team.

But Jerry wasn't just a team player. He was also what many people would call a "generational talent" at Greenville, leading the nation in passing yards and touchdowns. But he never let his statistics or leadership get to his head. He loved his teammates, coaches, and fans that showed up to every game.

Greenville entered the semifinals of the state championship game with a record of 13–1, yet the team they faced were the favorites for the title. After a hard-fought game, Greenville went home in disappointment, as they lost the game due to a last possession touchdown from the opposing team. The loss was crushing to both the players and Mike because they knew how hard they had worked and had come so close to a ring. However, once the initial pain had worn off, the coaches began to look forward to the next season, knowing their best players were coming back as seniors. On the ride home Mike sensed how much his athletes were hurting, so he decided to give them a talk of hope.

"Hey, guys. Listen up." The bus was already pretty quiet, so it didn't take long before Mike spoke. "I know this wasn't the result we wanted or expected today, but you all played your tails off, and I can't be anything but proud of what we've accomplished this

DOI: 10.4324/9781003375449-23

season. But we're not done. While I'm proud of our two seniors leaving the program, I'm excited about next year's team. Let's not forget the heartache of today but use it to motivate us to win it all next year. Keep your heads up!" Coach Lennon exclaimed.

While his talk did not make an immediate effect, it did give them a future hope and even more of a reason to work harder as a team and toward a goal that had never been accomplished at Greenville. Mike knew that with Jerry at quarterback, it was entirely possible.

Shortly after the season ended, the off-season began to pick up with workouts and meetings with the team about plans for the next season. A few players had begun receiving college offers with the opportunity for them to play at the next level, and no one on the team received more college offers than Jerry. It seemed like every school in the nation wanted him to play for their team. All of Jerry's teammates were extremely excited for him and couldn't wait to hear him announce where he was going to college. And, as name, image, and likeness (NIL) bills began to spread across the sporting landscape, there was plenty of interest to see where Jerry would go.

Coach Lennon also heard the news surrounding the NIL bill and decided that it would be a good idea to address his team and clarify the exciting news.

"Guys, I'm sure by now you've all heard about the new rules surrounding athletes' name image, and likeness, but I wanted to clarify it all for you. This will largely affect college athletes, but athletes are now able to accept compensation for endorsement deals that include their presence and name. There is only one issue; our high school association and state is not allowing athletes within our district to receive compensation and benefits from this bill."

There were a few groans around the room, and it was quite obvious that his news was not welcomed by some, but for most it wouldn't make a difference. They weren't superstars and were mostly excited about their near future.

As the off-season continued, Jerry took several visits to colleges and decided that it was time to choose where he would commit.

"Coach, I know where I want to go, but I want to have an event with my family, teammates, and coaches to announce and verbally commit for the college I want to attend and continue my career," Jerry said to Mike.

"Jerry, I think that is a great idea! I will make the announcement to the players and coaches, and you tell your family to be ready," he replied.

Throughout the next few weeks, Coach Lennon organized the players, coaches, and media to make sure Jerry received the signing day he deserved. When it finally came time for the announcement, everyone surrounded Jerry and was very excited to find out where he was committing.

"I would like to thank everyone who has gotten me to this point including my family, teammates, and coaches," said Jerry. "I'm excited to announce that I will be attending Florida State University after my senior season. Go Noles!" Jerry declared.

Everyone was excited about Jerry's decision, especially Florida State University, but after his commitment, life began to change. Although Jerry still had one season left in high school, he began to be seen as a celebrity within his community and on social media. His highlight became a regular post on ESPN and SportsCenter, and he was given special treatment everywhere he went. Most of these benefits were minor and deserved due to Jerry's hard work, but one offer came in that was far different from the rest. Powerade approached him about a seven-figure endorsement deal to participate in multiple commercials and attend two events that they hosted. This deal was not one that Jerry could overlook, so he discussed it with his parents before meeting with Mike. They met in Mike's office.

"Hey, Coach. I wanted to let you know that I've received an endorsement offer from Powerade that would pay me a million dollars. I know it sounds like an easy decision, but I wanted to get your opinion on the offer."

Mike couldn't help but look surprised. A million dollars to a teenager! It was crazy.

"Well, Jerry. I know you're probably very excited about this opportunity, but you can't take that deal."

"What do you mean? I thought you'd be excited for me. I thought you would be on my side!"

"Jerry, I'm not against you. It's just our county's football association; athletes in our district, county, and state can't accept endorsement deals, even with the new NIL bill. You just need to understand—"

"No, Coach, I don't need to understand anything!" Jerry interrupted. "I have given my all for you and this team and have never been selfish. This is the one decision I make for myself, and you just immediately shot me down. I'm done!" Jerry exclaimed, as he charged out of Coach Lennon's office.

Mike was left in his office feeling awful for the way Jerry felt and spent the rest of the week thinking about what he could have done differently. He didn't know what Jerry meant when he said he was done, but Coach Lennon was almost certain that Jerry wouldn't leave the team. "Thankfully, it was still the off-season and summer practices weren't starting yet, so this issue wouldn't make it to the rest of the team," Coach thought to himself. He figured that Jerry would soon come in to speak with him again to have a calmer conversation about the offer Jerry received.

As the weeks passed, Jerry never came in to see Coach Lennon. With only one week until summer practices began, Coach Lennon decided to hold a meeting with the team seniors and captains to set a standard for the season. He was extremely excited for the upcoming season and his conversation with his players, but Jerry didn't show. There were some queries about it from the other players, but Jerry quelled them and went on with the meeting as usual getting his leaders excited for the summer practices. However, going home that night, he couldn't help but think about why Jerry wasn't there and, later that night, texted Jerry asking him to meet him at his office the next day.

The next day arrived, and Jerry walked in supported by his father. Mike thought it was odd but didn't say anything about it.

"Hey, Jerry, thanks for coming. I wanted to talk to you about the upcoming season."

"Me too, Coach. There's something I'd like to get off my chest," Jerry replied.

"Of course. Go ahead."

"Well, Coach. My parents, sponsors, and I did some research and found that I can accept endorsement deals but not in Florida. So, I've thought it over, and we've decided to move to New Orleans so that I can play my final year at Cedarville High," Jerry explained.

Mike was stunned but tried to regroup.

"Oh. Well, I can't say I was expecting that, but I mean, is there anything I can do to convince you to stay?"

Jerry and his father stood up and prepared to walk out. Jerry stuck out his hand.

"No, Coach. I'm sorry this is my decision; this deal and opportunity is going to change my life. Thanks for everything you've done for me."

With that, Jerry was gone. Coach Lennon was stunned. He had spent so much time and effort changing the culture of the team to become a family and brotherhood, and Jerry had just walked away. Now he had to face the entire football team in just a few days to explain that their leader had chosen money over team. What had he done wrong? What could he have done differently to change the situation? What about their state championship run? Why was a teenager he had spent years developing now a millionaire, while he and his staff struggled to even raise money for basic program necessities?

"What am I going to do?" Coach Lennon thought to himself.

Questions for Consideration

1. Who are the stakeholders in this case?
2. Coach Lennon had a good culture within his team that quickly fell apart. Provide one example with a source (outside of the sources in References and Further Readings) that shows how this has happened in real life.
3. What is the value to the coach and the program when an athlete gets notoriety for his or her athletic success like this? Do you have any evidence to back up your reasoning?
4. If you are Coach Lennon, what do you do now? Rationalize your answer.
5. Is there anything Coach Lennon could have done in advance to perhaps avoid this situation from happening? If so, what?
6. If you were in charge of NIL legislation, how would you manage NIL in high school? Would you open it up or try to limit financial opportunities for athletes? What are the pros and cons of each option?

References and Further Readings

Casalino, F. (2022). Call to the bullpen: Saving high school student athlete name, image, and likeness rights. *Jeffrey S. Moorad Sports Law Journal, 29*(2), 263.

College Athlete Name, Image, and Likeness Act [Proposed New Name: College student Athlete Name, Image, and Likeness Act]. (2021). *National conference of commissioners on uniform state laws.*

Keller, B. (2022, August 21). *High school NIL: State-by-state regulations for name, image and likeness rights.* https://opendorse.com/blog/nil-high-school/

Rabinowitz, B. (2021, August 2). Top high school quarterback recruit Quinn Ewers skipping senior season to enroll at Ohio State. *USA Today.* www.usatoday.com/story/sports/ncaaf/2021/08/02/quinn-ewers-skip-high-school-enroll-ohio-state/5456975001/

Tao, A. (2021). New influencers on the block: The NIL and high school athletes. *Kentucky Law Journal, 110.*

Walsh, M. (2021). Commodification of college athletes' name, image, and likeness. *Creighton Law Review, 55*(1), 79.

Part II

College Sports

23 Scholarships

Who Gets What?

Coach Walt White leaned back in his office chair and rested his feet on his desk. Coaches Jessie Pinkerman and Guster Freng, White's assistant coaches, quietly sat across from him slumped on a small office couch. None of the men spoke and a sad melancholy filled the room.

White finally broke the silence.

"Always the bridesmaid, never the bride," he said. No one spoke.

White had coached his college baseball team, the Crocodiles, to yet another world series appearance, but unfortunately, as had happened five other times over the previous decade, they had come up short.

The Crocodiles had become one of the preeminent college baseball teams in the country. Each year multiple players were drafted into the professional ranks, and star high school players across the country flooded White's inbox each year with requests to play. He had created a culture in the locker room where everyone got along and pulled for one another. All the players saw Coach White as a mentor and role model, as he believed in treating every one of his players with respect and honesty.

"So, gentlemen?" White asked his two assistants. "What do you think? Why does this keep happening?"

Coach Pinkerman sat up, leaned forward on the couch, and spoke.

"Coach, a lot of people say that pitching and defense wins championships. We need better pitching."

Coach Freng chimed in and agreed.

"Yeah, Coach. It seems our arms were tired by the end of the season. Seems to be that way every year."

The Crocodiles had led the country three out of the past four years in hitting. During that time, they had achieved two world series appearances and a super-regional appearance in between. But their pitching had consistently finished in the lower half of their own conference. They had played a brand of baseball in which they outscored teams rather than outpitched them. That type of philosophy had worked fine during the regular season but had not given them the ultimate success they wanted in the National Collegiate Athletic Association's (NCAA's) tourney.

"You might be right boys," White said. "But all the best pitching prospects for next year have already committed to other schools. Not a lot we can do about that now." The three men sighed. "But that's certainly something we can look at for next year's

DOI: 10.4324/9781003375449-25

class," White continued. With that, they adjourned their meeting and agreed to meet again in a month to start prepping for the next season.

A week later, White had settled into a relaxing but short summer break. He had taken the family to the beach for some well-needed rest and relaxation. The intensity of coaching at a high-end division I program was extreme, and White had realized years ago that downtime to decompress was necessary. However, a week into his beach vacation, his cell phone rang. It was Coach Pinkerman and White felt obligated to pick up.

"Hey, Coach. I've got some news for you. I just got a call from Saul Gooden's dad. He wants to meet with us the day after tomorrow," Pinkerman said excitedly.

Saul Gooden was a local 4-star prospect who had played high school baseball just down the street from the Crocodiles. With over two dozen scholarship offers, Saul could have played anywhere in the country but had decided to leave the state. He had stated that not only was this a way for him to see another part of the country but also because he wanted to play for a school that put a premium on pitching. He had chosen Miami State University and, in his freshman year, had gone 7–3 with a low Earned Run Average (ERA) and a slew of strikeouts. He had been awarded freshman pitcher of the year for his conference.

White was confused. "What does his dad want to meet about?" he asked.

"Saul's mom has gotten really sick," Pinkerman responded. "He wants to come home and play for the Crocodiles! The NCAA has given him the option to move back to Preytonville to be close to his mom. The transfer portal allows him to play next year!"

Platt's heart started to skip. This was like a miracle had fallen into his lap.

"Okay, Jessie," White said. "I'll see you in a couple of days!"

Two days later, Coach White arrived back at his office refreshed and recharged. Coaches Pinkerman and Freng were already there waiting for him, and Todd Gooden, Saul's father, was there as well. White exchanged a handshake with Mr. Gooden and, after offering him a seat, sat down opposite him.

"So how are you doing, Mr. Gooden? I'm sorry to hear about your wife," White said. "How is she doing?"

"Thank you," Mr. Gooden replied. "She's doing better."

"Well, I'm so glad to hear that." They exchanged some other pleasantries for a few minutes before White broke the ice.

"So, I hear your son might want to play for us next year?" White asked.

"Yes, Coach. Saul would love to come home and play for you," Mr. Gooden responded. "He wants to be close to his mom while she's undergoing treatment," he continued.

"That would be terrific," White said with a big smile on his face. "We'd love to have Saul on our team. Let's make it happen."

"I appreciate that, Coach," Mr. Gooden responded and shifted in his chair. "There is something we'd need though to feel comfortable about making the move."

"Okay, like what?" White responded a bit confused.

"We'd want to be assured Saul would be on a pretty much full scholarship," Mr. Gooden said.

White rubbed his jaw. As a late, emergency-based transfer, he had assumed that Saul would play on a reduced in-state tuition for this year with some supplementary money for additional cost and would live with his parents. White had already signed letters of intent with all his new recruits. NCAA rules allotted 11.7 scholarships for D1 baseball teams. That had to be divided among 27 players on the team. Big-time recruits often got the few full scholarships. Platt had none left.

"Hmmmm. Okay, well, that's a tough spot we're in because of all the commitments we've already made for this season," White said. "Let me see what we can work out. I'll get back to you in couple of days."

"Okay, Coach," Mr. Gooden said. "I appreciate you trying to work it out. With the money I'm having to spend on my wife's treatments, we just don't have the ability to pay for any college right now. I'm really sorry to put you in a pinch."

"I understand," White said. "You don't need to apologize. You need to focus on your wife right now. Let me see what I can do."

With that, the four men exchanged handshakes, and Mr. Gooden left.

"So, what are we gonna do boys?" White asked.

"Good grief, Coach. This is going to be a scramble. I'm not sure," Coach Freng said.

"We have to figure it out and make it work," Coach Pinkerman chimed in. "Saul Gooden *has* to be on this team next season. He could be the difference maker we need to finally win this thing," he continued.

"I know, I know," White responded shaking his head. "Let's figure it out and make it happen. Call your families and tell them you're gonna be late for dinner. Let's get to work."

Over the next several hours the three men labored over various ideas. Shortly before midnight they had formulated a plan. They would reduce two position players' scholarships by 50 percent each and rescind their plan to award another 50 percent scholarship to a current walk-on player. This would make room for them to give a full scholarship to Saul Gooden. This was a gut-wrenching decision by three men, and they were fully aware it would be challenging to deliver this news to the three ballplayers. They agreed they would get together the next day and call in the three players individually to tell them of their plan.

The next day the three coaches assembled in Coach White's office. The players were in the gym doing off-season conditioning. White sent word to the strength and conditioning coach to summon the first player who was a part of their scholarship reduction plan.

The three players involved were all entering their junior year. Hank Shrater was the starting shortstop. As a sophomore, he had led the conference in fielding percentage. Although he was not a power hitter, he had batted near .300 in his sophomore campaign. He was a solid contact hitter who had a high on-base percentage. He had been on a 75 percent scholarship in both his seasons with the Crocodiles but was now going to see that reduced to a 50 percent scholarship.

Michael Ermentrot was the starting left fielder who had enjoyed a big sophomore year. Michael had double-digit homers and hit for a good average. He had huge hits at crucial moments throughout the season and the tournament. He had also been on a 75 percent scholarship but was now going to see his scholarship reduced by 25 percent.

The third player, Tuc Salmaca, had been a walk-on both his seasons with the Crocodiles. He was a local kid who had played with Saul Gooden in high school. Serving in a utility role, Tuc had only seen a couple dozen at bats his freshman year, but his sophomore year had seen a marked improvement in his play and his playing time. Apart from catcher and pitcher, Dennis had played every position in both the infield and the outfield. Tuc was a pesky hitter with an average over .300. He had also led the team in steals and runs scored. He had thought his junior year was going to be a dream come true with a 50 percent scholarship. Now that was not going to happen.

As the coaches matriculated through talking to each player, their hearts hurt with the reaction each player showed. The players had said the right thing that they understood why it was being done and that it would be best for the team. But it was obvious by their reactions that they were hurt.

After the players had all left, the three coaches sat quietly in the office mulling over what they had just done.

"That was pretty awful," White said.

"I feel like a heel," Coach Pinkerman said.

Coach Freng didn't say anything. He sat slumped over disconsolately staring at the ground.

"Guys," White said. "We did the best we could with an impossible situation."

After an hour of consoling one another, the three men agreed to go home. They would get together again the next day to talk more. As they were getting ready to leave, someone knocked on the office door. It was Gale Bottiker, the team's strength and conditioning coach.

"Coaches, could I have a quick minute of your time?" Bottiker asked.

"Sure, Gale," White responded. "What's up?"

Gale pulled up a chair and sat down in a position so that he could face all three coaches.

"I thought you guys should know," Gale started. "I was in my office, and I could hear several players talking about this scholarship issue. Some of them were pretty upset. I even heard a couple of them talking about leaving the program and transferring to different schools. It got pretty heated. Anyway, I just thought you all should know." With that, Gale said good night and left the office.

The three coaches stood staring at one another. What would they do now?

Questions for Consideration

1. Who are the stakeholders in this case?
2. Why was Saul Gooden allowed to transfer and begin playing for another school so quickly?
3. Do you agree with the coaching decision to reduce some players' scholarship delineations so that they could secure Saul Gooden coming to their team?
4. What approach(es) could the coaches have taken regarding the scholarships that might have lessened the discontent of players on the team?
5. If placed in the same situation, how would you have handled the situation?

References and Further Readings

DIY College Rankings. (2022). *11.7 Reality check: College baseball scholarships.* www.diycollegerankings.com/11-7-reality-check/475/

NCASA Sports.org. (2022). *How baseball scholarships really work.* www.ncsasports.org/baseball/scholarships

Winters, K. (2019). NSA: Are athletic scholarships guaranteed for four years? *USA Today High School Sports.* https://usatodayhss.com/2019/ncsa-are-athletic-scholarships-guaranteed-for-four-years

YouTube.com. (2022). *Uneven: College baseball scholarship issue.* www.youtube.com/watch?v=C7cKh4fo6Bg

24 Less Than Four

Jimmy Hopper had gotten the basketball head coach job at Draper State after a long and highly successful career as high school coach at Hawkins High School. He had amassed four straight district championships at Hawkins and two straight state titles. Over a ten-year career, Hopper had the highest winning percentage for a high school basketball coach in state history. But, somewhat unexpectedly, Coach Hopper left Hawkins and took a head coaching position at a small Division II school in West Virginia. In only his second year, he had won the National Championship.

Suddenly, Hopper was the talk of the town. Inquiries from Division I teams up and down the East Coast flooded in. One of those inquiries came from a Division I up-and-comer, Draper State. Hopper had eagerly decided to take the Draper State position largely because he was from North Carolina and wanted to stay close to friends and family.

When Hopper accepted the head coaching position at Draper State, he knew it came with expectations. The Draper State Banshees had burst on the scene as a National Collegiate Athletic Association (NCAA) basketball powerhouse 15 years earlier after a surprisingly successful season. Entry into and a long run in the NCAA tourney had put Draper St. on the basketball landscape. That first year they had made it to the Sweet 16. The next year, solid high school recruits around the country were calling upon the upstart program to play for them and their outstanding coach, Luke Sinclair. After over a decade of success, including ten straight invitations to the NCAA tourney, four trips to the Elite 8, and one season making it the championship game, Coach Sinclair left Draper State to take on another challenge.

Unfortunately for Draper State, Sinclair's departure had an almost immediate impact on the team's success. After a couple of .500 seasons, the team finished next to last in their own conference. The high-end recruits, which were only a few years earlier begging to get to play for the Banshees, were no longer calling. The program's precipitous decline did not set well with alumni donors. There was clamoring from sponsors and donors alike that something needed to be done. After a five-year run, Coach Sinclair's replacement, who had been one of his assistants, was fired and Coach Hopper was hired.

Hopper came to Draper State with much fanfare. His charisma and magnanimous personality made him a media darling. There was a renewed excitement in the program, and the high-end recruiting calls that had dried up reappeared. Sponsors and donors were elated and reveled at the hire.

DOI: 10.4324/9781003375449-26

Hopper's coaching philosophy centered on getting "his type" of players. He wanted athletes who participated academically and were good stewards both on and off the court. Over the course of his coaching career, Hopper had found that if he had solid guys playing for him, he was able to focus on coaching instead of disciplining or babysitting. He believed that a good group of selfless athletes led to team cohesion and comradery, which, in turn, led to success.

Despite the team's disappointing play for half a decade, Coach Hopper had a solid, if not great, first recruiting class. He had signed a few notable players. Bill Hargrove was a highly touted player who was coming off an injury redshirt year at another university that he had acquired through the transfer portal. The other player whom Hopper thought might make a splash was Dimitri Kaminski. Originally from Poland, he was considered a "can't miss" product. This was the makings of a great class, especially for a first-year head coach who got into the recruiting season late.

The Banshees' first season was typical of a rebuilding team. The team won 14 games while losing 16. As should have been expected, the young recruiting class had seen difficulties in their developmental first season. The highly touted transfer, Bill Hargrove, never really got on track as he battled to regain his pre-injury form. The other recruits had mixed levels of success too. Vick Creel had had an up-and-down season. Some games he scored 20 points; other games he went scoreless. Edward Munson, the other notable transfer, had done a good job rebounding but had struggled to get into double digits. Dimitri Kaminski, the young player from Poland, had struggled defensively and often found himself in foul trouble. This greatly affected his minutes in games.

The diamond in the rough that Hopper had identified, Michael Wheeler, had been the big surprise. He made the all-conference freshman team and was really playing strong at the end of the season. Despite the disappointing win–loss record, Hopper was happy with what his team had accomplished. There was a great team unity among all the Draper State players. Each player acknowledged their need for improvement and the areas they needed to improve. They agreed to a program of off-season conditioning, and optimism among the team remained high. Most importantly to Hopper, everyone on his team was doing well academically, and there were no off court issues.

The sophomore season showed even more promise as everyone's numbers had significant improvement. Hargrove had a much better campaign and seemed to trust that his injury had finally healed. Creel's game seemed to have found consistency, and he became an all-conference player, averaging 18 points and 6 assists a game while shooting a high field goal (FG) percentage. Munson had packed on a lot of muscle and had become a dominant rebounder and shot blocker. Dimitri had become a reliable starter and averaged double figures in rebounding and scoring. Wheeler, who had the best season among the recruiting class, had an even better second year. He too finished with both all-conference honors, and the team had seen pro scouts in the audience watching him play.

The Banshees' win–loss record was also markedly improved, rebounding from 14 wins the first year to 24 wins their second year. The season concluded with an at-large bid into the NCAA tournament and a first-round win. Even though the Banshees lost in the second round, the team had tremendous optimism for the next season as the year ended.

As the spring semester neared an end, Coach Hopper sat with his assistant coaches formulating off-season workout regimens for his players. The coaches were in a great mood as they joked back and forth with the hopeful anticipation they had for the next season. They were wrapping up their meeting when they heard a knock on the door.

"Come in," Hopper shouted. In walked two of his players, Vick Creel and Michael Wheeler.

"Coach," Creel said, his head hanging down while staring at the ground.

"What's up guys?" Hopper asked.

"Coach," Creel said again, "Mike and I need to talk to you about something."

Hopper's heart sunk as he suddenly had the feeling of impending doom.

"Alright then."

"Coach," Creel said, "we appreciate everything you've done for us, but Mike and I have decided to leave school and enter the pro draft."

This hadn't been completely unexpected to Hopper. Like everyone else, he had seen the visits and talked to several scouts who had come to the games to scout his players.

"Are you guys absolutely sure about this?" Hopper asked them.

"Yes, Coach. We've talked with our families, and we think this is best for us and them," Creel sheepishly said.

As much as it hurt that his players were leaving, Hopper knew he needed to support the two young men.

"Well, guys, we're gonna miss you both next year," Hopper said. "But I'm so happy and so proud of both of you."

And with that, he walked over and hugged both players. After a minute, the teary-eyed players left the office, and Hopper sank down into his chair.

"Well, gents," he said to his assistant coaches. "That puts a bit of a damper on things."

The next year, Hopper's third year at Draper State, the Banshees started out well. Hargrove and Munson came out of the gates firing on all cylinders, and the team jumped out to a 9–0 start. Dimitri was having a very productive junior season too. The team appeared to have responded to the loss of its two star players brilliantly. Hopper had the team playing with confidence and determination.

As the midway point of the season rolled around, Hargrove twisted his ankle and missed the next five games. Even when he came back, he was clearly hobbled, and his play took a precipitous dive. So did the team. The Banshees lost 8 of their final 15 games, and it was a major disappointment to everyone at Draper State when the team narrowly missed out on the NCAA tournament. Hopper, who had just a year earlier been the darling of Draper, was now getting beaten up by the local media and on online social sites, and he wasn't immune to criticism.

Shortly after the season ended, Coach Hopper received a call from his athletic director, Joy Boyers.

"Hey, Coach," she said. "I need you to come by the office today. We need to talk."

For the second time in less than a year, Hopper's heart sunk. His stomach churned. He had a bad feeling about what was coming next.

Questions for Consideration

1. Who are the stakeholders in this case?
2. Should Coach Hopper have tried to talk the players out of leaving school and entering the draft? Defend your answer.
3. Was there anything that Coach Hopper and his assistant coaches could have done to circumvent the team's quick decline?
4. Ultimately, was Hopper's philosophy appropriate in only getting "his type" of players? Is this philosophy even reasonable in college athletics anymore?
5. If Coach Hopper is ultimately let go, was the administration correct in how they handled the situation? Defend your answer.

References and Further Readings

D'Angelo, T. (2021). D'Angelo: Coaching carousel spinning out control earlier than ever. *The Palm Beach Post.* www.palmbeachpost.com/story/sports/college/2021/11/17/why-so-many-college-football-coaches-being-fired-mid-season/8638478002/

Forde, P. (2021). Ford-yard dash: Jimmy Lake's firing stands out for its swiftness. *Sports Illustrated.* www.yardbarker.com/general_sports/articles/head_coaches_and_managers_who_were_dismissed_soon_after_winning_a_championship/s1__33856985#slide_1

Garder, S. (2022). Head coaches and managers who were dismissed soon after winning a championship. *Yardbarker.com.* www.yardbarker.com/general_sports/articles/head_coaches_and_managers_who_were_dismissed_soon_after_winning_a_championship/s1__33856985#slide_1

25 Stats Get Me Drafted

Bobbie Keen was chomping at the bit. The young Eureka State small forward had spent the entire off-season hearing her name bantered about and discussed by the media. She was at the point of cringing every time she heard an analyst discuss her prospects in the pros. Keen had come to the Eureka State Hedgehogs as a five-star "can't miss" prospect. At 5 feet 11 inches tall, she was a little undersized for a small forward, but she made up for her height by being a chiseled specimen; she weighed 175 pounds and displayed a lot more muscle than the typical women's basketball forward. She was big and athletic, and as a solid rebounder and midrange shooter, she often "out physicalled" her competition. She was so much stronger than the players she was competing against that she generally wore them down over the course of the game.

Keen had played her entire high school career in the paint (the lane). At times, because of her physical size, she even played center. College had seen her transition her game to playing a little more outside. Even though she still dominated the paint, she had developed a nice short-range jumper. It was enough to keep defenders from camping out inside in an attempt to reduce her scoring. So why then was the media scrutinizing her prospects to play in the pros? It came down to her long-range shooting.

"In the NBA she's gonna be playing with the big folks," one critic said. "She's not tall enough to score underneath, and she can't shoot from the three-point line."

"This is a kid without a position," another critic chimed in. "She's never going to be anything but a deep bench player. No way she's a first-round pick."

"If only this kid could shoot," another analyst said.

The constant negativity had an impact on Keen. She began to wear a huge chip on her shoulder and developed an attitude of "I'll show you" in response to all the criticism.

Keen had been a basketball star her whole life. If she wasn't on the court playing, she was in the gym training. Strength and athleticism had always been a part of Keen. In college, she had started as a freshman and had improved significantly by her sophomore year. She was even named to the all-conference team averaging 19 points and 6 rebounds. Despite all the accolades, she was receiving only lukewarm interest from pro scouts. All the negative commentary had had a profound impact on her. She worried that her lifelong dreams of playing in the Women's National Basketball Association (WNBA) might be drifting away.

DOI: 10.4324/9781003375449-27

As summer neared end, Keen couldn't wait for October when practice would begin. The entire off-season, Keen had spent day after day shooting long-range shots. She was determined to show everyone that she was ready and could play in the pros.

A level of excitement engulfed the Hedgehog basketball court for the first day of practice. And why wouldn't it? Coach Trinity LaRusso and her assistant Coach Joanne Lawrence had all their starters back from the previous year. That team had gone 24–6, won their conference, and had surprisedly made it to the Sweet 16 in the National Collegiate Athletic Association's (NCAA's) tournament. Expectations were high for this year's Hedgehogs. The two coaches couldn't help but grin when the team walked on the practice floor and began stretching.

"Good grief. I've got butterflies," LaRusso said.

"I hear ya," Lawrence responded. "This is going to be an amazing year. Maybe a once in a lifetime kind of season," she continued.

Prognosticators had picked Eureka State to win their conference and be a high seed in the post season NCAA National Championship Tournament. These lofty predictions came because in addition to having all five starters back, the Hedgehogs had three players picked to the preseason all-conference team. In addition to Keen, point guard Miggy Diaz and shooting guard Toni Nichols were also picked as preseason first teamers. A playful meme trickled through social media calling them the "Gen Z Dream Team."

As the team finished their first practice warm-ups the players laughed and joked around with one another. Aside from talent, Coach LaRusso's team had real chemistry. These women were friends on and off the court and really supported one another. Practice began the same as it always did with a LaRusso coached team, a couple of minutes of meditation and centering. LaRusso had employed this philosophy from her own high school playing days when she was highly involved with martial arts. The players who played for her had thought the whole thing was hokey at first but had eventually bought in. On this day, Bobbie Keen was struggling to center. Her energy was so high that she was almost hyperventilating. She couldn't wait to show her teammates, coaches, and critics what she could do now.

After a few layup-line, passing, defense, and short jumper warm-up drills, the team split into two squads and prepared to scrimmage. LaRusso expected a bit of rust for his Hedgehog team the first day back. It always took a few practices to get everyone back in the flow. As the scrimmage progressed, LaRusso couldn't help but notice how much more active Keen's offensive game was. She was no longer simply setting up in the paint and looking to score with short shots. Keen was routinely sliding out to the three-point line and nailing jumpers. Coaches LaRusso and Lawrence as well as the players were surprised by this change in Keen's game. While she wasn't necessarily troubled by the evolution of Keen's game, LaRusso was concerned. LaRusso's star player was taking a lot more shots than she had taken in the previous season. After the scrimmage concluded, the two coaches adjourned to their office to discuss the team's first practice.

"So, what did you think about Keen?" LaRusso asked. "She was jacking up a lot of shots; a lot more than last season," she continued.

"I'd chalk it up to first day back excitement, Coach," Lawrence responded. "I wouldn't worry about it," she continued.

But over the next few weeks of practice, things did not change. LaRusso began to have serious concerns as the season's first game approached. More worrying was the fact that she and Lawrence had started to notice other players starting to show some frustration. They were not getting the same opportunities they had had in the previous season.

As the season began, the Hedgehogs looked impressive. They won their first five games in dominant fashion using their superior athleticism and talent to blow their opponents off the floor. Most notably, Keen had been incredible. Her scoring was up eight points a game from what it had been the previous season, and she was now the media darling. Prognosticators were now predicting Keen to be a lottery pick.

Winning had also seemed to cure much of the team's ills. The discontent that had shown itself during the previous few weeks of practice had disappeared. Nobody seemed to care anymore about how many more shots Keen was taking. The players seemed closer than ever.

Despite their hot start, LaRusso had developed serious concerns. Her Eureka State team was playing far less talented teams. They were bigger, stronger, and faster than their opponents and were getting wide-open shots and an abundance of turnovers by the less talented competition. This had led to tons of easy layups and free points.

"So, how 'bout that Coach!" Coach Lawrence excitedly said to LaRusso after the Hedgehogs' fifth blowout victory.

"Winning can eliminate discontented feelings," LaRusso responded, "but it can also hide team deficiencies."

"Come on, Coach. Enjoy the ride," Lawrence said.

LaRusso gave a half-hearted smile back to Lawrence. Her gut told her the early team success might be fool's gold. She hoped she was wrong but feared she was right.

As conference play began, the Hedgehogs were the prohibitive favorites. The Eureka State players were anxious to show the nation just how talented they were. They were ready to match up against the higher-level talented teams in their conference.

The first conference game matched Eureka State against Nichols University. A private university that required their student athletes to meet high academic standards, the Nichols University Gophers were picked to finish in the bottom of the conference. This was a team that the Hedgehogs were expected to handle easily.

However, instead of a blowout, the game was closely contested. Eureka State found themselves behind by double digits in the second half. Keen led her team to a furious comeback, taking 10 three-pointers in the second half and connecting on 7 of them. The game came to down a final possession by the Gophers in which they had a chance to win, but their last-second shot fell short, and the Hedgehogs prevailed. Keen was celebrated as a hero, and the local sports radio talk shows reveled over her talent.

The next morning, the two coaches sat in their office and analyzed the game film. Now even Coach Lawrence was able to see what LaRusso had seen during their early lopsided wins. The team wasn't playing as a team. Their trademark ball distribution and passing had defaulted to individuals playing one-on-one against the opposition. Keen was shooting the ball too much, which had decreased everyone else's opportunities to get their shots. Now, when players did get an opportunity to touch the ball, they were looking to shoot. Gone was their sharing the ball, making the extra pass, looking for the best shot. Instead of a "we" game, it had become "me" basketball.

"So, what do you want to do?" Lawrence asked LaRusso. "Should we say something to Keen?"

"What can we do?" LaRusso responded. "It's kinda hard to criticize them when they're undefeated. Hopefully, they'll learn from this and get to playing how we used to play. As far as Keen goes, how do you criticize someone that had 35 points in a game and led us to a magical comeback win?"

But things didn't get better. In the second game, Eureka State played Valley University. Valley had finished just behind the Hedgehogs the previous season in conference play. The game started ugly and stayed ugly for Eureka State, and Valley soundly beat them. In addition, Keen had had an off-shooting night. She was 3–15 from the three-point line and only shot three shots in the paint where only last year she had dominated.

Things continued to go downhill over the next several games. The Hedgehogs lost six of their next seven contests and found themselves sitting in the bottom of the conference with the worst record. The team's field goal percentage was awful. Keen, who was hot from the field in the early part of the season, had gone on a real cold streak, and the three-pointers that were falling early in the year were no longer finding the net. Grumblings among the team had come back to the locker room, and team morale was bad. Team chemistry that had included joking and friendships had been replaced with hurt feelings and sniping. After the most recent loss, LaRusso decided she had to address the team.

"What is going on?" she screamed at the team in the locker room after the game. "We're not playing as a team. We're playing like a bunch of individuals!"

"I think we know what's going on," someone said. Everyone looked back at the player who had made the comment. It was Eloise Moscow. Moscow, affectionately nicknamed Hawk because of her defensive prowess, was one of the few seniors on the team. During the recent losing streak, she had remained true to the team's original ball sharing philosophy. "Someone is playing for themselves," Hawk continued. "Their head is already out the door and into the pros."

Everyone knew who Hawk was talking about. Keen stood up scowling back toward Hawk. "Don't dance around it," she said. "Say what you wanna say."

At this point LaRusso interrupted the standoff between the two players. "This isn't productive. Assigning blame doesn't help the situation. We win as team and we lose as a team."

"Hawk's right," someone else chimed in. This time everyone looked back to see that was Terri Nichol, the team's point guard. "We got a player who forgot who she was. She's taking shots she shouldn't taking."

Now Keen was angry. "Screw this," she exclaimed. "I've been carrying y'all all year. I'm done." And with that, she threw her jersey, which she had changed out of, to the ground and stomped out of the locker room.

The rest of the team disconsolately got up in unison and left the locker room soon after. That night, LaRusso received a call from her athletic director.

"Coach, I just got a call from Bobbie Keen's dad. She's left school effective immediately to focus on preparing for the NBA draft. I also received a group letter from several other team members expressing their discontent with their place on the team. We need to meet with the players first thing tomorrow morning and then you and I need to sit down afterwards and talk about coaching philosophy and how to address this issue."

Questions to Consider

1. Who are the stakeholders in this case?
2. Could the coaching staff have done anything early on to circumvent the media banter, which ultimately led to Bobby Keen trying to change her game to be more draftable for the NBA?
3. Once it became obvious that Keen's change in play was hurting the team, what should the coaching staff have done?
4. The athlete padding stats to prepare for a professional career are becoming more prominent. What are some things that universities, the NCAA, and professional sports could do to help improve this trend?

References and Further Readings

Arthur, C. A., Woodman, T., Ong, C. W., Hardy, L., & Ntoumanis, N. (2011). The role of athlete narcissism in moderating the relationship between coaches' transformational leader behaviors and athlete motivation. *Journal of Sport and Exercise Psychology, 33*(1), 3–19.

DelVecchio, S. (2021). Mike Leach blasts sports 'selfish' players who sit out bowl games. *Larry Brown Sports.* https://larrybrownsports.com/college-football/mike-leach-blasts-selfish-Players-sit-out-bowl-games/588599

Roberts, R., Woodman, T., Lofthouse, S., & Williams, L. (2015). Not all players are equally motivated: The role of narcissism. *European Journal of Sport Science, 15*(6), 536–542.

Zinkula, J. (2019). *NBA basketball: Is sport losing too much talent early to the NBA?* https://bustingbrackets.com/2019/06/01/ncaa-basketball-sport-losing-much-talent-early-nba-draft/

26 Self Over Team

Coach Grant Stuck had been the head coach of men's wrestling for 13 years at Gresham Community College (GCC). There had been talks of a women's team more recently, which he was in favor of, but for now he worked with a group of tough, rowdy, but competitive men who were always looking to make the step up. For many, this would be the last stopping point in their careers. Some were at GCC because they just weren't good enough for one of the powerhouse universities. Some couldn't handle the academic workload, and some had experienced challenges at the upper levels; they were talented enough to make it to the major wrestling universities, but behavior or some other action had led them down the path of community college wrestling.

Grant had built a reasonably successful program with his band of brothers as he liked to call them. Some stayed for two years, and others were able to make it up and out to a division one university after a year. It was not uncommon to see wrestling scouts in the stands at his meets. He really had seen some talent come through his facility.

This year was not unlike many others. The team was talented, and it was Grant's job, along with his part-time assistant, to try to bring them all together to work toward team goals that led to the success of all of them. Of course, it was never easy. Everyone wanted to be on the mat, and there was the usual bickering about who got the starting spots. Add almost constant hunger into the mix as they tried to stay lean and make weight, and it was a challenge to keep wrestlers happy and focused on long-term goals.

Statistics were one way Grant tried to get his team motivated toward these goals. He used stats for all kinds of things. Team and individual records were plastered on the wall and mats, and he collated other stats such as takedowns, reversals, riding time, wins, losses, and even more for each meet, individual, and team. As years went by, statistics became a norm. Grant really pushed beating the stats and made it almost a tradition, believing it really helped to push his teams to better themselves and the wrestlers who had come before.

A new season brought new talent and challenges. Xavier Franks was a standout at 145 lb and had found his way to GCC by way of some poor decision making as a freshman at a major Division I university. Grant knew he wouldn't be staying at GCC for long given his potential, but once you have lost the limelight, it is always hard to get it back. But Xavier worked hard in practice and looked authentic. He'd already

DOI: 10.4324/9781003375449-28

achieved a couple of college preseason records, and Grant was excited by the potential of a very good team this season.

The season started well. A 7–3 record was comfortably within the margins for good seedings for most of his wrestlers heading into nationals. Grant's athletes were performing well and earning points when the team needed them. At times Grant asked his wrestlers to compete for the team above themselves. For example, if a wrestler was down near the end of the third period, he would ask them to avoid the pin or takedown rather than try one of their own. This would guarantee a loss to the athlete, of course, but it would avoid the potential for giving up bonus points for a big loss. It was a decision he hated making at times, but it was a team decision, not an individual one, and was based on the statistics.

Over the course of the season Xavier had done very well. A flashy wrestler, he enjoyed trying the big pin and flair move over steady points. Several of his matchups had not gone the distance, and his social media following had exploded with some of his clickbait moves. On a couple of occasions, Grant had noted Xavier not following his instructions. The team had not accrued as many points as Grant had wanted because Xavier had avoided the small but incremental points for the big one. They hadn't always happened. Yet, while this frustrated Grant, Xavier kept winning.

As the season neared the championships, Grant spoke to Xavier about it.

"Xavier, you've got to think about the team too," said Grant.

"I've got you Coach," responded Xavier. "I'm not going to let you down. You know that."

"I know, I know," Grant replied. "But sometimes we need the small points to add up. Last week you didn't hit your pin, and you could have earned bonus points if you'd at least hit your tech fall. But you didn't."

"But I still won, didn't I? That helps the team."

Grant sighed. "Yes, it always helps, but I want you to think of how this affects the team. We want to win a team national championship too."

"Gotcha, Coach. I'll try and listen more when I'm on the mat. I just love finishing them inside the time, you know?"

"I know. But this is for us, not you."

"Okay, Coach. I'll try and do better."

The team entered their final dual meet at home on a high. The athletes entered the mats to the blare of their music and the cheers from home support. And they started well in the 121lb and 128lb, winning both by small margins. But their 136lb was pinned in dramatic fashion, and GCC fell behind on points. Grant felt confident when Xavier stepped to the mat, but he'd seen his athlete waving to his girlfriend in the stands just before he walked on. His girlfriend waited with her phone ready. Grant suddenly didn't feel so confident.

The match went the typical "Xavier way" whereby Xavier toyed with his opponent through the first two periods looking for a pin. Xavier was up by one, having exchanged some stalling and escapes, but Grant bellowed from the sidelines for Xavier to grind out some points. But Xavier didn't listen. With 30 seconds to go, Xavier exploded into life and put his opponent into a near fall. He went for the pin but couldn't hold it; his opponent wriggled out of the move and escaped. As the official raised Xavier's hand at the buzzer, Xavier fist pumped to his girlfriend, but Grant was not as ecstatic. The team had suffered from his selfishness.

After the meet, Grant's assistant coach pulled him aside to show him Xavier's social media account. The hits, likes, and shares were climbing from the spectacular move Xavier had made in the third. What it didn't show was the finish, where his opponent escaped from it. Grant sighed and went to find Xavier.

"Xavier, we need to talk."

"About what Coach?"

"What happened to what we talked about? What happened about grinding out wins, looking for the tech falls and so on? I thought you understood we needed that for the team?"

Xavier shifted uncomfortably.

"Well?" Grant finally asked.

"Uh, it's like this, Coach." Xavier paused again, deciding whether to speak or not.

"Just tell me!"

"Well, you're always preaching about stats and how important they are. And I've realized they are. No one cares if I get a tech fall or if I grind out a win. I've got fans."

"What are you talking about?"

"Look, Coach. I'm in community college, and I don't know if I'll ever get picked up by a Division I university again after what I did to get me put here. I have to think about numero uno. And that's about stats. How many viewers I have, who liked my posts, how many shares I get. It's about stats, Coach. That's what the people are interested in."

"What people?"

"The fans! They don't care about boring stats. They want big-time stats. That's what sells." Xavier was getting increasingly animated. "Coach, I've been talking with my girlfriend and some others about going MMA after this year."

"Mixed martial arts?"

"Yeah, Coach. It's about what sells. I've got the talent, and I've been building my brand this year. I've talked with some reps, and they're interested in offering me a package. But I've got to get my profile up, and it's hard at GCC, you know? But when I put on a show, people like it. That's why I don't really care about stats, or at least your stats, anyway. They care about pins, Coach! Those are the important stats. And I care about the stats here." He raised his phone. "This is where I'm focused."

"I see," said Grant. He wasn't sure he did but wasn't sure what else to say. "Okay, Xavier. Thanks for being straight with me."

"Sure, Coach. Can I go now?"

"Yes."

With that, Grant left feeling perplexed and unsure what to do next. It was clear that while he had preached the value of statistics, he might have made a monster out of them. How could he convince Xavier to do the right thing for the team when his outlook was so self-centered? How could he keep the team focused through the season? What was he to do now?

Questions for Consideration

1. Who are the stakeholders in the case?
2. At what point do you think Coach Grant should have stopped Xavier from promoting himself over the team's goals?
3. If you were Coach Grant, and you decided to put an end to Xavier's showboating, what would you do? Would you enforce disciplinary action or something else? Justify your answer.
4. Provide some statistics on the use of varying platforms of social media. Which one is currently the most used/popular among 16- to 25-year-olds?
5. If you found yourself in Coach Grant's position at the end of the story, what would you do and why?

References and Further Readings

Donelson, G. (2021, August 15). Top NCAA athletes-turned influencers. *Tagger Media*. www.taggermedia.com/blog/top-ncaa-athlete-influencers

Lim, J. H., Donovan, L. A., Kaufman, P., & Ishida, C. (2020). Professional athletes' social media use and player performance: Evidence from the national football league. *International Journal of Sport Communication*, *14*(1), 33–59.

Park, J., Williams, A., & Son, S. (2020). Social media as a personal branding tool: A qualitative study of student-athletes' perceptions and behaviors. *Journal of Athletic Development and Experience*, *2*(1), 2.

Price, S. (2021, April 26). How Premier League starts can use statistics to boost their careers. *Forbes*. www.forbes.com/sites/steveprice/2021/04/26/how-premier-league-stars-can-use-statistics-to-boost-their-careers/?sh=2bbb3dab4399

Su, Y., Baker, B., Doyle, J. P., & Kunkel, T. (2020). Rise of an athlete brand: Factors influencing the social media following of athletes. *Faculty/Researcher Works*. https://doi.org/10.32731/SMQ.291.302020.03

27 The Job Carousel

At Oldstown University, a Division II school in Nebraska, the women's lacrosse team is led by head coach Jill Rutherford, assistant coach Erica Pelton, and volunteer coach Tommy Quan. Following a final four appearance, they were all excited by the team's returning talent despite losing two key seniors. With some new incoming freshmen with great potential, they were looking forward to trying to go one more round further next year.

Of course, everyone was dreaming of a national title, something Oldstown University could have only laughed at prior to Rutherford's arrival. Over a nine-year period, she and Erica had slowly built the program from a "lucky to get to .500" status into a genuine contender for a title.

Jill and Erica had an excellent relationship that had stood the test of time and trials. They complemented each other's strengths well, which had been a significant contributor to the program's improvement. In fact, the team might have even said that Erica was the real mastermind behind all the clever game plans that had contributed to the team's success.

Although not all assistant coaches are happy being number two, Erica was content. She knew Jill would at some point soon call it quits and hand over the reins to Erica. Jill had been intentional about preparing Erica to take over the team for several years. Perhaps, just perhaps, Jill was waiting for that one real shot at a championship before she hung up her whistle.

But you know when you're watching a movie, and literally the last thing you would expect to happen, happens? Well, perhaps someone could have written the script for what followed because it sure had the hallmarks of a classic plot twist movie.

Not two weeks into the off-season on a Monday morning, Jill called a meeting with the staff and team and announced her resignation. No forewarning; no heads-up; no courtesy call to Erica. Jill quite literally walked in, announced it was time for her to move on (not retire by the way; she never used the word "retire"), said her goodbyes, and was gone, just like that. One would assume that Jill would at least pack up her office, but that had been taken care of too. She'd apparently come in during the weekend and cleaned out.

"This was a very difficult decision for me," she said to them all. "I want you all to know this has nothing to do with you all. I really could not have asked for anything more from you. This decision was really about respect, and I'm not going to compromise one of my core values, even for a generous contract offer."

DOI: 10.4324/9781003375449-29

She delivered this announcement with directness, empathy, and sincerity. But with that, Jill was gone. Over the course of the next few minutes, Erica was pummeled by questions from staff and player alike. Not that she had any answers. They all felt an overwhelming sense of sadness, confusion, anger, anxiety, and hopelessness. How were they going to continue achieving success without their leader? How were the players going to develop and get that championship they all wanted so badly? Would the environment next year still be one they appreciated and loved? Who was responsible for Jill's feelings of disrespect? Why would anyone be disrespectful toward Jill, one of the most successful and admired coaches at the school and in all of women's lacrosse? How could the players and staff trust the administration to have their best interests in mind when the person they trusted the most could not apparently do so?

While Erica's plan was to take over as head coach in years to come, she did not expect that time to be pushed up to now. She'd learned a lot from Jill over the years and knew what good leadership from a head coach looked like. But could she lead a team that had been rocked to its core on such short notice? On the other hand, the team needed a leader, and this had always been what she had wanted to do. It didn't take long for Erica to start acting like a head coach, and she did her best to be honest and answer questions. Of course, most of the responses were "I don't know" and "I'll try and find out."

"Will you be our next head coach?" one of the players shouted above the hubbub that comes from the discussion of the shocking news.

"Yeah!" exclaimed a few others. "We want Coach Erica!"

Erica held up her hand and waited for silence.

"Look," she responded. "You know it's not my position to determine who becomes the next head coach. But I appreciate your support, and I think Coach Jill has prepared me well for this role. I want to be here for you all for in whatever you need, and I'm willing to step up if I'm asked to."

There were some cheers around the room at the thought of at least maintaining some continuity to the program. Recruits who weren't given stability might start thinking twice about a program in disarray. While the group was still present, her phone buzzed with a text from Athletic Director (AD) Roger Berry to let her know he was coming over to meet with the staff and then the athletes. Erica broke up the meeting and sent the players off with instructions to return in an hour. They left still buzzing with conversation.

Roger was new to Oldstown, having taken the position not more than six months prior, and Erica had never spoken to him beyond the perfunctory meet and greet when he was first introduced. Suffice to say, none of the lacrosse team, apart from the now departed Jill, really knew Roger. She and Tommy met with Roger and the rest of the lacrosse fitness and training staff in the conference room.

"I'm sorry we're really meeting this way for the first time like this," he began as he sat, "and I know this is a shock to you all. It's a real shock to us too. But you are all professionals, and I expect that you all act like it by seeing out the last couple of weeks of the semester as you are."

Tommy, the volunteer coach spoke up. "What about our own roles on the team?"

"For now, there is no change," responded Roger.

"You mean there's no one in charge? No interim head coach or anything?" asked Erica.

"No. Because this is so sudden and the season is over, we're going to just keep things as they are, and you will all hold the positions you're in until we have some time to look at the whole structure of the program."

"No one in charge . . ." Tommy muttered quietly but loud enough that everyone could still hear. Roger either hadn't heard or elected not to respond.

"Now if you'll excuse me, I also need to talk to the team," he said quickly getting up before anyone else could ask another question. "Can someone please show me to the locker room?"

As he exited Erica, Tommy, and the staff just looked at one another not sure what to say. They slowly rose and followed Roger out of the door and led him to the locker room to talk with the team. Once everyone was quiet, he spoke again. This time, there was nowhere to sit, and he shifted from one foot to the other, seemingly uncomfortable.

"I know this is an incredibly sad day for you all. I know Coach Jill meant an enormous amount to you. But I want to let you know that we're going to continue to fully invest in your program because you all are truly what makes this program successful. We'll move quickly to get a new head coach in place. I understand how important that is for stability of your program. I've already been on the phone making some calls, so I promise you we are moving quickly on this."

"What exactly does fully investing in our program look like?" one of the braver players asked.

"We're already working on a new scoreboard for you all. We're replacing your grass, and we have one of the top five highest coaching salary budgets in Division II for women's lacrosse. We plan to keep it that way."

There were some murmurs around the room with that response, and Erica knew why. Roger might not know, but she knew her team. The players hadn't come to Oldstown for the facilities or the money; they had come to be coached by Jill and were more concerned about who would replace her.

"How will you know if a candidate fits our style of play?" another player asked emboldened by her teammate's first question. "Will you ask for outside help to assist you with that element since you don't know much about lacrosse or our program? Can you just make Erica the head coach?"

There were some noises of support at that last question.

"Yes, I sure will ask for help. As for Coach Pelton, she will be seriously considered given the success she has helped to build here at Oldstown."

"We would love to have some involvement in the process, since no one knows this program better than we do. Will we be able to have a say in the matter?" The question came from the team's co-captain.

"My door is always open and I'll take your feedback anytime."

It was apparent to Erica that Roger had had about enough questions and was ready to leave. But one more question was quickly asked before he could escape, this time from their only international athlete, a walk-on from Israel who had quickly excelled at the sport. Her English was not proficient, but her sincerity was apparent for all to see.

"We have just witnessed our leader walk out of the door after nine faithful years with the program because of you. She did not say this directly, but we know. If you didn't respect her, that shows you don't respect us. So please tell us, how can we trust you to make decisions for us? How can we trust *you*?" She emphasized the last word.

Roger's eyes widened for a second, and his face passed from one of surprise to confusion to annoyance.

"I look forward to hearing your feedback," he finally said, his voice devoid of any empathy or understanding, before walking out.

The players all glanced at one another, mouths agape. With that, the meeting wrapped up. The players could not help but display their feelings of anger, frustration, and hopelessness. Erica said some platitudes but was in shock herself from it all. She had just caught a glimpse of what Jill had been dealing with for the past few months.

"Wow, I can see why Jill made the decision to leave," she thought to herself. "But maybe things will be different with me as head coach. Maybe he will change after going through all of this and treat me with more respect. Besides, the team needs me. The program needs me."

Erica continued to consult with some of the leaders of the team over the next few days to hear their concerns. It was clear they wanted her to become head coach, but she hadn't heard anything from AD Berry. There was little information she could give them. No news isn't always good news, and the days bled into a week. Erica began to fear the worst. She knew how important it was to get a coach named prior to the end of the semester in just a few weeks. Yet, the administration remained silent.

That next weekend, Erica got a call from a colleague at another program.

"Hey, John, what's up?" she asked.

"I called to ask you that same thing!" John exclaimed. "I just spoke with Desiree Haden, one of the associate ADs at your school, and they are chairing the search committee for Jill's replacement. They asked me to interview for the head coach position. I just wanted to call and let you know and see what you thought."

"Really? Well, I'm guessing they're interviewing a few of us to cover their bases. Did you say you will?"

"I said I'd give them a callback. I wanted to call you first and see what's really going on there. Why would Jill leave such a great job where she was so successful? It just seems off."

Without giving specifics, Erica told John that she didn't know exactly why Jill left but it was unexpected, she didn't know in advance, and that she hadn't talked to her since she made her announcement.

"Honestly, you'd be great for the job, but I'm kind of hoping I get selected for it," she concluded.

"Interesting. I asked them about you, and they said that you're fourth on their priority list, so I figured that was because you weren't very interested in the position."

"Wait, what? Are they even allowed to say things like that? Isn't a list like that confidential or something?"

"I don't know, but I'm probably going to tell them I'm not interested. I like where I'm at, and it sounds a bit dysfunctional if you ask me."

They said their goodbyes, hung up, and Erica was left to her own thoughts. Was she really only their fourth choice on the candidate list? Hard to believe maybe, but then again, not hard to believe given that she hadn't heard from the administration much since the hiring process started. Suddenly, the years of preparation and the plans Erica had envisioned for her future were looking bleak. Would she even be the head coach? Would she want to work for someone who put her fourth on the list and had acted like she barely existed? What if she didn't get the job? Did she still have a future at Oldstown at all?

Questions for Consideration

1. Who are the stakeholders in this case?
2. Could AD Berry have done anything to make the situation less problematic?
3. What would you do if you were Coach Erica and why?
4. Is there anything Erica could have done differently to help her and the team?
5. Do you think Coach Jill should have waited until the end of next season to resign? Why or why not?
6. What do you think will happen to the team if Coach Erica chooses to leave? Why?
7. What do you think the challenges will be in finding a new high-quality head coach?
8. Do you think the players should have any involvement in the hiring process? Justify your answer.

References and Further Readings

Dolamore, S., Lovell, D., Collins, H., & Kline, A. (2021). The role of empathy in organizational communication during times of crisis. *Administrative Theory & Praxis, 43*(3), 366–375.

Greenberg, M. (n.d.). University of Illinois assistant coaches controversy: A re-examination of assistant coaches' term of contract. *Marquette University Law School.* https://law.marquette.edu/national-sports-law-institute/university-illinois-assistant-coaches-controversy-re-examination-assistant-coaches-term-contract

Leccesi, J. (2017, July 12). The coach who recruited you leaves the program – now what? *USA Today.* https://usatodayhss.com/2017/the-coach-who-recruited-you-leaves-the-program-now-what

Mazzei, A., Kim, J. N., Togna, G., Lee, Y., & Lovari, A. (2019). Employees as advocates or adversaries during a corporate crisis. The role of perceived authenticity and employee empowerment. *Sinergie Italian Journal of Management, 37,* 195–212.

Schoofs, L., Fannes, G., & Claeys, A. S. (2022). Empathy as a main ingredient of impactful crisis communication: The perspectives of crisis communication practitioners. *Public Relations Review, 48*(1), 102150.

Soltanzadeh, S., & Mooney, M. (2021). Autonomy in the context of decision-making dilemmas. *TMC Asser Institute for International & European Law* (Asser Research Paper), *7.*

28 The Transfer Portal

Decisions, Decisions, Decisions

Coach Jasmine Russell sat back in her office chair and looked around. Her small office didn't reflect the success she'd had in the five years she'd been at Streetwood College, but less visible college sports like women's tennis didn't get the financial love or attention of larger, more prominent programs. Still, multiple conference trophies helped to brighten up the place. She figured she had to be doing something right. "So far so good," Jasmine thought to herself, although that national championship ring had still eluded her. "Maybe this year . . ." The season was nearing its conclusion, and the conference and national championship were in a few short weeks. One of her players had asked to meet, so Jasmine paused for a moment to reflect while she waited along with her assistant coach, Emily Power.

Jasmine always thought of herself as a player's coach. A former pro player herself, she knew what it took to make it. She also knew that her job was to develop each player so that they could succeed at the college and potentially the pro level. She worked hard to build individual connections and relationships with her players so that they would play hard for her. Jasmine was proud that only one player in five years had requested a transfer from her program, and that was because of a family situation at home. She had even helped the player transfer to another program. Transfer portal or not, players seemed to be happy and successful.

Liz Long was a third-year player who seemed to fit the mold of a talented player who could become something special. Jasmine remembered recruiting her and had been impressed by her desire to be challenged physically and mentally. But, at the time, there had been a problem.

"Emily, she's a great player," she told her assistant coach. "She's athletic, talented, and has a high ceiling. She could definitely help us, but we've already filled out our recruiting class for her year."

"I know," replied Emily, "but she's everything you're looking for in a player. If we want to be competitive, how can we turn a great player down?"

Liz Long was indeed a talented athlete, and Jasmine knew she had great potential. She also loved how much she wanted to attend and compete at Streetwood. So, Jasmine decided to make room for Liz Long on the team and offer her a partial scholarship.

Liz came in her freshmen year and worked really hard to make the starting lineup. But always being in the hunt for national championships means a stacked team, and Liz didn't get to play. Perhaps frustrated, Liz didn't continue her upward progression

DOI: 10.4324/9781003375449-30

in her second year. She failed several of the conditioning tests during training sessions and had to take a few mental health breaks throughout the year. She got sick before their first competition and never seemed to recover from it. Jasmine could see her struggle and worked with the team's athletic trainer to get Liz to meet with the school's psychologist. Although Jasmine wasn't exactly sure what they talked about, she was very supportive when Liz needed days off for her mental health, even if it was a challenge for the coaching staff and team dynamics.

"It's frustrating because Liz used to be the most mentally tough person on the team. How can we push her to be better on the court?" Jasmine asked her staff. "She's one of our best players but isn't showing up consistently to practice. With such a strong team, it's tough to keep giving Liz chances when we have others waiting for opportunities."

The coaches continued to give her space when Liz needed it, and Liz still had moments of greatness at times but never seemed to be able to put a string of consistent trainings together. However, by the end of the year, Liz seemed to have recovered and was back in the lineup for the national championship run. Jasmine, Emily, and all the staff were hoping that Liz would be the Liz from her first year and put together some good performances over the last week of the season. It wasn't meant to be, and Liz underperformed. With only 12 players in her roster of starters, when one fails in both singles and doubles it can't be hidden, especially against the very best. A team that had so much potential came home disappointed.

Even though it wasn't the season she had hoped from her, Coach Jasmine was excited for the next season and worked with Emily and her entire staff in the off-season to try and mitigate some of the challenges they had experienced. And the season started very well. Following a strong fall training season, Jasmine was feeling good about where the team was at going into the season. Liz had good practice days and bad practice days, but Jasmine knew that was all a part of being on a very high-level, competitive team. Everyone had to work for their spot, and nothing was guaranteed. This was one of the keys to their success, and players came to be tested and play against the best.

Liz was having a great preseason, but just two weeks prior to their first competition, she fell awkwardly chasing a ball and was diagnosed with a slight strain of the volar ligament in the wrist. The team doctor recommended a weekend of rest, but Liz kept complaining of continued stiffness, so she kept herself out of practice for six days. When the first competition rolled around a few days later, Jasmine did not think it was fair to the team to start someone who had missed so much practice. Plus, Liz had not exactly earned a starting spot yet. Jasmine met with Liz and told her she would get opportunities to start but not that weekend.

And she got those opportunities. The weeks rolled on, but no player really stood out to claim the final spot left in the starting lineup. Then, after several weeks, Liz did just that, coming up big in a few matches for the team. Excited to have a final starting roster, Jasmine announced the list to the team following their most recent success.

The following Monday, Liz sent Jasmine a text asking to meet both her and Emily, which Jasmine set up. Liz came into the office looking a little uncomfortable.

"Hey, Liz, what's up? What a great weekend you had! We're excited to build on that this week at practice," Jasmine said enthusiastically. "Let me pull up some video for you so we can see what we need to work on this week."

Liz twisted uncomfortably in her seat. "Uh, well, that's not why I am here." She paused before blurting out very quickly, "I wanted to let you know I'm entering the transfer portal. I do not feel valued here and want to see what else is out there."

Both Jasmine and Emily looked at each other shocked. Jasmine regrouped quickly.

"Liz, do you know what that means to the team? It would be really tough for us to play a player in the starting lineup that has said they don't want to be here and are looking to leave. You're a starter. I said that this weekend. How do you think that will make your teammates feel if we play you over players who want to be a part of this program in the long term?"

Liz looked down at the floor and didn't say anything for a while. "It's what I want, Coach."

"Can you give us some time to process this?" Emily chimed in. "Liz, we think you're a great player and you just earned your starting spot. We want you to stay but think about how this would look to the team."

"Well, I mean, I'm 100% still dedicated to the team while I'm here. I'm just saying that I'm going to start thinking about and looking into where I want to go. But I'll be fully into the team in the meantime."

The meeting quickly ended, and Jasmine and Emily sat for a moment. This hadn't been anticipated. After some discussion, they agreed to give it a week and see if they could change Liz's mind before they decided what to do. She wanted the best for Liz but felt that this decision to enter the portal was to get more playing time and be a bigger star on the team than she was.

Jasmine thought a lot about Liz that week. She thought she could look past Liz being in the transfer portal, but it was harder than she originally thought.

"I feel like I'm lying to the team," she told Emily a few days later. "They trust us, but if they find out that we're playing Liz knowing that she doesn't want to be here, it could really affect our team culture. I'm afraid they would lose trust in us!"

Emily agreed. She wanted Liz to stay too, but if players found out, Emily thought players would feel betrayed and themselves might try to leave. It could ruin the team.

Later that week they decided to bring Liz in and talk it through with her. After all, Jasmine recruited Liz and knew her well and thought she could be convinced to change her mind. It didn't work, and Jasmine closed the meeting by telling Liz that she and Emily would have to think about what was best for the team moving forward.

After Liz had left, they agreed to make a final decision after that weekend's competition at Thomastown University. Liz had several close friends on the team, and they were worried about the impact it would have on them if Liz was dropped immediately prior to an important competition. That weekend's outcomes would have major ramifications on ranking and tournament seeding.

The next morning at practice, the team seemed really flat. Several players, including Liz, had horrible body language and barely tried during warm-up. It got progressively worse after that, so bad that Coach Jasmine brought the team in.

"A lot of us look mentally unfocused today. I want you all to grab a drink and think about if you want to be at practice or not. If you don't, then please go home, and we will reset tomorrow. Coach Emily and I would like to coach the players that want to be here today. No hard feelings or repercussions if you don't want to be here."

It was a needed speech, and the team responded—all of them except Liz, who grabbed her bag and left. Jasmine texted her later to see if she was okay. Liz responded that her back hurt, and she would be back tomorrow for the trip to Thomastown. Jasmine told her to see the trainer and get any treatment necessary. Liz said she would.

The next morning, as Jasmine and Emily were preparing to leave, Jasmine got a text from Liz: "Will I play this weekend, or are you thinking of not playing me because I'm in the transfer portal? I still want to play." Jasmine hadn't yet decided what to do, and Liz had earned the starting spot from a week before. She made a quick decision and texted back: "I always want to play the best players who have earned their spot, and you have, but you need to get that back checked out before we go." Liz responded, "Okay." A few minutes later, Emily pulled Coach Jasmine aside and told her that Liz had decided not to come on the trip.

"What?" she exclaimed! "I was just texting her, and she was getting her back checked."

"Well," said Emily, "she just texted me and said she wasn't in the right mental space to travel with the team. Guess we are going without her this weekend."

Jasmine shook her head and sighed. What a mess! Here she was, taking her team to one of the most important in-season weekends away from home while one of her starters pulls out last minute. No doubt rumors would fly, and she had to get ahead of this. How did she ever get into this mess? What should she say? The team gathered ready to get on the bus.

"Hey, where's Liz?" asked Karolina, Liz's doubles partner.

Jasmine took a breath, looked at Emily, and took a breath.

Questions for Consideration

1. Who are the stakeholders?
2. Should Liz be allowed to stay on the team? Why or why not? Justify your answer.
3. What are the ramifications of a player entering the transfer portal during season?
4. What could Coach Jasmine have done differently throughout this situation?
5. Place yourself in the position of Emily, the assistant coach. Do you think it is your position to have a say in this situation? Why or why not?
6. The transfer portal also allows coaches to recruit new talent into their roster. What can you do to avoid recruiting a student-athlete who might be wanting to transfer for all of the wrong reasons?

References and Further Readings

Bextraordinary. (2018). Gossip destroys people, teams and workplace culture. *Bextraordinary*. https://bextraordinary.com.au/insights/f/gossip-destroys-people-teams-and-workplace-culture

Dellenger, R. (2022, February 2). As transfer portal overflows, the search for solutions is on. *Sports Illustrated*. www.si.com/college/2022/02/02/college-football-transfer-portal-free-agency-solutions

Linton, I. (2016, October 26). What is a stakeholder in sports? *Small Business – Chron*. https://smallbusiness.chron.com/stakeholder-sports-54584.html

McCarthy, C. (2022). Advisory board members share insights about transfer portal challenges. *College Athletics and the Law, 19*(4), 4–7.

Pifer, N. D., Huml, M. R., & Asada, A. (2021). Switching schools: Examining the networks, antecedents, and on-court outcomes of NCAA Division I men's basketball transfers. *Journal of Issues in Intercollegiate Athletics, 14*, 170–193.

29 If We Can Buy It, Why Can't We Use It?

It had been a long, arduous journey for Burt Goodwin. He had definitely done his time in the coaching business. He had sacrificed long-term friendships. He had held off getting married and starting a family. It had been a long and difficult journey. But Burt had done it because he loved football. He loved everything about it. He looked forward to practice and strategy sessions with his fellow coaches. He enjoyed watching game film and strategy sessions to develop game plans. Burt even liked working with strength and conditioning coaches to create off-season workout plans for players. Football was in his blood, and he couldn't imagine life without it.

Burt's meteoric rise had begun as a volunteer assistant when he was an undergraduate in college. Then he worked as an assistant coach in high school followed by a stint as a high school head coach. Finally, he had returned to college as a graduate assistant while pursuing his master's degree. After ten years of bouncing around from one coaching job to another, Burt had finally hit the jackpot: the head coach position at Lumin University. Burt had begun at Lumin serving as the offensive coordinator for four years. When Lumin's longtime head coach Seth Millick had retired, he pushed for Burt to get the job. The university accepted Coach Millick's recommendation, and Burt was hired. Burt had hit the ground running and had the Lumin Melons seeing success the likes of which they had never experienced in recent memory.

Coming off their first conference title in 20 years, the Melons brought back 16 starters. They were the prohibitive favorites to repeat as conference champions. Burt had become the university darling, and everyone in town and the surrounding area loved him. For the first time in his life, this 36-year-old coach could sit back, relax, and smell the roses. He had finally married his longtime girlfriend Helly, bought a house, and had a baby on the way. Life in this picturesque Colorado town was good, and Burt was happy.

As football season approached, Burt had butterflies like he always did. He was amazed that after all these years he still got as excited about football as much he did when he was a kid. He could barely control his energy level as he arrived at the coach's office to meet with his assistants in preparation for the upcoming season. As he got out of his car, he saw one of his assistants, and they walked together into the sports complex.

"So how you feeling, Coach Burt? Are you as hyped up as I am?" The questions had come from Rick Hale, Burt's assistant coach and offensive coordinator. Rick had

DOI: 10.4324/9781003375449-31

tracked a similar path that Burt himself had gone through. He had been the quarterbacks coach for the past several years at Lumin and had been promoted by Burt to the offensive coordinator after Burt took the head job. Burt felt like a mentor to Rick and wanted to help him achieve his coaching goals like his own had been fulfilled.

"Hyped as an eight-year-old kid at Christmas," Burt responded with a grin.

The two men laughed and sat down at a long table with the rest of the coaching staff. The season had officially begun.

A couple of weeks later, the players arrived at the sports complex for the beginning of spring drills. Burt had a great group of guys on his team. They were all fairly good students, had no off-field issues, and were supportive of their teammates, and almost all of them were open to being coached. Because of the character his players had purveyed over several seasons, Burt felt comfortable with not having to closely monitor them as he might have had to do with a group that might have shown less character. The lack of having to constantly monitor his players was a huge benefit for Burt. He and his assistant coaches could spend their time prepping for practice and games instead of babysitting 85 grown men.

Spring and summer practice went extremely well, and the Melons appeared poised for another run at the conference championship. The confidence coming out of the spring and summer practice sessions had the team feeling well prepped as they entered their first game against non-conference and nationally ranked Eagen State University. Burt had worried that such a tough opponent right of the gate was risky, but it brought a lot of notoriety to his program as it was nationally televised.

As the game played out, the Melons jumped out to a huge lead in the game and held on late to upset Eagen State. The Lumin Melons were no longer just competing for a conference title; the nation realized that they were competing for a national title.

The Melons' hot start continued through their first four games, and they found themselves 4–0 and a spot in the National Collegiate Athletic Association's (NCAA's) top ten football rankings. Always an optimist, the hot start had even exceeded Burt's expectations. He and Coach Hale were hitting all the right keys, and the team really believed that they could beat anyone they played.

The Melons had a bye week between their fourth and fifth game. On the Tuesday of the bye week Burt met with his team.

"Guys, I just got the notice. We have mandatory drug tests on Thursday," Burt said. His statement was met with a collective moan from his players.

"I know, I know," Burt responded. "Make sure you're here on time for your test, and don't do anything stupid before then," he joked.

The players chuckled. Burt was indeed joking, as he knew his players were stand-up kids and would never doing anything as foolish as taking drugs before their drug test.

As Thursday rolled around, Burt arrived at the sports complex with no concerns about the drug testing for his players. He scrolled through his phone as walked through the locker room toward his coaching office. As he passed through the locker room, Burt noticed out of the side of his eye that one of players' lockers was open, so he walked over to close it. The locker belonged to Mark Stout, Lumin's star quarterback. As he reached out to close the locker, Burt noticed a plastic drink bottle in the locker. "Quick Detox" it said on the side of the bottle. A bit puzzled, Burt closed the locker door and went to his office. A quick Google search revealed that "Quick Detox" was a drink designed to eliminate any trace of marijuana from someone's system and would allow an individual to pass any marijuana drug test. Burt's mouth dropped open, and for the first time, he felt butterflies in his stomach for a reason other than excitement.

That night, Burt told Helly what he had found in the locker. She convinced him to call his assistant coach, Rick Hale, and tell him too. Shocked, Rick convinced Burt to meet him back at the sports complex to investigate if they could find any more evidence of the detox drink's use by his players. A few minutes later, the two men met in the sports complex parking lot.

"So where should we look?" Burt asked his assistant coach.

"Right here," Rick replied. He was pointed at a trash can near the exit doors of the sports complex building.

"C'mon," Burt said. "They wouldn't be that stupid!"

"They're kids, Coach," Rick replied. "They think they're invincible."

The two men began to rummage through the trash can, and within seconds they found their first bottle of detox drink. Over the next 20 minutes they found five more. Burt and Rick lined up the bottles on the sidewalk and then sat down dejectedly on the curb.

"What now?" Rick asked Burt.

Burt sighed. "We need to talk to the team tomorrow," he said. "Contact the team tonight and tell them to be at the complex tomorrow morning at 7 A.M. sharp. We're gonna get to the bottom of this before they start their classes tomorrow! Let's keep this between us for now."

With that, the two men said good night and went wearily home.

The two coaches met back in their office conference room at 6 A.M. Neither one had slept well, and both wanted to make sure they arrived before any of their players. Shortly before 7 A.M., the players started meandering in. The concerned look on the coaches' faces let the players know that this meeting was over something big. As the players sat in their desks in the conference room, muffled whispers permeated the air. Everyone was wondering what this was all about. After all the players had arrived, Coach Burt walked in and sat on a table that was positioned in the front of the room. He held one of the bottles over his head that he and Rick had found in the trash. The room went silent.

Burt spoke. "Gentlemen," he said. "Yesterday, Coach Rick and I found several of these bottles in the trash can outside. These are drinks used to mask marijuana use. What the heck is going on? You all sit here, and Coach Rick and I are going to call each of you into my office. You're going to be honest and tell me if you've drunk one of these."

Both coaches left the room and walked to their offices, which were down the hall. Before they made it to their office, they heard someone behind them say, "Hey, Coach." The two men turned back and found Dylan Gorge walking toward them. Dylan was a star wide receiver for the Melons. A senior, experts were predicting him to be a high second round draft pick.

"Dylan," Burt said. "Do you have something to tell us?"

"Could I speak with both of you in your office?" Dylan continued.

The two coaches nodded, and the three went to Burt's office and closed the door.

"Coach, I'm really sorry about this," Dylan began. "We weren't doing this to get you or anyone else in trouble," he continued.

"How many players do you mean by 'We'?" Burt retorted. "How many are we talking about?"

"Maybe a couple of dozen. Maybe more. I don't know for sure."

Burt put his head in hands and rubbed his head. "Good grief, Dylan! Who are some the guys we're talking about here?"

"Me, Mark, Irving, Ethan, and . . ."

Burt cut him off. "Stop. I don't need to hear any more right now." It was devastating to hear the names that Dylan had just given. Irving Bailiss was the starting running backs for the Melons. He could have gone pro after his junior season but had come back to improve his draft stock and help his team contend for another conference championship. Ethan Fower was the starting left tackle for the Melons. A mountain of a man, he was responsible for protecting his quarterback from a blind side hit. Only a sophomore, he was already getting scouting reports from the National Football League's (NFL's) teams.

"Why, Dylan?" Burt asked. "Why would you guys smoke pot and jeopardize everything we've been working for?"

Dylan looked at Coach Burt with a confused look on his face.

"Smoke? We didn't smoke anything! We took gummies."

"Gummies? I'm confused!"

"Yeah, Coach. We wouldn't smoke. That would hurt our performance."

Burt was getting frustrated. "What are you talking about, Dylan? What is going on? Why were you ingesting gummies?"

Dylan took a deep breath and started to explain.

"Coach, some of us were having a lot of pain issues from some nagging injuries. Others on the team were having terrible performance anxiety. A low dose of the THC gummies is really effective."

Burt rubbed his head again. "Where did you even get these gummies? Did you just walk into a dispensary and buy them?" Years earlier, Colorado had passed legislation making it legal to purchase marijuana from licensed dispensaries.

"No, Coach."

"Then how, Dylan?" Burt asked. "How did you purchase them?"

"There's a doctor here in town. We went to him, and he legally prescribed them for us for pain and anxiety," Dylan answered.

"You mean you all got real prescriptions?" Burt asked.

"Yes, Coach!" Dylan said. "Since it's legal in the state and since we got a prescription, we thought it would be okay. The only reason we did the detox drinks is because at the last second before the drug test, a few guys got nervous."

Burt remained silent for a couple of minutes pondering all he had just been told. Finally, he spoke.

"Okay, Dylan. Thank you for coming forward. Please go back to conference room and tell your teammates to head to class. I need to talk to Coach Hale. Tell everyone to meet back in the conference room at the beginning of practice this afternoon."

As Dylan left the two coaches looked at each other, both waiting for the other one to talk.

"Good grief," Rick sighed. "What do we do?"

"It seems we have two choices," Burt began. "We can do another surprise drug test and kick everyone off the team that shows up positive, which would effectively end our season. Or we could roll with this, and if comes to a head and the players get busted, we could argue that it's legal in the state and the players even had legal prescriptions; so, they shouldn't be penalized for that."

"I don't know," Rick responded. "There's no way that argument would work; would it?"

"Rick," Burt said. "A few years ago, no one ever thought that players could earn money off their likeness or transfer to another school without a penalty year. Now look at the rights to athletes. Maybe we should make a stand here too, on this issue? Whatever we decide, we need to decide now and back each other regardless of what choice we make."

The two men sat in Burt's office contemplating what to do next. This might be the most crucial decision either one would make in their lifetime. Burt felt the butterflies starting up again.

Questions for Consideration

1. Who are the stakeholders in this case?
2. What steps could the coaches have done early in the process to circumvent the situation they found their team in?
3. At the end of story, the coaches are left with two decisions on how to address the situation. If you were a coach in this scenario, which direction would you go? Defend your answer.
4. Looking into the future, where do you see the issue of sport and marijuana use ending up?

References and Further Readings

Abrams, J., & Ganguli, T. (2022). Why pros like Britney Griner choose Cannabis for their pain. *New York Times*. www.nytimes.com/2022/08/01/sports/basketball/brittney-griner-athletes-cannabis-marijuana.html

Hanna, J. (2019). It's time to get real about Marijuana and professional sports: Part 1. *American Bar Association*. www.americanbar.org/groups/litigation/committees/jiop/articles/2019/marijuana-professional-sports/

Malcolm, K. (2021). An Olympic controversy: Do marijuana and athletes mix? *Michigan Health*. https://healthblog.uofmhealth.org/bones-muscles-joints/an-olympic-controversy-do-marijuana-and-athletics-mix

Marshall, L. (2021). Should marijuana still be banned from sport? *CU Boulder Today*. www.colorado.edu/today/2021/07/07/should-marijuana-still-be-banned-sport

30 It's Not Who I Am

"Okay, everyone, let's bring it in and hit the road," Coach Pauline Raven shouted above the splashes and noises that reverberate around any swimming natatorium. It was the end of the conference championships, and while none of her swimmers would be heading to nationals, it hadn't been a bad season. Finishing fourth at conference was commendable given their budget and the challenges of recruiting to a smaller college. Arkadoo wasn't exactly a destination location for swimming, or anything for that matter, so Pauline was proud of what they had done that year with the group that they had. Her swimmers headed toward the bus, and she waited at the steps to the bus to do a head count before their 6-hour ride home.

As the coach hit the interstate, Pauline settled into her seat to reflect on a season well done. But her reverie was soon interrupted by a tap on the shoulder. She turned to see Liam Manuel. Liam was a good student-athlete who attained decent grades but hadn't had a good season in the pool, if it must be said.

"Hi, Liam. What's up?" she asked.

"Uh, hey, Coach. Can I meet with you sometime soon? I need to talk to you about something private."

"Yeah, okay. Can you give me an idea what it's about?"

"Well, I need to talk to you about something I'm going through. It's pretty personal. I'd prefer not to say more on the bus."

"Okay, sure. But I'd like Coach Reed to be there too," responded Pauline, nodding her head toward her longtime assistant, Lonnie Reed, already asleep on the other side of the aisle. "That okay with you?"

"Uh, yeah. Sure. I guess so."

"Alright. Well, let's get back to campus and will figure out a good time. Okay?"

"Thanks, Coach."

A couple of days later, once the student-athletes had settled back into spring classes and the coaches had recovered a little from the grueling trip to the conference championships, Pauline set up a meeting with Lonnie and Liam in her office. Liam shuffled in looking nervous.

"Hi, Liam. How's it going?" Lonnie asked as he walked in.

"Good, I guess," responded Liam.

"Take a seat, Liam," Pauline said, gesturing to the seat available next to Lonnie at the coffee table. She got up from behind her desk and moved over to the chair opposite

DOI: 10.4324/9781003375449-32

them bringing a pen and paper to take notes. She hated talking to people from behind a desk, especially when things might be sensitive. Note taking had become a norm because you never knew when you'd need evidence of what actually took place. It was rare, but it did happen. She'd learned that much in her coaching education. Liam fidgeted and looked nervous, so Pauline spoke first to break the ice.

"So, how do you think the season went for you?" she asked.

"Not great at all," Liam responded.

"A little harsh maybe, but I wouldn't disagree with you entirely," Lonnie chimed in. "But if you could put your finger on it, what do you think caused you to have a season below your expectations? Looking at your times you seem to have dipped this year."

"Yeah, that's kind of why I wanted to talk to you." Liam paused as if deciding before taking a deep breath and continuing. "Look, only my parents and brother know about this, but over the last year or so I've been seriously considering transitioning to a female."

Pauline tried to maintain her look of surprise, but there's no doubt that had a camera been in that room, a poker face she would not have had. Lonnie couldn't hide his surprise either, and the gaping mouth gave that away. Pauline quickly rallied from the surprise.

"Well, uh, Liam. I've got to be honest. That was not one of my top ten things I was expecting to hear." Lonnie nodded his head in agreement. "Perhaps you can give us a little backstory to fill us in with what's going on?"

Liam nodded his head and looked up to the left, a tell that he was accessing his memories.

"Even as a kid I've always felt uncomfortable about who I was. I have an older brother, but I never wanted to do things he wanted to. And in high school I really didn't feel right. I didn't fit in. It was like my mind didn't sync with my body. It's really hard to explain."

Liam paused, but neither coach spoke.

"When I came to college, I wanted to swim my best. But I felt so weird swimming as a woman in what I felt was a man's body. After a while, I went and got some counseling from someone in the counseling center, and I finally began to understand who I was. This has been going on for three years now, and I've finally accepted that I'm transgender. This past year has been awful for me. I mean, it's nothing to do with either of you. You've been great. But I've felt depressed. I haven't been sleeping well. I've missed some classes I shouldn't have. I've gotten to the point where I realized that if I didn't do something I'd be messed up as a swimmer, student, and person. So here I am."

Pauline spoke first. "Thanks for sharing, Liam. Or is it Liam? I guess I don't know what to call you now. I'm sorry. I don't want to be awkward, but I don't want to offend you."

"That's okay. Liam is fine for now. I'm still trying to figure things out too. I've talked to my parents, and I'm going to start hormone replacement therapy, or HRT, in the off-season. But my question to you is, can I still be on the team as a transgender athlete? What about my scholarship too?"

Pauline sat back and looked at Lonnie. Lonnie shrugged his shoulders; he didn't look too comfortable with any of this conversation.

"Well, Liam. I honestly have no idea. Coach Lonnie and I will have to discuss it, of course, and we will need to discuss with the university probably about what legal requirements are necessary for you to compete on an athletic team. And, while we haven't had much time to digest this, obviously, assuming you can be on the team we'll need to think about how we tell the rest of the team."

Liam nodded. "Yeah, Coach. I know this is unusual, and I get that I might not be able to swim again on a team. But this is more important to me than swimming."

Lonnie finally spoke. "Look, Liam. Are you absolutely sure you want to do this? Can you wait another season and finish out your career? I get that you've had a bad year, but maybe we can help you more? Forget your times and performances for a second. I'm just thinking of the ramifications of what this might mean. People are going to go nuts. And I'm just trying to tell you the truth here. And when I mean people, I'm not just talking about the locals. This is media worthy stuff. You'll be in the news, maybe even in national news, and with that comes unbelievable scrutiny. Is that what you want?"

"Lonnie," Pauline interrupted.

"No, hold on, Coach. He, I mean she, I mean Liam . . . sorry Liam, I'm . . . this is weird."

"It's okay, Coach," Liam said.

"There's also going to be pressure in the university. You're going to be stared at in class. People will look at you differently. You may lose friends." Liam was beginning to look despondent, and Pauline could see that Lonnie's words, albeit true, were hurting.

"Lonnie, hold off a minute."

"No, Coach. Liam needs to hear this. If . . . Liam can't handle this, then what's it going to be like in an environment where people don't support this? Liam, I'm just trying to be real. Assuming you can swim, it's going to really affect the team. I have no idea how they will respond. Some are probably going to be really against it. You'll be taking the spot of someone else on the women's side. We'll probably get backlash from parents and donors too."

"Lonnie, enough!"

"But . . ."

"Enough," Pauline said a little more quietly but forcefully. Lonnie stilled.

"Look, Liam," Pauline said turning back, "while this is hard to hear, what Lonnie is saying is true. I'm sure you've thought about all of this already."

Liam nodded, looking down at the floor.

"This is hard for us to digest, but your welfare is always more important than anything else. Okay?"

Liam nodded again.

"We just want to be sure this is what you want to do. If it isn't, this conversation never leaves this room. If it is, then we'll support you however we can, even if you can't be on the team. Okay?"

"Okay, Coach. Well, I have thought a lot about it. And I've been thinking about it for years. I want this change. I'd rather change than remain on the team. I don't want to have to choose between who I am and the team though."

"Then it's settled. Give us some time to talk to some people about the best way to approach this. I'll need to talk with our Compliance Officer and probably our

Communications Director first. I'll ask that they keep this all confidential until we develop a plan to figure it out."

"Thanks, Coach. You both mean a lot to me."

"You're welcome."

"And I'm sorry for how I took it," Lonnie responded. "I wasn't expecting it and really wanted to make sure you knew what you were doing."

"I get it, Coach. I'm guessing you won't be the first person I surprise." For the first time, Liam had a slight smile.

With that, Liam stood up and left, closing the door to a silence that only comes from the feeling of knowing what upheaval might be coming. Pauline looked at Lonnie; Lonnie looked at Pauline. Neither spoke for a several seconds.

"Well," Pauline said, "strap yourself in Lonnie, because this crazy train is about to get real."

Lonnie groaned, leant back, and looked to the ceiling. "I didn't sign up for this," he muttered quietly. "This isn't right."

"Times, technique, and training," Pauline thought to herself. "That's what I studied to do. That's what coaching is. Why do I have the feeling that I'm going to be doing way more than that this year?"

Questions for Consideration

1. Who are the stakeholders in this case?
2. What did Pauline do right in this situation?
3. Pick a side and defend your answer with support: transgender athletes should or should not be permitted to compete in male–female competitions that are the opposite of their birth sex.
4. Considering the sport that you play or coach, what are the laws or policies associated with transgender athletes? Research them, and share what you learned. Do you agree or disagree with them? Why or why not?
5. Coach Pauline appears to be a little more willing to understand Liam than Coach Lonnie, who might be very much against this transition or allowing Liam to be part of the team. As the head coach, how do you balance the feelings of Lonnie with the wishes of the student-athlete? How do you ensure that you don't bring your own personal feelings about transgender into the situation?
6. Some organizations have discussed the idea of having "open" competitions, where there is no gender, and all compete against one another. Others have suggested that transgender should have its own category. What do you think about these ideas? Back up your answers.

References and Further Readings

Barnes, K. (2022, May 31). Former University of Pennsylvania swimmer Lia Thomas responds to critics: 'trans women competing in women's sports does not threaten Women's sports'. *ESPN*. www.espn.com/college-sports/story/_/id/34013007

BBC. (n.d.). Fina bars transgender swimmers from women's elite events if they went through male puberty. *BBC Sport*. www.bbc.com/sport/swimming/61853450

Roan, D. (n.d., June 20). Transgender athletes: Lord Coe hints athletics could follow swimming in banning trans women. *BBC Sport*. www.bbc.com/sport/athletics/61865789

Sanchez, R. (2022, March 3). 'I am Lia': The trans swimmer dividing America tells her story. *Sports Illustrated*. www.si.com/college/2022/03/03/lia-thomas-penn-swimmer-transgender-woman-daily-cover

Part III

Professional Sports

31 The Salary Cap and the Boss

The words stood out in huge, bold print. This might be one of the great coaching jobs in the history of the league! The headline was splashed across the front of the *Alexandria Gazette*, and they were not an exaggeration by any stretch of the imagination. Over the past four decades, the Alexandria Walkers had been the laughingstock of the National Football League (NFL). Terrible management, faulty coaching, and a string of terrible draft picks and free agent signings had kept the team mired as bottom feeders to the rest of league. The Walkers hadn't seen the playoffs, much less a winning season, in modern times. Gone were the talented players of past championship seasons, and the team had really fallen on hard times. Neegan Morgan, the team's general manager, knew that the reputation of the Walkers would keep away most splashy coaching candidates so that he had to think creatively. He needed to hire a diamond in the rough that no one else in the league was privy too. He decided that coach was Darryl Ditson.

Coach Ditson had been a huge surprise hire by the Walkers. An innovative offensive-minded college coach, Ditson had only been a head coach for three years before Morgan hired him. Before ascending to the head coach position at Commonwealth University, Ditson had splashed onto the scene as an unconventional offensive coordinator. Having created an exciting brand of offensive football at Commonwealth, he was the obvious choice to replace Commonwealth's head coach Gabe Stokes when he retired. In his short stint as the Commonwealth head coach, Ditson had won two conference championships with three bowl appearances. The media and college football experts all anticipated his move to a bigger, more prominent university, but no one thought he'd move to the professional ranks.

Ditson was given a lot of freedom to determine the direction of the team. He could cut players he didn't think worked in his scheme and was also given much of the decision making regarding the draft. And he was allowed, within very tight salary constraints, to pick a few lower-tiered free agents to make out his roster. The team had been so bad for so long that yearly attendance had dropped to exceptionally low numbers. The low attendance combined by the fact that few sponsors wanted to sponsor the team and their antiquated stadium meant revenue was incredibly low. Merchandising for the team was almost nonexistent; not a lot of people wanted to show their team pride by wearing Alexandria Walker shirts.

Coach Ditson came to the Walkers with a concise plan. Upon taking the job, he immediately released or traded away many of the older veterans with inflated salaries.

DOI: 10.4324/9781003375449-34

He then turned his attention to the draft. Aided by his longtime friend and defensive coordinator from Commonwealth, Rick Grines, they meticulously poured over draft reports and college film to find the type of players they wanted to run their team. Ditson often reflected on his first draft with Grines and their conversations prior to that draft because it created the blueprint for them to use with all their drafts in the future.

"So, what do you think, Rick?" Ditson had said. "We need players, a lot of players on both sides of the ball. How do you wanna go about setting up our draft board? What do you need on defense? Guys are a lot bigger and stronger at this level than they were when we were coaching in college."

"Darryl," Coach Grines replied. "I've always thought you said it best eight years ago when I first met you at Commonwealth. You can teach a guy how to get bigger and stronger, but you can't teach them to get faster."

"So, you're suggesting getting quicker players and then beef them up while keeping their speed?" Ditson asked. "You really think that'll work at this level like it did in college?"

"I think it's our best option to become relevant fast," Grines replied.

Darryl nodded, and the two men began creating a comprehensive draft board to search for players to make their team relevant—fast players whom they thought they could pack muscle on. They both hoped this philosophy would work.

Their strategy had immediate success. The team drafted a young, skinny kid as their future quarterback out of a small institution, Hilltop College. Glen Ree had a cannon of an arm and wide receiver speed but had only played against lower-level tier schools and talent. At 6 feet, 1 inch and a scrawny 175 pounds, most scouts predicted that Ree wasn't big enough to play at the pro level. Because of that fact, the Walkers were able to get Ree far lower in the draft than his talent probably deserved. As soon as Ree was drafted, Ditson connected him with his newly hired strength and training coordinator, Abe Ford (nicknamed "Captain America"). Abe immediately began working with Ree to bulk him up. He created a program for the team's new quarterback, which included intense workouts, high-protein diets, and a stretching routine that would allow Ree to add muscle without losing his athleticism and flexibility. By the time preseason rolled around, Ree weighed in at almost 200 pounds. His body was now far more suitable to play in NFL.

But Ree wasn't the only transformation project that Coach Ford had fostered. Ditson and Grines drafted several other smallish players who possessed elevated levels of speed. Tight end Shane Wals, offensive lineman Al Jerry, defensive end Gene Porter, and wide receiver Carl Grines, Rick Grine's son, were all examples of lighter but quicker players that Ford helped mold.

The transformed draft picks along with a sprinkling of good locker room veterans, most notably, linebacker Morgan Joenz, created a different and more optimistic team environment than the Walkers had seen in a long time. Success under Ditson's tutelage came quickly. Taking a team that had won just one game the year before he took over, the Walkers won six in the first season with Ditson. The steady improvement continued the next season with a 10–6 record and a wild card playoff berth. That first draft class that Ditson and Grines fashioned had paid tremendous dividends. Ree had been rookie of the year in his first season. Wals had made a pro-bowl in his second season, and Grine's son, Carl, had burst onto the scene and had led the league in receiving yards in his second season.

Season three saw the Walkers sell out their season tickets for the first time in 40 years. General admission tickets that once sold for $10 were now selling for $50. A ticket to see the Alexandria Walkers had become the hottest in town. The team finished season three with another 10–6 season and a first playoff win in modern memory. The team's quarterback Glen Ree made his first pro-bowl and finished third in the league for the Most Valuable Player (MVP) Award. Wals, Jerry, and Porter had all made second team all-pro. Carl Grines had made first team all-pro while again leading the league in receptions and touchdowns. The Walkers had become media darlings, and no one had anything but acclaim for Ditson's coaching job. He was now considered one of the best young minds in the NFL.

As the off-season began of Walker's fourth season under Ditson, expectations were extremely high. The Walkers were not only the preseason favorites to win their division, but many prognosticators were also picking them as Superbowl favorites. The team had become very profitable. Merchandising and licensing money had skyrocketed, and there was even talk of the city building the team a new state-of-the-art stadium. The team and its ownership were riding a tremendous wave. Coach Ditson was the toast of the town, and the news outlets' headlines sang his praises.

A few weeks into the off-season Ditson got a call from Neegan, the team's general manager.

"Hey, Coach, we need to get together to talk about a few things regarding the off-season," Neegan said. "Can you meet me in the morning?"

Ditson felt the tenor of the conversation was a bit odd but agreed to meet with Neegan the next day. He arrived at the team facility the next morning feeling a bit pensive. He brought his trusted assistant Coach Grines with him, as he'd had a huge role in putting the team together. The three men shook hands and exchanged pleasantries before they all sat down at a large table to talk in Neegan's office.

"So, what's up, Neegan?" Ditson asked. "We usually don't start planning personnel stuff for another couple of weeks."

"Well, Coach, I wanted you to hear it from me first," Neegan said. "Ownership has instructed me to look into seeking trade offers from other teams for your quarterback Ree," he continued.

Ditson and Grines sat still, quite stunned. Both their mouths would have hit the floor if it weren't for the tabletop stopping them.

"What are you talking about?" Ditson asked. "What's going on?"

Neegan sighed deeply. "Well, as you probably know I've been in contract extension talks with Glen's representatives for weeks. Ownership doesn't want to pay him anywhere close to what they're asking."

Ditson and Grines sat still in their chairs in complete shock.

"There's more," Neegan continued. "Of the rest of that core group you originally drafted, ownership is telling me that we can only pick two of those five to retain."

"But all those guys are still under contract for another year!" Ditson exclaimed. "Why move them now?"

"Management wants to build up some draft picks and keep costs low. They feel it's better to trade them now and get something back for them than let them leave next year for nothing."

The Walkers had always been family owned by the Michonne family. Recently, Maggie, the oldest daughter, had taken control of the team and sold some controlling shares to a conglomerate company, known as the Peletier Group. The Peletier Group had an ownership stake in several sports teams around the world. Although they were focused on winning, their primary goal was to run a profitable team. With the quick success of the Walkers, Peletier saw the team as a tremendous investment opportunity, especially with a new stadium in the works.

As the reality of the situation sank in, the three men poured over depth charts and free agents on other teams. The three finally decided on signing Jesus Rovea, a ten-year veteran journeyman who was currently a free agent for the Hillside Whispers. Jesus had had a fairly good season for the Whispers. It was nowhere near the season Glen Ree just had, but Jesus was a serviceable quarterback. Most importantly to management, Jesus would cost them less than half the price Ree would have.

Ree, Grines, and Neegan ultimately decided to keep Grines's son, Carl, and their defensive end Porter while letting go of their tight end and offensive lineman. The unsigned players were replaced by two players who were nearing the end of their careers but came at a very discounted price.

Ditson's fourth season did not go as well as he had hoped. The loss of the all-pro offensive lineman Al Jerry had made the line porous. Quarterback Jesus did not have the same speed and agility as his predecessor. Jesus was under constant pressure, which led to many more turnovers than the team had had in recent seasons. The loss of the tight end Wals took away the offense's safety valve. This caused a lot of drives to stall, and the team suffered. Expectations that had been so high before the season started had gone up in smoke. The team went from a 10–6 season the previous year to a 6–10 season. The once-packed stadium began to see a lot of empty seats at the end of the season.

Ditson and Grines were dejected and felt powerless. As they sat in their office pondering the team's future, Grines decided to break the monotony by turning on the television. A local news network was interviewing Maggie Michonne, the team's owner.

"We're extremely disappointed with our team's performance this year," Ms. Michonne said. "Our ownership group has lofty expectations for this team. Our fans deserve better," she continued. "Everyone bears some responsibility for our disappointing season, from the players to the coaches to the management. As ownership, we will have to evaluate our team, and changes will be made."

A local reporter in the audience shouted out a question. "Could some of those changes include coaching?" they asked.

"Changes could come at any level," Ms. Michonne replied.

Ditson felt his blood pressure rising. His face flushed, and he began to get intensely angry.

"Turn that crap off," Ditson barked. "I've heard enough."

Ditson had no idea was coming next.

Questions for Consideration

1. Who are the stakeholders in this case?
2. What are some things the coaches could have done early on to mitigate the disintegration of the team's talent and possible loss of their jobs?
3. What steps might management have taken to keep the team together?
4. If you were Coach Ditson, what argument might you make to stay the course and keep your job? Defend your answer.

References and Further Readings

Lingerman, M. (2017). European soccer clubs shouldn't be eager to sell top talent for big money. *The Daily Collegian*. www.collegian.psu.edu/sports/men_soccer/european-soccer-clubs-shouldn-t-be-eager-to-sell-top-talent-for-big-money/article_bbeb2780–929e-11e7–13b-d34de740447d.html

Parcells, B. (2020). The tough work of turning a team around. *Magazine*. https://hbr.org/2000/11/the-tough-work-of-turning-around-a-team

Paresh, D. (2013). By deferring some earnings, athletes can help themselves and their teams. *Los Angeles Times*. www.latimes.com/sports/la-sp-worst-sports-contracts-20131117-story.html

32 Drafts, Management, and the Coach

Coach Frank Cassel was ready! After three years of waiting, his time was almost here. Coach Cassel had taken over as the head coach for the professional football team, the Columbus Punishers, four years earlier. At the time he took over, the team was saddled with several huge salaries for older players who were well past their prime. Even more troubling was the fact that the Punishers had acquired these players by giving away numerous draft picks to acquire them. This had all been done before Coach Cassel had become head coach, but he still had had to endure the mistakes made by the previous general manager (GM) and coach. But now, this year, the team had finally cleared those salaries, and for the first time in his tenure as coach, they had a first- and second-round draft pick in the upcoming draft. Better yet, Cassel and the new GM, Curt Hoyle, had traded away some players to move up in draft to really improve their first- and second-round picks. They were now near the top of each of the rounds and had several picks in the third and fourth rounds.

Bill Russou had bought the team 20 years ago and had seen little success during his ownership. An extensive list of coaches and GMs had been hired only to fail at turning the team around. Russou had always been a hands-off owner. He hired a GM and coach and stepped back to let them do what they do. The problem was that he had not been particularly savvy when it came to hiring management or coaches. However, Russou had been pleased with the progress that Cassel and Hoyle had made. Although the team had yet to make the playoffs, they had been in contention the past two years. And now, without the expiring guaranteed contracts of the aging players looming over them like an albatross, the Punishers finally had a real opportunity to upgrade their team talent and seriously compete.

The team was desperate for an influx of fresh players. Cassel and his assistant coach Lieberman knew that the team needed help on both sides of the ball. Cassel not only was the head coach but also served as the defensive coordinator, while Lieberman served as the offensive coordinator. The two men had poured over countless draft sheets, college game video, testimonials from coaches, and stat sheets to try to fill as many needs as they could.

Lieberman had received a master's degree in statistics while working as a graduate assistant for his college football team. He was an expert at sports analytics and had created a series of tested mathematical models that helped determine best matchups and what players might be the best to draft. Despite his tried-and-true formulas, the draft

DOI: 10.4324/9781003375449-35

prep was always a laborious task. To aid in this endeavor, as they had done in previous years, the two men had called in several other assistant coaches on their staff to assist in the process. Jon Pilgram, the offensive line coach, and Stan Stein, the defensive backfield coach, were there to offer their opinions and try to help rebuild the team through this high-stake draft. After weeks of preparation, they had identified the direction and players they wanted to go for in the draft. What made it even more exciting was the fact that this was a draft loaded with talent at almost every position the team needed.

A week out from the draft, Cassel and Lieberman met with GM Hoyle and the owner Bill Russou to go over the plan for the draft. As they arrived at the team complex, their heads swirled at the enormity of what was coming. But they were prepared; they had done their homework and were ready. Upon entering the administrative conference room, the two coaches noticed that several other people were already sitting at the long conference table in the room. Of course, Bill Russou, the team owner, was there along with GM Hoyle. But there was someone else there too, someone they didn't recognize. A young woman was sitting next to the team owner.

"Gentlemen," Russou said. "I want to introduce you to my granddaughter, Dina Mitani." The young woman stood up with the introduction and shook hands with both the coaches. "Guys, Dina just graduated with her MBA from Harvard! She's sharp as a whip. I've asked her to sit in with us today to help sort this draft thing out. You know the draft has never really been my thing. Dina has been doing her homework, and I think I'm going to let her take over any input I might have here."

"Oh, Grandpa," Mitani said blushing. She was obviously a little embarrassed by her grandfather's praise. "Gentlemen, I'm not here to rock the boat. I'm just here to give my input and ideas regarding the team direction."

Cassel and Lieberman sat in shocked silence. Finally, Cassel broke the awkward silence. "It will be a pleasure working with you, Dina," he said. With that, he and Lieberman opened their paper file folders and began laying out the stacks of documents that they, along with their other assistants, had meticulously labored over. As the coaches arranged their documents on the long conference table, Mitani, who had brought a folder of her own, began to lay out her documents on the table opposite of the coaches. The coaches were not only a bit surprised but also a little impressed.

For the next several hours Mitani, the two coaches, and the GM compared notes. Both groups vigorously argued their positions on which players made the most sense to draft. The foursome did agree on some prospective players, but Mitani and the two coaches had quite different opinions on who to select for the coveted first- and second-round draft picks. All the while, Russou sat off to the side answering some emails on his phone and looking glowingly at his granddaughter. Late into the evening the group agreed to call it a night.

"Guys, look," Mitani said. "Ultimately, the decision on who to draft in the early rounds is yours to make. I stand by my assertions, but the final decision is yours."

Cassel and Lieberman took a huge sigh. "You don't know how much we appreciate hearing that, Dina. We respect you and your input too. Thank you for allowing us the opportunity to make our selections in those early rounds," Cassel said.

The five people at the table shook hands and left the complex. Cassel and Lieberman, who had driven over to the meeting together, debriefed as they drove home.

"That was some kind of a crazy, unexpected day," Lieberman said a bit exasperated.

"Yes, it was," Cassel responded. "Thank goodness, it turned out all right in the end. If we hadn't gotten to draft the players we wanted after finally getting some top-round picks . . . well, luckily, we don't have to worry about that."

Other than a few generalized emails, there wasn't any meaningful communication between the coaches and the management in the past few days leading up to draft day. The coaches met again several times to sure up contingency plans in case their primary choices were taken ahead of their draft position.

On draft day, all the coaches, the GM and his assistants, the owner and his granddaughter all met in a decked-out strategy room. Cameras and camera crew covered every angle in the room. Everyone was in an upbeat and excited mood. Mitani hugged Cassel and Lieberman and told them she hadn't been able to sleep the night before because she was so excited.

The Punishers had the fourth pick in the first round. It was the first time in five years the team had had a first-round pick and even longer since it had a pick in the top five. They also had two early selections in the second round. Although this was a talent-rich draft, Cassel and Lieberman really had their eyes on one of two players. The first player they prized was a defensive end named Wilfred Rollins. Rollins was considered a "can't miss prospect" by the experts. In college, he had been unstoppable, piling up 14 sacks and 65 tackles in just 12 games. Opposing coaches said he was unstoppable even when he was double teamed. Many draft experts tagged him as the best defensive line prospect in 30 years. He was a beast. The second player the coaches had identified for the first round was a linebacker. Brett Maloney possessed both size and speed. He had the football IQ of a quarterback and would be the perfect captain for their defense. Maloney was also considered a "can't miss prospect." Both players would be expected to make an immediate impact on any team they went to. The problem was that the Punishers were not the only team who wanted these players. Any one of the three teams picking ahead of them could grab either of these coveted players. Cassel and his assistants had resigned themselves that both these picks might have gone when it came their turn to pick. This is why the contingency selections they had developed were so important.

The draft began. The Jigsaws had the first selection. They were coming off a terrible season and needed help on both offense and defense. The League Commissioner came to podium and read off the Jigsaws selection.

"With the first pick in the draft the Jigsaws select Arrey Bendex, offensive lineman." Cassel was surprised and elated. "One team down, two to go," he said to himself.

Amazingly, the next two teams passed over both the players the Punishers coveted. When Cassel realized that both their choice players were available, he grabbed Lieberman, Pilgrim, and Stein in astonishment.

"Holy cow, guys," he screamed. "Who do we take?"

As the four coaches huddled, they could hear the commissioner's announcement on the screen.

"The Punishers are now on the clock. They have 10 minutes."

Suddenly, Cassel felt a tap on his shoulder. He turned around to find Bill Russou standing there.

"Coach," Russou sheepishly said. "Could I have a quick word?"

"Sure, Bill," Cassel responded. "But we need to hurry. We're on the clock."

"Coach, I know you and the other coaches are really high on a couple of defensive players, but my granddaughter really feels we need to select a wide receiver she's researched," Russou said.

"What?" Cassel responded in shock. "She said it was ultimately our decision. What's changed in the last few days?"

"Nothing really," Russou continued. "It's just that Dina is so certain of this player. What if we go with the receiver in the first round and you guys pick both the second-round players? What are your thoughts?"

Cassel stood still and in a complete disbelief of what was happening. What should he do now?

Questions for Consideration

1. Who are the stakeholders in this case?
2. What were some mistakes the coaches made leading up to the draft?
3. Should the GM have been more involved in the drafting process? How might that have helped the outcome?
4. If they had it to do over, what do you think the coaches might have done differently to get the outcome they wanted?

References and Further Readings

D'Andrea, C. (2019). Kliff Kingsbury once said he'd draft Kyler Murray No.1 overall. *Good News Kliff!* www.sbnation.com/2019/1/10/18176792/kliff-kingsbury-Kyler-murray-2019-nfl-draft-no-1-overall-good-news-kliff

Gabriel, G. (2014). A front office guide to draft day. *The Bleacher Report.* https://bleacherreport.com/articles/2054904-an-insider-guide-to-draft-day-and-the-nfldraftroom#:~:text=On%20draft%20day%2C%20there%20is,some%20cases%2C%20the%20owner

Nanavati, R. (2020). *Whose decision was it to make Tua Tagovailoa the starting quarterback in Miami?* https://phinphanatic.com/2022/01/07/stephen-ross-forced-tua-tagovailoa-grier-flores/

Pompei, D. (2016). How NFL teams really make their draft picks. *The Bleacher Report.* https://bleacherreport.com/articles/2631445-how-nfl-teams-really-make-their-draft-picks

33 I've Got the Power

Or Do I?

It was a routine training session on a Wednesday afternoon in September at the Seattle Admirals practice facility. With just a few weeks to go before the preseason started, Head Coach Andy Warrick was looking forward to a successful campaign. The roster had remained relatively intact from last season and Kyle Pendergraft, the team's general manager (GM), had done some wizardry to bring a couple of players who would certainly strengthen their starting five.

Denzel Williams was a real coup. With a few trade picks to the Kansas City Tornados, a power forward and one of the top five scoring players in the league was now joining a squad that had made it to the semifinals of the Western Conference Championships last year. Nothing was easy in the National Basketball Association (NBA), so attaining a top eight finish was something Andy was relatively pleased with. Of course, all the management, staff, players, and fans wanted the NBA championship in the trophy case, but it wasn't that simple.

"But maybe, just maybe, we have a real shot at taking out the Renegades," Andy thought to himself, as practice continued under the guidance of his assistants. The Renegades had taken out his Admirals in five games in the playoffs, but each had been close. Perhaps the missing pieces were now in place.

Practice ended and Andy called them all in.

"Good practice, everyone. Remember that details matter. What were we working on this afternoon specifically?"

"3–2 zone, Coach," responded Paul Gublez, a 7-footer with a wingspan of an albatross.

"Right. We want pressure on the wings. We know most of the teams we're going to play in our conference will have serious three-point shooting power, so we need to be on the perimeter to shut them down. That's why we're spending so much time on the 3–2. Anybody have any questions?"

As might be typical of any practice where the players just want to hit the showers and head out, there were none. But then Denzel spoke up.

"Well, Coach, 3–2 is a good zone, but when I played for the Tornadoes, we played a 2–3 mainly. I mean, it worked out pretty well." He spoke with a slight smile on his face, and when he had finished, he looked around the team and pointed to three digits on his fingers where his championships rings would normally rest. There were a few

DOI: 10.4324/9781003375449-36

chuckles around the group, and Denzel gave a little head nod in acknowledgment of his status, which had been growing quickly on the team.

"Sure. 2–3 is a common zone to use, and it's effective if defending the interior and baseline. But like I said, we're trying to cut down the threes this season mainly. We got torched by several teams in the West, and we lost to the Renegades in part because we couldn't shut down their three-point shooting. That's why we're doing the 2–3."

"Yeah, Coach. But we've got Goobes and Mac. They can block everything that can come their way." Denzel gave high fives to Gublez and MacDonald, the team's primary centers.

"That's right!" said Gubles.

"Look," said Andy trying to calm things down. "We know we've got great interior play, but this is the best method for getting those wins in the playoffs. Let's break it down and continue tomorrow."

The team huddled, and then each went his separate way. Denzel, however, did seem to have a few players huddled around him. Andy figured the star power wasn't a bad thing, and no doubt some of the practice squad and younger players would be keen to learn from his experiences, but he didn't like to be questioned like that in front of the team.

Preseason went well, and the front office was excited by the team that had been put together. Kyle Prendergraft was particularly pleased with his acquisition of Denzel Williams, who had looked the part of a champion. However, the season did not begin too brightly. Some early issues with chemistry between the old and new players led to a .500 start over the first 20 games. Andy wasn't too worried, but no one wants to drop below .500 in a league where one losing season can cost you a job. Fans and management have short memories when it comes to winning.

Although Denzel was putting up big numbers each night, he was lackluster on defense, and it frustrated Andy. For example, in an away game on the East Coast, Denzel at times didn't even try to sprint back on defense. And the effect seemed to trickle into the rest of the team who lacked that fire and cohesion needed for championship-winning teams. Finally, in the third quarter, with the team down by 28, Andy pulled Denzel and kept him on the bench for the remainder of the game. Although the team still lost, they made a good run near the end and closed the gap to 12.

It wasn't until after the game that Andy was approached by his lead assistant coach, Jeremy Thumas.

"Not a great game, huh, Jeremy?" Andy started.

"No, not great at all," responded Jeremy. "It's not really the game that's bothering me though."

"What do you mean?"

"Once you benched Denzel, the team played better."

"Yeah, odd isn't it? The best player on the bench and the team performing better."

"True, but that's not the worst of it. Once you benched Denzel, he started sniping at you."

"What do you mean sniping?"

"He was muttering under his breath to those next to him about how you didn't know what you were doing and how it was obvious that the 3–2 zone wouldn't work and a 2–3 zone is better. Of course, he was also complaining about being benched and didn't mind letting anyone around him know. His attitude was awful to be honest. And the problem is that most of the team follow him now. It's hard not to. He's a champ."

Andy sighed before replying.

"Okay. I think that has been brewing for a while. I knew once I benched him things would kick off, but it looks like I need to do something about it sooner rather than later."

The next day after game film review Andy asked Denzel to stay behind.

"Denzel, Look, I know you weren't happy about being benched, but the film shows that your effort on defense wasn't great. I love how much you're putting into scoring, but to win we need the defensive effort too. I know the guys follow you, and if you set the example, they will follow. What do you say?"

"I don't know, Coach. I'm not as young as I used to be, and my personal trainer says I need to be more careful about how much effort I put in and when. Everyone knows I can score, so I think it's better that I put that effort into putting up points rather than wearing myself out on defense. Besides, we've got other guys who are way better on D."

"So that's why you're not playing D hard? What if I limited your minutes more? Maybe gave you more breaks instead?"

"Nah, Coach. If you do that, I won't get my chance to rack up points. There's a scoring leaderboard I've got to think about too."

"I see. Well, we can't have it both ways." He paused and let Denzel think about it. He waited a few seconds. Then he waited a few more.

"I guess I can do more on defense," he finally conceded.

"Thanks, Denzel. We need it. We definitely have a great team, and I know you can lead it."

"Sure, Coach." Denzel got up and left.

Andy wasn't entirely convinced that Denzel had bought into his need, but it was a start.

The season slowly ramped up toward playoffs, but the Admirals were stuttering toward the finish line. Seventh place in the West was not exactly championship material, but Andy hoped for a final push over the last few games to get out of the 7–10 spot and perhaps push for an easier first round matchup.

But things had not been going well. Although Denzel Williams had been putting up big numbers when he played, he had missed a number of games through apparent niggling injuries and continued to give limited effort on defense. The team could sense it too, and there was disharmony within the ranks. Denzel, not one to shy away from the camera, had made a few cryptic comments during media interviews that alluded to locker room disharmony, disagreements with the coaching staff, and a general unhappiness with how things were going.

Andy and his staff had tried a variety of methods to change things up. Rotation changes, extra days off, extra practices, whatever they tried didn't seem to work. It was one of the most frustrating things Andy had ever dealt with in his 15+ year career.

Denzel had become more overtly controversial in the locker room too, particularly when it came to defense, talking to the team behind the coaching staff's back about the 3–2 zone. Andy knew it was the best defensive strategy in general, but he had been willing to try other ideas too. At times, he felt like Denzel was trying to cause problems on purpose, but Andy couldn't believe that. Why would Denzel sabotage a team that could potentially win it all? It didn't make sense.

After another rough loss at home, Andy was called to Kyle Pendergraft's office, the GM. It wasn't a good sign. Kyle's assistant let him in, and Kyle waited behind his desk.

"Andy, good to see you. Have a seat."

"Sure. What's going on?"

"Well, as you know things haven't been going as well as we would have liked this season, so I wanted to just pause and take stock. I know we've had some chats over the past couple of months about the team, and I just wanted your take."

Andy paused and wondered how much to say. He was frustrated and decided to tell it like it was.

"If I'm honest, a large part of the problem is Denzel."

"Really." Kyle didn't really ask a question but said it as a statement. Andy didn't really notice and ploughed on.

"He doesn't play defense. We've tried all kinds of things. Rest, different defensive assignments, time off, tried talking to him, spoke to his agent, his personal trainer, the counselor, you name it. We just can't get him to push like we know he's capable of."

"I see."

"He's a great, great player. Enormously talented. But his attitude and effort are bringing down the whole team."

"Have you considered that you might be part of the problem?"

Andy was taken aback.

"What do you mean?"

Kyle walked from behind his desk and looked out of the window.

"There's been a lot of skepticism about your insistence on running basically running a 3–2 zone."

"Wait. Skepticism from whom?"

Kyle ignored him and continued.

"You know Denzel was a big deal for this organization. We invested a lot of resources to get him here, and if he's not on the court, he's not scoring points. If he's not scoring points, he's not selling shirts or putting butts on seats. You see the problem here."

"And if he's not playing, he's making you look bad as well," Andy thought to himself.

"I still want to know what you mean about the defensive plan," Andy responded, getting a little irritated by the conversation. "You know that coaching is my job."

Kyle turned back to face him. Andy couldn't help but notice the power differentials taking place. First the big desk and now the boss standing and the employee sitting below.

"Yes, I know. But my job is the overall performance of the team, which isn't great at the moment." Kyle sighed. "Look, Andy, let me make it plain."

"Please do," Andy said pointedly.

"We need to see a change in performances. Denzel thinks a 2–3 zone is best on defense, and if it makes him happier, which makes the team happier, then good things will happen for everyone."

"It's my job to make these kinds of decisions. Not players!"

"Sure. Sure. But if we're being straight, then let me be straight with you. Denzel isn't going anywhere. We've put way too much into getting him here. Results aren't good. If they don't improve, then we'll have to consider making some changes at the end of the season. Of course, if they do improve, then we can just forget this little conversation ever happened." Kyle smiled. "Okay?"

Andy didn't really know what to say. He rose, said something noncommittal, and walked out.

"How does a player have more power than a coach?" he wondered to himself. "How did Denzel get access to Kyle like that to talk strategy behind his back? And how can a player determine whether a coach does or does not have a job?"

As Andy walked back down to his office, he decided to call a coaches' meeting asap. He had a decision to make: acquiescing to Denzel and Kyle, accepting he had virtually no power anymore, or fighting for the system he believed in.

Questions for Consideration

1. Who are the stakeholders in this case?
2. How much or how little say should a head coach have in draft picks or selecting which players come to a professional team? Does it differ by sport? Justify your answer.
3. Present three examples where it appears that the player or players might have more power than the coach in professional sports.
4. Throughout the story, what could Andy have done to ameliorate the situation or at least limit how bad the situation got?
5. At the end of the story, Andy is placed in an exceedingly difficult situation. What would you do and why?
6. Find one academic article about player and coach power and read it. What did you learn from it?

References and Further Readings

BBC. (2021, December 30). Romelu Lukaku 'not happy' with role under Thomas Tuchel at Chelsea. *BBC Sport*. www.bbc.com/sport/football/59833820

Gould, D., Nalepa, J., & Mignano, M. (2020). Coaching generation Z athletes. *Journal of Applied Sport Psychology*, *32*(1), 104–120.

Press, A. (2022, May 23). *Mbappe insists he has no say in PSG coach, player signings*. www.si.com/soccer/2022/05/23/kylian-mbappe-psg-coach-player-signings-power

Siddiqi, D. J. (2016, July 23). James Harden gives reason for not playing defense. *Houston Rockets*. https://247sports.com/nba/houston-rockets/Article/James-Harden-gives-reason-for-not-playing-defense-46389839/

Zeegers, M. (2020, January 22). How many coaches has Lebron James gotten fired? *Sportscasting*. www.sportscasting.com/how-many-coaches-has-lebron-james-gotten-fired/

34 The Assistant

Coaching a professional team is the pinnacle of most coaching journeys, and Coach Billy Kempish was about to get his chance. Coach Kempish had a highly successful career at the college level and was one of several coaches being interviewed to take charge of the newly established expansion team, the Tallahassee Titans.

Kempish's teams had always been known for being very disciplined and playing fundamental baseball. He was conservative with base runners and methodical with his strategy; his teams relied on everyone doing their jobs because nobody was bigger than the team. The owners of the Titans had been clear that this was a culture and philosophy they wanted to build into their new team. After a tense wait while other candidates were interviewed, they ultimately offered Kempish the job.

Kempish was offered a one-year contract. The owners justified this because it was an expansion team after all, and the future was less than certain. But they made their expectations for the season clear. Kempish was told that the team needed to make the playoffs; if they didn't, the expansion would look like a failure, the team would lose local support and sponsors, and financial ruin might soon follow. The realities of the risks as well as potential rewards were made truly clear.

Without much input from Kempish, the owners hired others on the coaching staff. Kempish felt disconcerted by this controlling behavior by the owners, but it was a new team, and this was his first year. One of the hires was John Jackson, a young coach who had found remarkable success as a head coach at a junior college before becoming an assistant coach last year for the Nashville Nighthawks. It was clear to everyone that Jackson had a very bright future and, at some point, would undoubtedly earn a head coaching position in the pros. In fact, Jackson was one of many coaches interviewed by the Titans owners, but the owners told Jackson that while he was an excellent candidate for head coach, they felt that he could benefit from working with a well-established coach.

Coach Jackson believed that he was ready for a head coaching job now but was excited for the opportunity to be on the coaching staff of an expansion team. The challenge came to the coaching philosophies of Jackson and Kempish, who had vastly different approaches to the game. Jackson was much more focused on individual play and relying on the stars of the team to carry them to victory. He was also extremely aggressive, especially on the bases. He loved to call hit-and-run plays, double steals, and had no issue calling for a squeeze play or bunting with the cleanup hitter.

DOI: 10.4324/9781003375449-37

Spring training began, and the team was preparing for their first season. They had a well-rounded group of players, and the coaches were optimistic for the team. Kempish held a team meeting early to discuss expectations for the players during spring training. Everything seemed to be going smoothly, and the Titans finished their spring training with a record of 14 wins and 7 losses. Kempish held another team meeting as they prepared to kick off their first regular season. He told them that his expectation, as well as the owners', was for the team to make the playoffs. He told the team that he believed they had all the talent required to make a great run for the playoffs if they continued to play as a team and everyone did their job.

The first game of the season was the home opener, and fans were extremely excited to see their new team. They got off to a great start and immediately jumped into a 2–1 lead, maintaining it through the seventh inning. In the eighth inning, Kempish watched as the runner on second began to steal third base. The batter hit a line drive to second base, and it was quickly turned into a double play ending the inning. Kempish couldn't understand why the runner left for third because he was already in scoring position. It was unnecessary and far too aggressive, especially when they had the lead. The ill-timed hit-and-run would come back to haunt the Titans, and they ended up losing their first game 3–2.

After the game, Kempish approached Jackson to ask what happened with the eighth inning hit-and-run. Jackson told him that he thought that it would catch their opponents off guard so he made the call. Coach Kempish wasn't happy that Jackson didn't stick to the game plan, but he let it go because the season was still young, and they had a lot of baseball left to play.

Over the next few months, the Titans played relatively well, and heading into the all-star break, they were only four games out of first place. There were more instances where Jackson called plays that Kempish didn't agree with. Kempish would have been angrier about the calls Jackson was making, but they did work sometimes, and they were still in the playoff hunt. Kempish did have another conversation with Jackson, and he explained that he did not want to be as aggressive on the bases, wanting to continue playing fundamental baseball. Jackson said that he understood, and things got better for a while.

The second half of the season was a bit of a roller-coaster ride as the Titans bounced in and out of playoff contention. Their hopes for a spot in the playoffs would come down to the last three games of the regular season. They were playing their in-state rivals, the Orlando Orcas, and needed to win two of the next three games. All season long, games with the Orcas had come down to the wire.

The first game was just like the others, very close all the way to the end. The game was tied heading into the ninth. The Titans had a runner on second with two outs with the top of the order coming up. The Orcas had their star closer in the game, but he had struggled with the top of the Titans' batting order all season. His first pitch was outside for a ball. The next pitch came in a little low for another ball, and the count was 2–0. As he began his next delivery to the plate, the runner on second base tried to steal third. The pitch was yet another ball, but the runner was thrown out at third by the catcher. Inning over, the Orcas had escaped a very bad situation. The Orcas' second batter of the inning hit a solo home run that ended the game, and the Titans were one loss away from missing the playoffs. Kempish was furious!

As soon as they were alone, Kempish asked Jackson why their runner tried to steal with the top of the batting order up and the opponent's pitcher struggling. Again, coach Jackson defended his decision, stating that he understood that the pitcher was struggling and he wanted to put more pressure on the pitcher.

"If it had worked, we wouldn't be having this discussion," said Jackson.

"But it didn't work!" Kempish responded, walking away still furious. The Titans would have to take the next game if they still wanted any chance of making the playoffs.

The next game was also close, and the score was back and forth the entire game. Titans took the lead back in the bottom of the eighth inning and needed to make a defensive stand in the ninth. They got into some trouble when they walked two Orcas batters, but a timely double play ended the game and kept their dreams of the playoffs alive. Kempish and Jackson were still not seeing eye-to-eye on things, but their team was either on the edge of their first postseason or ending their season in what the owners would deem a failure.

Kempish thought about what would happen if the Titans were to lose and miss out on the playoffs. "Would the season truly be a failure if the team didn't make the playoffs in their first year?" Kempish thought to himself. "The owners have said so, and they're the ones signing my paycheck. And what about some of the calls that Jackson has made during the season? They weren't bad decisions, but they were terribly timed and far too aggressive for the situation. Could Jackson be doing things to make the Titans lose on purpose? No! Coach Jackson is a professional, and he wouldn't do something like that." He shook the thought of his assistant coach intentionally throwing games, and he headed out of the ballpark.

The last game of the regular season arrived sooner than anyone could really be prepared for. The entire season, and potentially Coach Kempish's job, was on the line. The Orcas held the lead heading into the bottom of the ninth, but the Titans were down by only one run with bases loaded. But there were two outs. The Titans' cleanup batter was up to bat next. He was 3 for 3 this game and was riding a 9-game hitting streak. Just like the day before, the Orcas' star closer had been struggling with the top of the Titan order, so things were looking promising for the Titans. It was a nervous time for everyone in the Titans' organization.

The Orcas pitcher continued to struggle and plowed his first pitch into the dirt. His next pitch was high, and the count moved to 2–0. The third pitch was inside for ball three. He seemed to be incapable of throwing a strike, and Kempish was ecstatic. He gave his batter the sign to take the pitch and look for the walk to bring in the tying run and gave them another chance for the win.

The fourth pitch was what can only be described as the most perfect pitch a batter will ever see, a fastball right down the middle of the plate. The batter swung, and the crack of the bat could be heard throughout the sold-out stadium as the fans went silent. The ball left the bat with such velocity that it would be near impossible for the outfielders to react in time to make a play, but luckily for the outfielders, the ball went straight at the second baseman. Whether it was a great play or just self-defense, the ball was caught; the game, along with the Titans season, was over.

Kempish couldn't believe what had just happened. He'd given the sign to take the pitch, not wanting the batter to swing because the pitcher was struggling so badly.

After the handshakes, he found his batter to find out what he was thinking and why he didn't listen to the call.

"Sorry, Coach," said the player remorsefully. "I would normally never swing at a 3–0 pitch, but Coach Jackson gave me the sign to swing away. Coach had told me before I went up to bat that the team needed me to close out the game. Coach saw your sign, but he signaled me to swing. I wasn't sure who to follow and when the ball came straight down the middle, I had to go for it."

Kempish walked off the field and could see the team owners standing in a group down the hallway. As he got closer, he saw Coach Jackson speaking with the owners before shaking their hands and walking away. As he approached, they all turned and walked away not saying a word. Kempish went to find Jackson and confront him and was surprised to discover him cleaning out his office. Before he could say anything, Jackson spoke.

"Coach," Jackson said, before Kempish could say a word, "I enjoyed working with you, but the majors aren't for everyone."

"Excuse me? Are we fired?"

"Well, not exactly. I just talked with the owners. They've asked me to take over the team for next season. Looks like I'm moving office," he said it with a smile hefting a box onto his shoulders. Kempish was too stunned to offer up a retort, and before he could speak Jackson had walked out the door.

Kempish slumped into an empty chair and thought back to when he had questioned if Jackson was losing games on purpose or not. Maybe he should have called Jackson out then. Maybe he should have pushed the owners harder to allow him to choose his own coaches. Maybe he should have been firmer about controlling Jackson's brazen calling. Where had it all gone wrong?

Questions for Consideration

1. Who are the stakeholders in this case?
2. What could Coach Kempish have done differently when working with Coach Jackson?
3. What was one of the major characteristics of an assistant coach that Coach Jackson was missing?
4. What could Coach Kempish have done when he first suspected Coach Jackson of losing on purpose or undermining him?
5. In your opinion, was hiring a coach who was interviewed for the head coaching position as an assistant coach a good or a bad idea on the part of the team owners?
6. Who is at fault for the season ending early?

References and Further Readings

Better Coaching. (n.d.). Assistant coaches. *Betteryouthcoaching.com*. www.betteryouthcoaching.com/assistant-coaches

Coaches Education Platform. (n.d.). *World association of basketball coaches*. https://wabc.fiba.com/manual/level-2/l1-coach/4-management/4-1-coachs-responsibilities/4–1–1-working-with-assistant-coaches/

Hoch, D. (2020). Working with assistant coaches. *Coaches Toolbox*. www.coachestoolbox.net/professional-development/managing-assistant-coaches

Rathwell, S., Bloom, G. A., & Loughead, T. M. (2014). Head coaches' perceptions on the roles, selection, and development of the assistant coach. *International Sport Coaching Journal, 1*(1), 5–16.

Sabock, R. J. (1981). Loyalty and the assistant coach. *Journal of Physical Education and Recreation, 52*(3), 46–46.

35 To Coach or Not to Coach, That Is the Question

"Honey, I'm home," said Ben Tunas, as he walked through the door. It was a cheesy movie quote, but Ben and his wife, April, had been using it for years.

"Hey, Babe," shouted April from the laundry room. "There's food still warm in the oven."

"Okay, thanks." It had been a long day, and Ben hated coming home so late in the evening. But as a personal trainer and racquetball coach, you worked when your clients could, not when you wanted to. He pulled the plate from the oven and trudged to the dining room to eat another meal alone.

After several minutes April walked in and sat down.

"Long day, huh?" she asked.

"Can you tell?"

"Yeah."

"You know I never wanted this right? I never planned on being a PT." Ben held out his hands exasperated.

"I know, Babe, but this is where we're at. One day it won't be like this. This is temporary."

"Yeah, I know. I just wish I could do what I really love all the time. I get the bills have to be paid, but never seeing the kids and being away from home early in the morning, the evenings, and weekends are just brutal."

"Something will happen. It will. Just keep doing what you do, and in time people will notice."

"I know." He finished quickly and gave her a kiss. "I'll be back down soon. I've got a client online tonight."

April was always so positive. It was one of the things that attracted Ben to her, and he needed to hear it. He'd always wanted to coach racquetball at the highest level. A former professional player, he had done okay on the tour, but the tour wasn't a massive income earner. He'd been lucky to pay the bills, let alone make a decent living. But an 11-year run on the tour had allowed him to develop great relationships with many people, and he had translated that into in-person and virtual racquetball coaching.

Racquetball was what he loved, but he just didn't have enough clients to provide a decent income. While the sport may have been big time in the 1980s and 1990s, it didn't have the same name recognition anymore, and finding clients wasn't easy. Therefore, as a supplement to his income, Ben had completed his certifications in personal training and

DOI: 10.4324/9781003375449-38

worked at a local gym. The combination of lessons and training, in combination with April's part-time job, paid the bills, but it meant a lot of time away from home.

There was some job satisfaction though. Ben was intent on making a difference and spent a lot of time looking for new ways to help his clients, whether in the gym or on the court. And he had been successful. Some of his amateur racquetball clients had medaled on the national stage in their respective divisions, and some of the more talented juniors he'd worked with had represented the United States in junior competitions. A couple had even begun to test the waters of professional play. He was proud of that, but in the grand scheme of the sport, he wasn't a big name.

A few weeks later during his lunchbreak at the gym, Ben's phone began buzzing. He looked at the caller ID, and a look of surprise crossed his face. It was Michael Walden, Executive Director of the US Racquetball Organization (USRO). He picked up.

"Hi, this is Ben."

"Hi, Ben. This is Mike Walden from USRO. How are you?"

"Good, thanks. You?"

"Good. Good. How's the family?"

"Fine, thanks. Uh, so this is an unexpected call. What can I do for you, Mike?"

"Well, as you probably know Brandon Pritt recently stepped down as the US team's junior coach. The Board of Directors would like you to consider replacing him."

There was silence.

"Ben?"

"Uh, yeah. Yeah. Sorry. I just wasn't expecting this. I mean, I put my name in the hat and did the interview and all, but I never really imagined that you'd be seriously considering me given that the likes of Francis Dover and Jen Wonder are available. They're legends in the sport."

"Well, that's true. But neither of them applied, probably because they coach international athletes now and would have to give up those contracts. Anyway, the board was extremely impressed with how you've developed some of your athletes from juniors into seniors. We've asked around, you know, and you have a great relationship with kids. And you're experienced as a player too. We think that helps."

"Uh, I don't know what to say."

"Well, don't say anything yet. I'll email you the details shortly and talk it over with your wife and let me know by the weekend. Sound good?"

"Yeah, yeah. That's great! Thanks for the opportunity!"

"You deserve it, Ben. Bye."

As soon as Ben hung up the phone, his mind began to race with all the possibilities and variables. This would put him on the map. It would increase his access to top-level players, and maybe, just maybe, he could give up his personal training with the new clients and income from being an international coach. He wanted to rush home and tell April, but he had after-school lessons to teach. Instead, he sent her a text.

"Exciting racquetball news! Can't wait to tell you."

"Can't wait to hear it!" came back the reply.

That evening, Ben practically bounced through the front door.

"Honey, I'm home," he shouted from the doorway. The kids raced to say hi, and April followed quickly after.

"Well, what's this big news?" she asked in the middle of the shouting and screaming of three young kids racing around.

"I'll tell you once the kids are in bed," he replied, enjoying the secret he knew.

"Okay, fine. Well, help me get them to bed then."

After a good hour or two of baths, tears, more food, and stories, it was finally quiet. Ben pulled out his laptop and sat down with April in the living room.

"So, I got a call from USRO today," he began and then paused.

"And? Come on!" She smiled!

"Okay, okay. They've asked me to be the head coach of the junior international team."

The look on April's face was priceless. It was one of wonderment and excitement.

"What?" she screamed. "That's awesome, Ben!" Ben couldn't stop grinning.

"I know, right? Apparently, they liked the work I've done with the juniors I've been working with and think I'll be able to help grow the team."

"That's amazing!" April paused. "So, what are the details?"

"Well, I haven't looked yet, but Mike Walden said he would send me the details."

"Come on then. Let's take a look." April scooted over to look at the laptop as Ben opened his email. They read it together.

Dear Ben,

On behalf of the Board of Directors of the United States Racquetball Organization, I would like to formally offer you the job of head coach of the junior national team for the next three years. The primary responsibility of this position is to attend and coach our athletes at the annual international world championships. Other additional duties are outlined in the attached document. For your services, we will pay the travel and expenses of your trips to these events. In addition, we will pay you a $2,000 stipend. I hope you will accept our offer and I look forward to working with you over the coming years.

Sincerely,
Mike Walden

Both Ben and April finished reading almost at the same time. Neither wanted to speak first. Finally, April was the bravest.

"$2,000? That's it? How long is this event?"

"Depending on travel, it's about a ten-day event," he responded, in a tone much less enthusiastically than he had a few minutes earlier.

"10 days? For $2,000? And 10 days away from home? Not to mention the other duties we haven't even looked at. That sounds cheap to me. Doesn't it to you?"

"Well, yeah. It does. The other problem I have is that those 10 days I won't be earning income at the gym or with my clients. You know what I make. It's not a great deal, but at $50 an hour, that's 20 clients in 10 days. I see way more than that. Way more. I'll be losing decent money, not to mention perhaps losing clients to other trainers." He shook his head. "But on the flip side, I will get a ton of visibility around the U.S. that could lead to more business. It could be a stepping stone to other things. I mean,

I don't want to be a personal trainer for the rest of my life. It's never been my dream. Racquetball has always been. You know that."

"I know. I know. But $2,000? It seems like you're being taken advantage of perhaps. By you gaining a title and some visibility, we might become poorer. It's not like we're flush." April gestured around the living room. It certainly wasn't anything special, and living month-to-month on the whims of clients who could stop at any minute wasn't exactly a comfortable lifestyle. He sighed and put his hands on his head. April put her arm around him.

"Look. You know I'll support you with whatever you want to do. I know this is a wonderful opportunity for you to do what you've always wanted. If you want to do it, then go for it. We'll make it work. Okay?"

"Okay. Thanks, Babe." He gave her a hug back.

"I'm heading to bed. Don't stay up too late." She got up and walked toward the stairs.

"I won't. I promise." But he knew he would. A chance to do what he loved but at the cost of his finances and considerable time away from home when he wasn't there enough already. He sighed again. Who would ever imagine that becoming an international coach would cause someone to lose money? This would be a hard decision to make.

Questions for Consideration

1. Who are the stakeholders in this case?
2. What could Ben do to help make his decision?
3. Who could Ben speak to in order to help make his decision?
4. Is becoming an international head coach a lucrative job?
5. If you were Ben, what would you decide? If you were April, what would you recommend? What's your rationale for this decision?
6. One of the components of this story that is not financial is that of time. As a coach, how do you measure the value of time? In what ways might you quantify its value? Do you think that its value changes as you age or advance in your career? Explain.

References and Further Readings

Andrzejczak, W. (2022, September 14). Interview with Wojciech Andrzejczak, tackle analyst and international football coach [Video]. *YouTube*. www.youtube.com/watch?v=VLDamu9ZPwY

Dominy, W. (2020, July 20). Interview with Wyn Dominy, owner of Mile High Blaze and director of ops, women's football alliance [Video]. *YouTube*. www.youtube.com/watch?v=hRqIfUWShFA&t=4s

Palmer, D. (2022, August 31). Interview with Douglas W. Palmer, athletic director of the University of Guam [Video]. *YouTube*. www.youtube.com/watch?v=yJiVIZvT_IE

Radcliff, J. (2014, October 1). Poor pay turning prep coaching into 'dying profession'. *Sport Digest*. http://thesportdigest.com/2014/10/poor-pay-turning-prep-coaching-into-dying-profession/

Varley, C. (2021, January 20). Interview with Harry Varley, head coach of women's soccer, Grenada Soccer Association [Video]. *YouTube*. https://youtu.be/2W8x23tvmAY

36 Titles Versus $

"Hello?" Nate Locus picked up his cell and answered. He'd been waiting for this call for a few days.

"Hi, is this Nate?" A male voice asked through the speakerphone.

"Yes, speaking."

"Hi, Nate. This is Dr. Samuel Fengwe calling from the Juberian National Sports Federation. How are you?"

"Good, thank you."

"Good to hear. I'm sure you know why we're calling, so I won't waste time. Our committee met yesterday, and we're delighted to offer you the position of Head Strength and Conditioning Coach for our national teams."

"That's fantastic! Thank you for the opportunity." Dr. Fengwe couldn't see the ecstatic look on Nate's face.

"Yes, we're very excited to have you. Our teams struggle. We have coaches, but we don't know too much about strength training, and I think you can really help us. Now, I know there are a lot of details to work out, but I wanted to let you know that we want you start work in Juberia as soon as possible. The salary is not what I would like to give you or what you deserve, but we are a small federation in a developing country, and our government does not have the financial support of other nations."

"I understand. As I said in the virtual interview, this is more than a salary for me. I want to return to where my parents came from many years ago. And the chance to work with a national team is a good opportunity for me."

"That's great to hear. I will email you the contract, and we can discuss travel and living arrangements and so on."

"Thank you, Dr. Fengwe."

After the pleasantries were over and Nate had hung up, he sat down on the couch in his small apartment. This is the job he'd been dreaming of since deciding to pursue a career in strength and conditioning in college. Reality had hit after college. Working as a personal trainer and part-time strength coach at a local training facility wasn't exactly filling the bank account, and he wanted more.

Two months ago, through a friend of his family, Nate had heard of an opening in the Juberian National Basketball Federation. Although he'd traveled to Juberia to visit relatives a couple of times growing up, Nate's home had always been the United States. His parents had immigrated when he was young, and while Nate

DOI: 10.4324/9781003375449-39

knew the struggles of Juberia, he'd only seen the poverty and corruption at surface level on his trips.

After speaking with his family and friends, Nate had applied for the position. While the financials weren't going to be great, the opportunity to put international experience on his resume was very attractive. He knew he had a good chance; ties to Juberia combined with a strong strength and conditioning education from the United States was a good fit, he thought. And he'd been proved right. He was moving to Juberia!

The next month flew by, as Nate packed his small apartment into storage, said his goodbyes, and, with a couple of suitcases, headed across to the other side of the continent. He'd not traveled to Juberia since he was a teenager, so the memories had faded. He spent what time he had doing research on the country, culture, and the federation. But what hit him in the airport was nothing any book could have taught. It was pandemonium. Hot, humid, with no air conditioning, the small baggage claim was swamped with humanity all scrambling for their luggage or to make some quick cash from an inspecting tourist.

Nate knew better than to fall for a scam and, after a 45-minute wait, was able to snatch his bags and escape through customs. Dr. Fengwe had promised that someone would meet him at the airport, but after a 20-minute search and wait, no one appeared. Nate checked and double-checked his email with the confirmation he'd printed out, but no one showed. Without cell phone service and no Wi-Fi in the airport, he had no way of contacting anyone to check. Thinking they might just be late, he waited for a further hour, continually pushing away anyone who might be looking to help, for a fee of course. Eventually, exhausted from jet lag and the stress of the journey, Nate gave up on his ride and negotiated what he hoped was a decent price to the Federation's headquarters.

After a bumpy taxi ride across the country's capital, Nate exited at a nondescript building with an old sign above it: Juberian National Sports Federation. All around him were broken streets, old buildings, and trash. With a cough of exhaust, his taxi staggered away, and Nate hauled his suitcases through the front door.

A security guard was stationed at an old desk in the main lobby. Nate approached.

"Yes?" asked the guard, looking up from his newspaper.

"Hi, I'm Nate Locus. I just arrived from the United States. I'm looking for Dr. Fengwe."

"Dr. Fengwe isn't here," the guard responded quite curtly.

"Oh, well, I was supposed to be picked up from the airport by someone from the Federation, but nobody arrived. Do you know when he will be back?"

"No."

"Uh, okay. Is there someone else I can talk to?"

"No. If you want to speak to Dr. Fengwe, then you need to wait for him."

"Well, will he be back today?"

The guard shrugged and went back to his newspaper.

"Okay. Well, I guess I'll wait over there." Nate pointed to some chairs.

The guard seemingly wasn't listening anymore. Nate slumped onto a chair and sighed. This wasn't how it was supposed to go.

"Wait, do you have Wi-Fi?" Nate asked hopefully.

"Not for visitors," the guard grunted. Nate sighed.

After about 30 minutes, Nate's eyes couldn't stay open, and he drifted off. His slumber was interrupted a couple of hours later by Dr. Fengwe.

"My goodness, Nate! It's so good to see you! I'm so sorry no one came to pick you up from the airport. Please, let me help you with your luggage, and we will go to my office."

Nate, relieved he was now getting help, picked up his bags and followed Dr. Fengwe down a hallway, not too dissimilar to the old, faded décor of the entrance. Dr. Fengwe opened the door to his office that was in stark contrast to everything Nate had seen so far. The carpet looked new, the desk long, and the chair leather.

"Come in, come in," said Dr. Fengwe, as he sunk into his plush chair. A window air conditioner hummed in the background. Nate sat.

"Well, I'm so glad to be here," Nate started. "I wanted to come here before I went to my apartment. Of course, I'm guessing you have my key anyway."

"Well, yes," Dr. Fengwe shifted in his chair. "Unfortunately, we have a problem with the apartment we had assigned for you, so I'm glad you came to see me."

"What do you mean 'problem'?"

"Uh, there was a problem with the previous tenant, and the property owner says there is a problem with payment. I don't really understand the whole situation."

"Okay, so where will I be staying?

"Yes, I don't know yet. We are working on it."

Nate wasn't sure what to say. This wasn't what was supposed to happen.

"I guess I'm confused. The contract provides me with a salary and an apartment."

"I know, I know. But you must understand that this was not expected. We cannot control these situations, and sometimes in Juberia these things happen. We will find you something."

And they did find him something. The water barely worked—not that you could drink it—showers were a luxury, and at times power would cut for hours. Nate knew what a developing country was, but this was something else. But he was persistent and had vowed to give it a go. There was culture shock, no doubt, but he dedicated the next few weeks to fitting in, getting along, and doing good work. The Federation's training facilities were limited, but Nate adapted. If a piece of equipment wasn't available like it would have been in any gym in the United States, he made modifications and did his best. And the athletes and coaches were appreciative. He was enjoying the challenge even if in trying circumstances.

At the end of the month, Dr. Fengwe called him to his office. Nate couldn't help but notice the stark contrast between his office and the rest of the facility.

"Please sit," Dr. Fengwe stated, and Nate sat.

"What's going on?" Nate asked. "Is everything okay?"

"Nothing, nothing. I just wanted to make sure you're settling in okay," Dr. Fengwe responded.

"Well, yes. I mean, it's a real adjustment, and I know I've made a lot of mistakes, but things are going okay. I'm learning a lot about the teams and coaches, and I think we're doing good things."

"So, you're happy here?"

"Well, I suppose so. I like my work."

"That's very good to hear." Dr. Fengwe paused and pursed his lips.

"What is it?" Nate began to get concerned.

"Nothing, nothing. It's just that we've had some problems with the funding for your position."

"What?"

"Yes, it's not a problem. Nothing to worry about. But funding from the government has been hard to get. The Federation is struggling financially."

"Okay . . . so what does this mean exactly?"

"Well, I must tell you that we don't have the money to pay you the full price of your contract. I know you get paid each month, but we cannot pay you the full amount."

"What does this mean? What are you paying me?" Nate sat up more alert. Dr. Fengwe didn't look comfortable, but it didn't look like he hadn't done this before either. There was something about him that gave the sense that this speech had been made before.

"You see, the government has reduced its funding, and so I must find ways to save costs. And I know how much you like it here and that you love your job. So instead of telling you that you can't work here, I can pay you 60% of what you were offered in the contract."

"60%? That's crazy! I mean, I can probably barely buy food with that let alone save anything."

"Yes, I know. I'm sorry. But I think you should consider it. This is an excellent job for your career, and I know we cannot pay a lot of money. But it is a good opportunity for you. We do want you to stay here. I think you should consider it."

"But you're basically asking me to work for free!"

"Well, no, you get an apartment and some money."

"Dr. Fengwe, this is crazy. I don't know if I can do this."

"Of course, of course. I understand if you cannot. But these are tough times, and we must work and do our best in them. Maybe you can let me know tomorrow."

He got up, indicating the meeting was over. Nate got up too and walked out of the office and down the old hallway. He couldn't believe what had just happened. How could the Federation have no money when Dr. Fengwe clearly did? How could they just change his contract at whim? What would his family say if he came home after just a month? What would his resume look like after this? What would he go home to? It wasn't like he had a job lined up. Nate took a deep breath and sighed. He had decisions to make.

Questions for Consideration

1. Who are the stakeholders in this case?
2. What mistakes might Nate have made early in this story? What would you do differently?
3. Juberia is a fictional country, but there are over 130 developing countries around the world with sports federations of some kind. What are ten challenges you might experience as a coach in a developing country?
4. Corruption is evident in many ways in developing countries, but it can also exist in sports in developed countries. Provide some evidence to support this.

5. What are some ways that Nate could have better prepared for coaching in another country?
6. If you are Nate, what would you do and why?

References and Further Readings

Andreff, W. (2006). Sport in developing countries. In W. Andreff & S. Szymanski (Eds.), *Handbook on the economics of sport* (pp. 308–315). Elgar.

Chappell, R. (n.d.). Sports development in Botswana. *The Sport Journal, 25.* https://thesportjournal.org/article/sports-development-in-botswana-africa-2/

Coetser, J. (2020, May 5). Interview with Jeanne-Marie Coetser, VP for South African wrestling federation [Video]. *YouTube.* https://youtu.be/3e3WOrOWIBo

Palmer, D. (2022, August 31). Interview with Douglas W. Palmer, athletic director of the University of Guam [Video]. *YouTube.* www.youtube.com/watch?v=yJiVIZvT_IE

Varley, C. (2021, January 20). Interview with Harry Varley, head coach of women's soccer, Grenada Soccer Association [Video]. *YouTube.* https://youtu.be/2W8x23tvmAY

37 A Clash of Ideologies

Personal Perspectives From a Journal

Background

This is a true story. It started at the United Soccer Coaches' convention where I met the head coach in this account through a mutual friend. We met and talked soccer over the next few days, discussing the importance of standard setting and clear guidelines of behavior within a team culture. On the fifth day of the convention, we had dinner along with other coaches we met at the convention. While at dinner, he offered me the job of goalkeeper coach at his USL 2 summer league team. The timing was excellent, because I had no coaching commitments between June and August, and there was nothing stopping me from going to another state and coaching for a USL 2 team for a three-month period. The coaches were all my age as well, so there was no generational gap. After considering the opportunity for a few days, I called him and let him know that I'd be more than happy to join his staff. He was as excited as I was because I was the last missing piece of his staff. What follows are some highlights of what I wrote in my journal during those summer months.

Day 1

As the goalkeeper coach and performance analyst, I was excited to meet with the rest of the staff to discuss the approach to the new season. The team competed in the "path to pro" tier of the professional soccer pyramid in the United States. Players for this team were recruited from college soccer programs nationwide. The rest of the staff consisted of the head coach, an assistant coach, and a volunteer coach.

Upon the coaches' arrival to our new apartment, prior to unpacking, they suggested we go to a bar. A little surprised, I agreed but asked if we could discuss what our game model would look like going forward. I wanted to know our recruitment policy and the thoughts of everyone on what type of culture we were going to promote to the team that summer. I should have known better, but as soon as we got to the bar the coaches ordered a few beers and remained on their phones all evening. I didn't have social media accounts, but the rest of the coaches immediately pulled out their phones and started posting and tagging one another across various accounts. I tried to fit in, but without access to these apps I felt a little left out, and there certainly wasn't any discussion about the team and our goals for that

DOI: 10.4324/9781003375449-40

summer. I went back to the apartment a little discouraged but blew it off as a first night initiation of sorts.

Day 7

Alarm bells were going off in my head on the training field when Head Coach Matt Tumbler had not conducted or participated in any training during our first week of practice. Worse still, he did not discuss with us as staff or the players any of his values, what he stood for, and what standards he was setting for the team on both individual and collective levels. Instead, Remy Jasper, the assistant coach, had led all the week's sessions.

None of the coaches had talked about their "why" or what the purpose of each training session was. Every session started with "Alright, everyone get 5 laps in," without talking to 'the players about the objectives of the session, principles of play, or the identity of the team. This worried me, as I'd always learned from my professional player days and the coach education, I had taken that coaches should create clarity, overcommunicate clarity, and reinforce clarity around values, principles, and the desired behaviors for on and off the field.

Day 13

After two weeks of training, I had realized that the coaches wanted to rule through fear. There was constant swearing and shouting in training, and both Remy along with Tom, the volunteer assistant coach, were quite happy to ridicule or punish a mistake. "Soft, mentally weak, entitled" were words mentioned over and over during practice by the coaching staff. A casual observer watching the training sessions that week hinted to me that the coaches' behavior reeked of insecurity and fragile egos, which was hard to disagree with. Players were always scolded, and the coaches had a stereotypical view of what a tough player looked like. In their eyes, none of the players fit that mold, which created resentment. Head Coach Matt had still not led a single training session.

Day 17

By this point, I'd given up trying to fit in with the coaching staff. Their focus was on sampling as many local bars or breweries as possible, which was not my scene. I just stayed home. It was 11 P.M. of day 17 of my "adventure" that I was awoken by a phone call from the volunteer assistant, Tom. I could almost smell the alcohol through the phone as he slurred his way into asking me to come and pick up the coaching staff because they had drunk too much. "I'm not a coach anymore," I thought to myself. "I'm just a glorified water boy." I got out of bed, put my shoes on, and drove over to the bar. When they got in, all were wearing their club gear. Every night out, the coaches wore their club gear, not even attempting to be professional or ethical in representing the institution that hired them for the summer.

Once they had all bundled into the car, they insisted on a stop at a fast-food joint to sober up before heading back to the apartment. Drunk and somewhat out of control, the coaches made explicit sexual jokes and gestures in full view of everyone in the restaurant.

Day 24

After the first three games, it was clear to me the type of people I now found myself working with. On every away game, the coaches would go out drinking at the local bars and strip clubs until 2 or 3 A.M. Players were aware of this behavior and had expressed dissatisfaction and resentment that the coaches were not adhering to the rules they themselves placed on the players.

Two players approached me to complain about this double standard. Unfortunately, as a new and junior member of the staff, I did not have a helpful answer to their legitimate concerns. Coaches would return to the hotel room stinking of alcohol and completely drunk. Their behavior on the sideline during games would be described by the casual observer as abusive, erratic, and lacking in composure and discipline. I did not speak on the touchline and had no interaction with the coaches whatsoever. Encouragement and positivity were a rare occurrence on the touchline. In addition, the level of abuse aimed at referees from our coach's bench was constant throughout every game.

Day 32

The coaches' discussions at the apartment were mostly banter, constantly joking around, talking about women. Every time I tried to steer the conversation toward decisions for the team or certain ideas to improve performance and growth in the team, they showed no interest. In their eyes, they already knew everything they needed to know and had no curiosity or urge to test their assumptions. The rare moments where they did talk about the team, it was almost always critical and negative.

Day 40

I discovered that the coaches have a group chat without me. Head Coach Matt had his phone connected to the company car through Bluetooth, and I discovered in the car through its touchscreen that they are communicating with one another on a private group chat. I didn't know what to think, but "angry" and "frustrated" were two words that came to mind.

Day 52

One of the players reached out to me indirectly through the athletic trainer and requested to speak with a mental health counselor. I brought this to Matt who immediately discounted it. When I brought it up to him again, his assistant coach stepped in and said, "Mental health is a sham. It's not real and these players are just weak." I found it hilarious that these coaches discount mental health and have the nerve to judge the players, especially when they themselves commit seriously unethical and destructive behavior. Although the irony was laughable, at the time I felt hopeless and completely dejected.

Day 78

The team headed to Canada to play two consecutive games, but I was required to remain home because I was ineligible to travel to Canada because of green card restrictions on my US residency application process. I receive text messages from players throughout the five-day trip, all talking about the coaches' unprofessional behavior, going out the night before the game, and lambasting the players for trivial issues.

I felt sorry for their struggles, but from a selfish point of view, I was glad I have breathing room from the coaches. The team drew their second game there, and upon returning to their home training field, the team was told by Matt to attend training for the sole purpose of shaming the players for a tied game. It was cringeworthy and pathetic; the players' body language told me they did not take what the coaches had to say seriously.

Day 100

By now, I was counting the seconds until the season was over. I had had it with the coaches constantly abusing and berating the players in training. There was no attention to periodization, so the players were overworked and overtraining the entire season. Multiple times I was approached by the athletic trainer who said to me, "Kyle, training should have ended 20 minutes ago. This is the reason we keep getting muscular injuries and why the players are completely exhausted on game days."

I asked her if she had mentioned it to the coaches previously. She informed me that she had brought it up many times. She expressed her feeling of being unvalued because the coaches ignored her advice and told her that back when they were players there was no such thing as periodization. As a result of this ignorance and arrogance, the players suffered mentally and physically throughout the summer, many opting to leave us midway through the short season.

Day 112

Two friends I had met locally showed me videos on social media of the coaches out at a bar until 2 A.M. in the morning. The coaches continued to wear the club gear when on a night out. I chose not to confront them about it, as I have no confidence in my ability to persuade them to adopt more subtle and respectful habits.

Day 135

After qualifying for the playoffs, a knockout-style competition, I recommended that we start working on penalty kicks and determine who our top five penalty kick takers are. I also suggested we evaluate out who is confident and who isn't and discuss the intricate details needed to boost our chances of winning a shootout.

Matt tells me no. "We'll be all right. When I was a player, I never worked on penalty kicks." At their response I was completely stunned but, more importantly, powerless. So, the week went by, and we won our round of 16 and quarterfinal games over the course of the week in regulation.

Day 142

It was the conference final; if we win, we get a trophy and qualify for the semifinal of the national tournament. The game goes to penalties, and many players choose to avoid volunteering. Our first two kickers missed their penalties. The opposition do not miss any of theirs. We lost the game; the season is over.

I walked over to the 7,000 fans and applaud them for supporting us, not just this evening but the whole season. I encouraged all the players to go and show their gratitude as well, but none of the coaches replicate the gesture. They do not thank the fans, they do not console the crying players who missed their penalties, nor do they show any compassion, empathy, or leadership. Instead, they went to the corner of the soccer field and sulked.

On the drive home later that night, the coaches had the nerve to start criticizing the players. "This player completely bottled it this season." "It's going to be hard for me to speak well of that player when he goes on trials to the pro clubs."

I couldn't help but think to myself. "You scum of the earth spend ten hours every day on Instagram, Snapchat, and Tik Tok. You don't tell the players you're proud of them, you don't work on their individual development, and you demean them. You're lazy, arrogant, thoughtless, refuse to give the players an opportunity to work on penalty kicks during the week . . . and you have the audacity to criticize the players for losing the game?"

The same night, the coaches headed to a strip club with the players. As always, they were wearing the club gear. In the early morning hours, they got a share ride service home and left the company car outside the strip club. Later that morning, each coach traveled back home to their college teams (without saying goodbye) and did not tell me or anyone that the company car was still parked outside the strip club downtown. This is important because that car was my only means of transportation, and they had chosen to leave it parked downtown overnight. The car was eventually picked up by an intern, who told the managers of the club that not only was the car left downtown overnight but it was also filled with beer cans.

What Did I Learn?

- I learnt you are only as effective as your partnerships; teamwork trumps individual talent.
- I learnt the importance of psychological safety within a leadership team.
- I learnt to stick true to my own values and not be persuaded by the three main groups in society that influence behavior: the close, the powerful, and the many.
- I learnt that no matter how horrible the experience, there are always opportunities for growth and development.

- I learnt that God did not put me in this planet to be friends with everyone. I now know that there are certain people in my profession whom I must stand up to and confront when people abuse their power and authority.
- I learnt to be grateful for the players' effort, determination, and resilience, no matter how poor the coaching was.

Reflection

In reflection, I felt ashamed that I was part of that coaching cohort. But I could not quit; I was tied to the team because of my visa status. Here are a variety of things I learned through this process. I did not consider approaching upper management at any point. I felt as though that would only make the situation worse. I believe conflict is only healthy when it's based on a foundation of trust, and I didn't feel trusted by the coaches or by the general managers, whom I barely interacted with.

I do believe I should have confronted the coaches about their secret messaging group. I don't believe it would have had a profound positive impact on the relationship. However, if I expect others to be transparent, I have to do the same and practice what I preach. I live by the principle of "do hard things, all the time."

It does not surprise me that this behavior goes on in the professional setting, but it's no less disappointing. When people gain more power, it rarely makes them more humble or introspective. Only few coaches can gain authority and roles of responsibility and still respect their surroundings and practice each day with gratitude and professionalism toward the people who report to them.

I definitely feel I should be blamed for some of what transpired. I should have confronted the coaches far earlier in the season. I also should have pushed harder for the team to practice penalty shootouts prior to the conference final loss. Bravery comes in overcoming and navigating not just uncontrollable obstacles such as bad luck, injuries, bad weather, referees, and so on but also internal obstacles and bad actors that hinder performance and team culture. I must be more assertive in what I believe should be done in a respectful but direct manner. Holding things in did not help myself or the team. It's a strong lesson for myself for future roles.

Questions for Consideration

1. Who are the stakeholders in this case?
2. Would you have approached the upper management at any point? Why or why not?
3. Would you have confronted the other coaches about their secret messaging group? What would you have said if you did?
4. This is a true story. Does it surprise you that such behavior goes on in coaching professional sports? Provide three examples from media outlets or literature.
5. The author confesses to holding some of the blame. What could/should the author have done to help change what he experienced?
6. If you were the author experiencing this coaching behavior, how would you have handled it differently? Justify your response.

References and Further Readings

ABC News. (2003, May 2). Iowa coach suspended amid partying reports. *ABC News*. https://abcnews.go.com/GMA/story?id=125196&page=1

Cruickshank, A., Collins, D., & Minten, S. (2013). Culture change in a professional sports team: Shaping environmental contexts and regulating power. *International Journal of Sports Science & Coaching*, *8*(2), 271–290.

Gearity, B. (2009). *Athletes' experience of poor coaching*. [Doctoral dissertation], University of Tennessee. https://trace.tennessee.edu/utk_graddiss/17

Lever, K. (2022, May 24). 'A mental health battle': How abusive coaching impacts college athletes. *Global Sport Matters*. https://globalsportmatters.com/culture/2022/05/24/mental-health-battle-how-coach-impacts-college-athletes/

Shields, D. L., LaVoi, N. M., Bredemeier, B. L., & Power, F. C. (2007). Predictors of poor sportspersonship in youth sports: Personal attitudes and social influences. *Journal of Sport and Exercise Psychology*, *29*(6), 747–762.

Whitley, D. (2015, August 25). USC is late to Sarkisian's party. *Orlando Sentinel*. www.orlandosentinel.com/opinion/os-usc-is-late-to-sarkisians-party-20150826-post.html

38 Who Do You Work For?

Trey Williams had coached professional soccer for a long time. He had lived and coached in a half dozen cities over the years. From lower-level leagues in Greece to the Polish second division, and his latest stop in France with many points in between, he had seen it all. Over that time, Williams had certainly had his share of ups and downs. His teams had sometimes earned promotion, sometimes avoided relegation, and sometimes they had not. Coach Williams had won coach of the year and also been fired before finishing even one season.

But his last four seasons in France with Diarritz had been a turning point in his career. He molded them into a top three team, to qualify for the UEFA Champions League in each of those seasons, and then made them Ligue 1 champions the last two seasons. Diarritz had never seen such success, and it landed Williams his dream job: manager of an English Premier League club. And it wasn't just any club but his hometown club, Covington City, which Williams had supported as a boy.

His dad regularly had taken Williams and his brothers to Covington City matches while they were kids. However, Williams knew that he didn't have the talent to play professional soccer, but he still dreamed of being associated with a Premier League club one day. This dream began with coaching youth club teams and continued through his long, winding professional coaching career. And now, he had arrived. Williams was returning to his hometown to coach the team he had grown up supporting—a dream come true.

The team Williams was taking over had avoided relegation the previous season, which is a win for a small club, and they had a good young core of players that had the city bursting with excitement about a new season with new opportunities. The previous manager, Ray Kent, had been encouraged to move on, according to the gossip columns, but both sides had been a bit hush-hush on why he had abruptly left at the end of the season. Most pundits assumed that it was the next transition in Kent's career, but nothing definitive had been reported.

Kent's abrupt departure didn't concern Williams. He was just happy to have this opportunity and brought his longtime assistant coach with him. Milton Hawthorne had been Coach Williams' assistant coach for almost two decades and had married his sister. Williams was the fiery, enthusiastic coach who was rightly tempered down when needed by the more subdued Hawthorne. They had shared this journey together, and now both men were seeing the fruits of their labor.

DOI: 10.4324/9781003375449-41

"I still can't believe this is happening," Hawthorne said to Williams. "I've got to be honest. I never thought we'd see this day."

"Believe it," Williams responded. "We've worked like no one else to get here. I couldn't have done it without you."

Hawthorne started to get a little emotional, and his eyes started to well up with tears. "Thanks," Hawthorne stuttered out.

Trying to keep his brother-in-law from getting too emotional, Williams moved on.

"Okay, enough of this stuff," he said. "Let's talk about the team. What do you know about this assistant coach, Rupert Mansion, whom the owner wants to retain from the last staff?"

"Rumor is that the owner and Coach Mansion are in a relationship," Hawthorne answered.

Kelsey Jones had inherited the Covington City team from her deceased husband. She wasn't a particularly huge soccer fan but enjoyed the pageantry that owning a team afforded her. She liked to do interviews about the team, and she appreciated when she was recognized in public. It made her feel like a celebrity. Over the last couple of years Kelsey had begun seeing one of the team's assistant coaches, Rupert Mansion.

Mansion had played professionally in England's lower leagues and came to Covington City as an intern. A young man himself, Mansion related well with the young players on the team, and the former head coach Kent had eventually made him a full-time assistant coach. When Kent left for the club, Kelsey Jones had made it a point to any potential new manager whom Mansion would remain with the team. Although Williams and Hawthorne hadn't had an opportunity to spend much time with Mansion, their brief encounters were positive. Mansion talked positively about Williams's coaching philosophy and methods and seemed eager to work with the two new coaches. Thus, Williams had little concern over any issues with his new assistant coach.

Professional soccer has very little off-season, which left little acclimation or prep time with his new team. A week after arriving in Covington City, Williams, alongside his two assistant coaches, met with his players.

"Lads," Williams said to the players, "I'm Coach Williams. This is Coach Hawthorne, and most you know Coach Mansion," he continued. A collective cheer was heard when Mansion was introduced. This made sense as he was the only returning familiar face from the previous coaching staff. "Alright, lads, let's get on the pitch so we can see what we've got."

Williams clapped his hands and the team divided up and began scrimmaging. Williams' teams were known for their aggressive offense, pushing the ball quickly down the field in crisscrossing, side-to-side fashion that kept the other team off balance and created openings through the middle. This was a cornerstone of his coaching philosophy and has been very effective for him throughout much of his career. After a few weeks of practices and friendlies, and methodically installing his new offense, the team was ready to begin Premier League play. The season opened with a bang with a match against the previous year's league champion, Monton United. In order to compete with Man U, Covington City would need big performances by their two young stars.

Beginning their third year in the league, striker James Weatherall and midfielder Sam Obisanka had burst onto the scene as immediate impact players for Covington and were largely credited with the team's relegation survival. They both gave a lot of credit to Mansion with their quick development and had developed a close relationship with him. The three of them often went to dinner together after practices and games. Aside from his relationship with the team's owner, it was also speculated that Mansion had been retained because of his ties with the team's two young stars.

Williams had noticed that during practices both Weatherall and Obisanka would confer with Mansion for guidance. This was not completely unusual on a team, but Williams was a bit concerned because the players seemed reluctant to follow any of his directives during scrimmages. Rather than pushing the ball up the field in the manner his offense schemes scripted, they would on occasion play more of a two-man game, which always ended with one of the two of them taking a shot even if it was not the best option available.

The day of the first game against Man U, Williams huddled the team in the locker room to give final instructions. "Alright, lads. Remember what we've practiced. Defenders get the ball out wide to your midfielders. Midfielders cross it over to your strikers. Front-line players, if you don't have a shot, pass it back out and work it around."

Most of the players seemed focused and attentive to Williams' instructions. However, Coach Hawthorne couldn't help but notice Mansion making eye contact with Weatherall and Obisanka. The three did their best to conceal their grins. After Williams finished talking to the team and they began leaving the locker room and heading to pitch, Hawthorne pulled Williams aside.

"We might have a problem with Weatherall and Obisanka," Hawthorne said. "I think they're taking their lead from Mansion."

"What?" Williams said puzzled.

"I caught the three of them grinning and almost smirking during your instructions," Hawthorne responded.

"Nahhh. I wouldn't worry about it," Williams said. "They're pros and know what they're doing. They'll stick with the plan. And as far as Mansion goes, he may be a bit aloof, but he knows his stuff. He won't go against me. We're alright, Hawthorne."

And with that Williams ran down the stadium portal and onto the pitch. Hawthorne, shaking his head, slowly followed.

As the game began both Hawthorne and Williams shouted instructions from the touchline to the players. They were reinforcing their match plan and urged their team to move the ball from side to side and up the field. All the while Mansion stood stoically on the sideline rubbing his chin watching the game.

It became clear early on that the team's two stars were not following Williams's philosophy of play. The two of them controlled the ball and generally kept it away from the rest of the team. The pleas from the touchline seemed to fall on deaf ears as the two continued to ignore the ball movement strategy and kept possession to themselves as much as possible. This resulted in an array of wild shots that didn't come close to scoring. It was obvious their Covington City teammates were getting frustrated.

On the other side of the ball, Man U's methodical movement resulted in two goals. Then, right before halftime, Weatherall cut the ball back to the center of the field instead of along the sidelines as instructed and found himself surrounded by defenders.

Quickly dispossessed, the ball made its way to a Man U striker who put a dagger into any hope that might have existed of a comeback: 3–0.

As the teams left the pitch and headed to the locker room for halftime, Hawthorne and Williams stayed on the field for a second to talk.

"What is going on with those two?" Hawthorne asked. "They're playing as if they're on the field by themselves!"

"I dunno," Williams replied. "Looked intentional to me. Let's get inside and give them what for."

As the two coaches neared the locker room, they could hear what sounded like someone shouting inside the room. Upon entering, they found Mansion shouting and reprimanding the team. Mansion was scolding the team for not looking for Weatherall or Obisanka.

"Get them the ball!" he screamed. When Mansion noticed the two coaches standing behind him, he stopped talking and stepped back. "I was just talking to them until you got back," he sheepishly said.

After reinforcing their game plan again to the team, Williams sent the team back to the pitch, but he pulled Weatherall and Obisanka back.

"Lads, I know how talented you both are," he said. "But I need you guys to follow the script and move the ball the way we've practiced."

"Okay, Coach," Weatherall replied. Obisanka nodded in agreement too, and the two players left the locker room. Waiting for them was Mansion, and the three walked back to the pitch together.

The second half started much the way the first half had started. Poor movement and ill-advised shots by the two star players. Another turnover, this time by Obisanka, led to another near goal by Man U. Williams had seen enough. He substituted the two young stars out of the game, and they indignantly stomped off the field and walked straight over to Mansion to bitterly complain in full view of the watching fans.

Mansion immediately stormed over to confront Williams and Hawthorne.

"What are you doing?" Mansion screamed. "Have you lost your mind?"

"Not *now*," Williams sternly responded. Mansion retreated to the bench to sit next to the players who had just been subbed.

Covington City lost the game but looked better after the substitutions. They scored a goal and didn't concede anymore, finishing on the losing side of a 3–1 result. After the game Williams addressed the team.

"Lads," Williams said, "Understand this. No player is ever free to do as they want in the game. You will stick with the plan or you will sit. Does everyone understand me?" The team sheepishly nodded.

As the last players filed out of the locker room and headed home, Mansion angrily burst back into the room and confronted Williams and Hawthorne.

"Who do you think you are?" Mansion bellowed. "What do you think you were doing out there? Have you lost your mind?" he continued.

"I was trying to win a match," Williams responded back angrily. "If you ever question my authority again, you'll never set foot in this stadium again. Do you understand me?" he sternly asked.

"Oh, is that right?" Mansion retorted. "Well, we'll see about that. You don't know who you're dealing with. We'll see who's allowed back in this stadium." And with that, he stormed out of the locker room, slamming the door behind him.

Williams and Hawthorne sat down beside each other on a bench. Both men sat silently wondering what had just happened and what would happen next.

Questions for Consideration

1. Who are the stakeholders in this case?
2. Before accepting the position, what were some things Coach Williams should have done?
3. What interaction should Williams and Hawthorne have had with Coach Mansion early in the process and before the season actually kicked off?
4. Would you have conducted the team's practice sessions differently? Describe what you would have done differently.
5. How should Williams and Hawthorne have approached the team's stars, Weatherall and Obisanka, that might have circumvented their poor attitude and direction both early on in the process and during the actual game?
6. As the final encounter with Mansion in the locker room concluded, what could Williams do in regard to addressing the team owner Jones to circumvent a negative outcome?

References and Further Readings

Terranova, J. (2022). Bruce Arians' surprise departure fuels Tom Brady conspiracy theories. *New York Post.* https://nypost.com/2022/03/31/bruce-arians-surprise-departure-fuels-tom-brady-conspiracy-theories/

Tivic, F. (2021). When Magic Johnson got his coach fired only a year after demanding the Lakers to extend his contract. *Basketball Network.* www.basketballnetwork.net/old-school/when-magic-johnson-got-his-coach-fired-only-a-year-after-demanding-the-lakers-to-extend-his-contract

Zeegers, M. (2020). How many coaches has Lebron James gotten fired? *Sportscasting.* www.sportscasting.com/how-many-coaches-has-lebron-james-gotten-fired/

39 Not My Fault

Coach Robert Singer walked into his team's locker room. His Lebanon Demons hockey team had just had another brutal defeat to close out the season. But when he entered the locker room his jaw dropped. He knew his outmatched team had been beaten up by the Lawrence Angelfish, but what he was now seeing was carnage. It looked like a medical trauma center. Players were strewn about the room. Some were on tables moaning and wrenching in pain. Others sat on benches covered in bandages. Medical staff and assistant coaches tended to the injuries. The Demons had struggled all year. They were young and talented, but they didn't have the size or power of their competition. Injuries, some of them major, had been frequent occurrences in almost every game of the season. But this was the epitome of season of horrors. Singer felt himself getting emotional seeing his players so physically wrecked.

Singer had just finished his second season as the Demons head coach. Previously, he had served as an assistant coach for the Salvation Wendigo's for seven years. A newly added team to the National Hockey League (NHL), the Demons were an extremely young team and with little experience. Comprised primarily of college players who had just finished their eligibility, they had some raw talent, but they were young and inexperienced. He knew that taking the head coaching job for an expansion team was risky, but he also knew that head coaching opportunities didn't come around often and had jumped at the opportunity. Plus, Singer firmly believed that the way to build a team was through the draft with "his type" of players. He was not keen on signing a bunch of free agent veterans. But in his second season with the Demons, he was getting a real reality check.

As Coach Singer stood in the locker room doorway, his assistant coach Mish Castiel walked up behind him.

"Good grief! What just happened?" Castiel said. "This is awful."

"I know," Coach Singer responded surveying the scene. "It kills me to see this. Something has gotta change."

After taking a few moments to compose himself, Singer decided he had to address the team. Moving to the front of the room, Coach Singer got everyone's attention and started to speak.

"Hey, everyone, listen up." He waited for silence. "Seeing what I'm seeing hurts me. You guys gave me everything you had this year. Obviously, you left everything on the ice. I want you all to know how proud I am of each of you. I love you guys. Let's go

DOI: 10.4324/9781003375449-42

home, take the weekend to rest, and we'll get together next week and figure out what to do next."

Monday morning, Coaches Singer and Castiel, their strength and training coordinators Kevin Tran and Jolie Mills, and their team nutritionist Jack Klime met to discuss the off-season and what they might do as a group to help the team improve.

"Okay, everyone," Coach Singer began. "I appreciate y'all coming in this morning. Coach Castiel and I thought it was important to have you three to join us to evaluate what we need to do this off-season to stay healthy and improve our performance for next year. The table is open, and I welcome your thoughts."

Kevin Tran had been hired right before the past season started. He been an assistant athletic trainer for several years with Salvation Wendigo's. He and Coach Singer had become friends while they were both there. Jolie Mills had been an intern with the Wendigo's under Tran. As a college graduate student, she had impressed the team coaches with her knowledge and disposition as an intern, so they brought her with them to the Demons as assistant athletic trainer. Tran was the first to speak.

"I appreciate you asking for our input. Clearly, we don't have the physical prowess that our competitors have. We need to have our players to aggressively invest in an off-season bulking strength training program. It's obvious we need to get bigger and stronger, and we need to do it quickly."

Jack Klime was next to chime in. Klime had been a private nutritionist for athletes for over a decade. Every athlete who had worked with him raved about how he adapted eating regimens specifically for an athlete's individual genetics and was able to adapt it for just about any sport. Despite his career success as a personal nutritionist, Klime wanted a new challenge in his life, so he jumped at the opportunity when Singer asked him to join the team.

"If we want to pack some weight on our guys, it needs to be the right type of weight. We need to create a nutrition plan, which includes high levels of protein and supplements, to help aid in recovery after these heavyweight bulking workouts. With your permission, I'd like to create individual regimens for every player to maximize their gains. They need to closely follow my nutrition plan."

Finally, Jolie Mills spoke.

"I'd like to think out the box a bit. Kevin and I have been talking, and we'd like to call in an outside consultant. There's a guy we met who is a master at workouts that pack on muscle quick. His name is Chuck Shorley. He's a former bodybuilder that's been working as a training consultant with groups that range from cross-trainers to the navy seals. He's got a master's degree in exercise science and is the ultimate motivator. He's famous for quickly packing on muscle while keeping body fat low. He might be just the spark we need."

Coach Singer rubbed his chin.

"Hmm . . . What do you think about Jolie and Tran's idea, Mish?"

"It couldn't hurt," Castiel answered. "We have to do something significant and fast. We can't go into next year the way we finished this year. This might be best option we have. Jolie was right; we got to think outside the box. We don't have two years to gradually bulk these guys up. We have to do it now."

"Okay," coach Singer said. "Let's do this. Bring this Shorley guy in, and then I want everyone to work together to come up with a plan in the next week that includes strength training and diet plan for our team. Let's meet in a week and then get the team together before their vacations and tell them the plan and what we expect from them." With that the group adjourned.

A week later Coach Singer summoned the team to meet at their athletic complex. Once everyone was seated, Singer talked to them and explained the off-season training and diet regimen. The athletic trainers both spoke as did the nutritionist. After they had laid out their training and eating regimens, Chuck Shorley was introduced. This was the first time that Coaches Singer and Castiel had met Shorley. He was a massive human being. He stood 6 feet 2 inches and weighed 250 pounds. With his level of muscle and low body fat, Singer thought he looked more like a Marvel action figure than a human. As he introduced himself, his big voice and demeanor had the athletes mesmerized. He was extremely charismatic, and by the end of his talk, they were fired up and ready to get started on their summer regimen.

As the meeting wrapped up and the players began to file out of the room, Singer noticed that a couple of the more talented players had stayed around to talk to Shorley. Sam and Dean Westchester had been huge stars in college. The brothers came from a long line of professional hockey players. Their father, John, had had a long and successful career in the NHL, and their mom, Mary, had played hockey too. She was a member of the first international women's hockey team. She had represented the United States in a couple of Olympics and some other international competitions. You could say that hockey was in the Westchester brothers' blood. It was like the family business. Although Sam was a few years older than Dean, Sam had stayed in college for a couple of extra years, while Dean had entered the draft a year early. It had worked out that they were drafted in back-to-back drafts, and as luck would have it, both players had ended up on the same professional team.

Although skilled, both the brothers were a little undersized, and both had taken a beating during the season. Singer had a personal connection to the Winchester family. He and John Winchester had played together while they were both pros and had become fast friends. Robert considered John's family like his own, and he had a close relationship with both the sons. He was like an uncle to the boys.

Coach Singer walked up to the group and introduced himself to Chuck Shorley. "Mr. Shorley," Singer said. "I'm Coach Robert Singer. It's a pleasure to meet you." Shorley smiled and shook Singer's hand.

"It's a pleasure to meet you too, Coach. I really appreciate you giving me this opportunity."

"I'm looking forward to seeing what you can do with these guys during the off-season. My athletic trainers say you're something of a miracle worker. We could use some miracles," Singer joked. "Looks to me like you already got some eager students for your tutelage," he continued.

Shorley laughed, and the two players got a little embarrassed.

"You're not even gonna recognize these two by the time the next season starts," Shorley said. "This I can promise you."

Coach Singer excused himself from the group and went to find Castiel. The two coaches went home, feeling good about how the meeting with the players had gone and what their prospects might be for the next year.

As preseason training camps rolled around, Singer and Castiel were eager to see what kind of progress the players had made in the off-season. The coaches had received regular updates about the players, including strength and weight status reports on the players, but stats never give a true indication of individual improvements.

As the coaches walked into the locker room, they were stopped in the tracks. The team was almost unrecognizable. The team that had once resembled skinny kids now looked like huge men. Everyone had put weight and muscle. As Singer and Castiel moved about the room welcoming players back to the team, they felt a tap on their back.

"Coach," Singer heard behind him. "How's it going?"

As Singer and Castiel turned around to see who was addressing them, they realized it was Dean and his older brother, Sam. The two brothers were almost unrecognizable. Each had packed on what looked like 30 pounds of muscle. They were a presence!

"Good grief, guys!" Singer exclaimed. "I hardly recognized you two. It appears someone took their off-season training seriously!" he continued.

"Yep, Coach, we really got into it. Chuck was incredible! He took us under his wing. He trained us hard, but it was great," Sam Westchester said.

"We were all in with everything Chuck was selling," Dean continued smiling broadly.

As the two coaches talked with the players, Chuck Shorley walked up to them.

"So, what do you think Coach?" Shorley said. "Didn't I tell ya that you wouldn't recognize these two the next time you saw them?

"You weren't lying! This is amazing. You really are a miracle worker!" Singer replied.

After the group of four men dispersed, Castiel walked up to Singer.

"What do you think, Coach?" Castiel asked. "Impressive as it is, this all seems to be a little too good to be true, don't you think?"

"Just go with it. Let's enjoy it and quit finding things to worry about. This is a good thing, Mish," Singer said as he patted Castiel on the shoulder. Castiel shrugged, and the two men continued to roam the room chatting with the team.

There was a marked difference in the team's play during the preseason. Players were faster to the puck and didn't tire nearly as quickly as they previously had. The power on their shots and passes was an amazing upgrade. Singer and Castiel could hardly contain their excitement for the upcoming season. This on-ice improvement was especially apparent with the Westchester brothers. Although they had always been skilled, the extra muscle they now possessed seemed to give them a newfound confidence. Both players were among the league leaders in points—Dean more from scoring while Sam led the league in assists.

As the early part of the season progressed, the Devils were turning heads with their play. Other league teams remarked about how much different the Devils looked and performed. After six games, the Devils found themselves 5–1. The Lebanon residents were excited about their recent expansion team, and tickets to games became a hot commodity. Everyone was talking about the Devils.

A couple of weeks into the season, Coach Singer received a phone call.

"Coach Singer," Singer said.

"Hi, Coach. This is Billie." Billie was someone Singer vaguely knew from the team's admin office.

"Hi, Billie. What's up?"

"Well, we just got back a report from USADA."

"USADA?"

"Yes, the United States Anti-Doping Agency."

Singer felt a drop in his stomach, and his heart skipped a beat.

"Uh, okay."

"I wanted to let you know that they found some discrepancies in their most recent randomized drug test of the team," Billie continued.

Coach Singer's heart skipped another couple of beats. "Billie, would you mind if I put you on speaker phone and had you repeat that so my assistant coach could hear that?"

Billie agreed, and as Coach Singer put his office phone on speaker mode, she repeated the news.

"As I said, they found some discrepancies on your players' most recent urine sample tests. The test indicates the use of performance-enhancing drugs for several of your players."

"You gotta be kidding me," Castiel said, dropping his head into his hands.

"Which players are you talking about here?" Castiel asked.

"I'll send you the list over email," she replied. "We'll need to discuss this in more detail as soon as possible."

Singer thanked her, and the call ended.

A few seconds later the list revealed four players who had had a positive test. Most notably, both Winchester brothers' names were on the list.

"Castiel, get Sam and Dean in my office. *Now*!" Singer said angrily.

A few minutes later the two brothers walked in sheepishly to Singer's office. After staring at the players for a few minutes Singer finally spoke.

"What's going on here, guys? What did you do?"

"I'm sorry, Coach," Sam said. "Chuck said we could get to where we wanted to be by taking a boost drug. And boy was he right. The results were so quick. We kinda got swept up in excitement of it all. Chuck swore that this was a designer drug and wouldn't be detected by drug tests. We're really sorry."

"How many players are we talking about who did this stuff?" Singer retorted.

"I'm not sure," Dean replied. "I know we weren't the only ones."

"You guys understand that you're going to be suspended now, don't you?" Singer said. "You and everyone else who went this direction have jeopardized our entire season."

"I get it now, Coach," Dean continued. "We just really wanted to show you that we could improve to the level you wanted us to. We regret that now."

A few minutes later the players left the office. Castiel flopped down onto a small couch in Singer's office. The two coaches exchanged no words and sat in silence trying to comprehend what had happened, what they could have done differently to circumvent this situation, and what they were going to do now.

Questions for Consideration

1. Who are the stakeholders in this case?
2. Do you agree with the approach Singer and Castiel took to improve the physical ability of their players? What are some alternate methods they could have done to improve the stature of their team?
3. How did Singer's team building philosophy impact the current situation?
4. What was the key mistake Singer made early on regarding Chuck Shorley?
5. How should Coach Singer have reacted when he first saw the physical changes in his players?
6. If you were the head coach of the Devils, what steps would you take to mitigate such issues in the future?

References and Further Readings

Blackburn, P. (2017). Bill Belichick has reportedly banned Brady's trainer from the Patriot's plane, sideline. *CBS Sports*. Retrieved from www.cbssports.com/nfl/news/bill-belichick-has-reportedly-banned-bradys-trainer-from-the-patriots-plane-sideline/

Carrol, W. (2014). Undetectable: The new PED that could be in the Olympics, NFL and MLB now. *Bleacher Report*. https://bleacherreport.com/articles/1955231-undetectable-the-new-ped-that-could-be-in-the-olympics-nfl-and-mlb-now

Draper, K. (2022). Ringworm? Tatis's explanations stretch common sense, experts say. *New York Times*. www.nytimes.com/2022/08/26/sports/baseball/fernando-tatis-jr-baseball-steroids.html

Stephens, M. (2022). Honey baker winner accepts six-month suspension over doping violation. *Hockey News*. https://thehockeynews.com/news/hobey-baker-winner-accepts-six-month-suspension-over-doping-violation

Wells, A. (2017). Alex Rodriquez says PED suspension cost him his reputation, more than $40M. *Bleacher Report*. https://bleacherreport.com/articles/2738639-alex-rodriguez-says-ped-suspension-cost-him-his-reputation-more-than-40m

40 Forgive and Forget?

It had been an up-and-down tenure for Coach Jade Carter as head coach of Eureka. She was hired to coach the Eureka Fusion professional women's basketball team three years earlier. When Carter took over the team, it was embroiled with infighting and inner turmoil. Players didn't get along with one another and were upset with management and team ownership. Their star player, Bev Barlow, had been frustrated over contract negotiations with management and was demanding a trade. In addition, the former coach of the Fusion, Nat Stark, had been ushered out after a scandalous affair with an intern. This had left Carter many fires to put out.

Carter's first season had been a success. Holly Martin, the team's longtime veteran and perennial all-star, had had a great season. Carter had managed to calm Barlow's discontent over her contract and get her to buy into her coaching system, which allowed Barlow great offensive freedom. Players got along and seemed to like their new coach's approach. The team had gone to the playoffs and advanced to the third round.

However, despite putting up Most Valuable Player (MVP) level numbers, management had come nowhere close to what Barlow felt she deserved. Her discontentment boiled over during Carter's second season. A hold out by Barlow before the season started, and a questionably long stint on the disabled list, led to an eventual trade away from the team. Her departure coupled with Holly Martin experiencing several injuries during the season had spelled doom for Carter's Fusion team, and they finished slightly below .500 and missed the playoffs.

This season, Carter's third, had been an abject disaster. Barlow had been traded for a couple of, what turned out to be, average draft picks. Holly Martin's retirement had been particularly hard on the team. A Fusion lifer, she was considered the soul of the team. Martin had played with the team for over a decade, and her name was synonymous with the Fusion. She had been a part of the team back to the days when they were good. But Father Time and scar tissue in her knees from several anterior cruciate ligament (ACL) operations had convinced her that it was time to call it a day. Now with no Beverly, no Martin, and with several young draft picks who had not produced like Carter and management thought they would, the team was in last place. Whispers of Carter's job security were starting to be heard.

The negative dynamics from the last two seasons had brought Carter and the Fusion to where they were today. The organization teetered on the precipice of reverting back to where they were a few seasons ago—a team entrenched in the bottom of their division.

DOI: 10.4324/9781003375449-43

A few days after the season ended, Eureka's general manager (GM), Heather Deecon, walked into Carter's office and quickly shut the door. Heather and Jade had been friends for a long time, rising up through "B" level developmental basketball leagues together. They had spent several working together, Carter as an assistant coach and Deecon in low-level management. When Heather got the job with the Fusion, she had been the catalyst to get Carter hired as coach.

"Jade," Deecon said. "I've got something to tell you, and it's big. Before I tell you, I need you to know that it's not a sure thing. But there's a strong possibility that the team might be getting a huge upgrade in talent."

Carter was intrigued and arched her back as she attentively sat up.

"Give me a second, Heather. Let me get Doug in here to hear this too."

Doug Fargo was Carter's assistant coach. He had actually coached Carter's daughter, Zoe, in college and had given her a graduate assistantship after she finished up her playing eligibility. After leaving college ball, Carter hired him to be her second on the bench. After a quick phone call, Coach Doug Fargo shuffled into Carter's office.

"Do tell, Heather," Carter said. "What big talent might be headed our way?"

Heather grinned. "Ownership is in talks to trade for Josephine Lupo!" she exclaimed.

Carter struggled to speak.

"You're kidding me."

Josephine Lupo was a generational talent. Still at the pinnacle of her career, Lupo was superbly talented. Just 26, she had already won three league MVP awards. The tallest player in the league, she possessed ball skills that resembled a point guard. She was able to shoot outside, drive to the basket, and post up underneath like a traditional center. Her height, strength, and quickness made her virtually impossible to defend. She had led her Portland Planets team to a championship last season.

"How in the world is Josephine Lupo available?" Fargo asked doubtfully.

"So, here's the scenario," Heather said leaning forward. "Her leaving the team and possibly coming here aren't without some baggage. It hasn't come out yet, but she is in a bit of legal trouble. Looks like she beat up both her boyfriend's sister and the sister's 18-year-old son. Apparently, this isn't the first time something like this has happened with her. Evidently, the Planets and her representatives have been covering up acts of violence for a while now. It looks like there might have been some cover-up back when she was in college too. She got angry in a game and intentionally elbowed a girl in the nose breaking it. She also got into a fight with a player on her own Planet team. Evidently, she grabbed this player around the throat. It left marks. There's probably more too. Team reps from the Planets say she's matured and doesn't behave that way anymore, but the stuff happened."

"And with all that, ownership is still open to bringing her in?" Carter asked.

"Yep," Heather said nodding. "They want to know your feelings on the matter and whether you'd sign off on it."

Carter sat back in her chair and looked up. She felt bad for still being excited about bringing her to the team. She wasn't a violent person, and with a daughter of her own, she had always stood up against violence against anyone in any form.

"Let me think about it, Heather," Carter said.

"Don't think about it too long, Jade," Heather retorted as she stood up to leave the office. "Things are in motion. If we don't get her someone else will."

That night Carter went home to talk to her most trusted confidants, her husband, Jake, and her daughter, Zoe. Zoe had played college basketball herself and later worked as a grad assistant for her college team. After she graduated with her graduate degree, Carter had hired her as a consultant and team scout. Carter's husband, Jake, had been a collegiate gymnast, and after his college eligibility was completed, he had gotten a law degree. The firm he partnered for often took on cases that centered around women causes like sexual harassment and pay equality in the workplace. These two often served as her sounding board for a variety of issues on the team.

As the family of three sat down for dinner, Carter shared with them what was happening with the team.

Jake was the first to respond. "Jade, I think this is a bad idea. As a family we've always supported protection of women. We've preached how you cannot allow them to be abused or taken advantage of. We must apply the same standard, as is in this case, when a woman is the abuser. I don't see how you could in good conscience welcome such a person on to the team."

After Jake had finished giving her opinion, Carter looked at Zoe as she chimed in.

"I get it, Mom. We need a very quick infusion of talent to the team. Aside from the ethical side of it, I'm concerned about the blowback we'd get from the public and press."

For the rest of the evening the three analyzed every side of the situation. As it started getting late, the three decided to table the discussion and talk about it the next morning. The next morning at breakfast Carter brought the situation back up.

"I thought about everything you said last night after I got in bed. Ultimately, I've come to the same conclusion you both had at dinner. I don't know how I'd be able to really live with myself if I went along with Lupo being traded to the team."

Both Jake and Zoe hugged Jade and acknowledged how proud they were of her. Carter said goodbye and headed to work. As Carter arrived at the team facility, she saw Fargo waiting for her by the front door to the complex. The two walked into the building together.

"So?" Fargo excitedly asked. "What did you decide?"

"I just don't think I can do it," Carter said shaking her head. "It would be hard to look at myself in the mirror if I endorsed her being a part of our squad."

"I get it. I had misgivings about it too. As great as it would be to have her talent on the team, somehow it just doesn't seem right."

As they arrived at Carter's office, Heather Deecon was waiting for them.

"Good morning. Not to rush you, but we need to come up with a decision quicker than I thought. Ownership wants an answer by this afternoon."

"I don't need to wait that long, Heather," Jade said. "I can tell you right now. As tempting as it would be to get Lupo on the team, I'm gonna have to decline."

Heather seemed a little surprised.

"Okay. So what pushed you to decline?"

"Well, of course, the ethical stuff surrounding her violence is the biggest factor, but I'm also concerned with the reaction we'd get from the press and the public," Carter answered.

"I understand. As GM, I had a lot of worries about how such an acquisition might be reacted to in the public. It could get dicey. I'll let ownership know your decision. I respect your decision and will back it."

Later that day, Carter and Fargo were reviewing some game film together when they heard a knock on the door. Fargo opened the door to find Heather Deecon standing there.

"Hey," Deecon said a little breathlessly. "Turn off the game tape and turn on the news."

Puzzled, Carter did as Deecon had asked. The local news was breaking a special report. The cameras shifted to a press conference in the Fusion team complex. Standing at the podium was Kevin Blake, the sports information director for the Fusion.

"Today with open arms and excited hearts the Eureka Fusion announce that we have acquired Josephine Lupo in a trade from the Portland Planets. We think that Ms. Lupo exemplifies those virtues that the Fusion hold dear: hard work, team centered, and high character. Additionally, we have just signed Ms. Lupo to a new long-term contract. Ms. Lupo is a generational talent that doesn't come around very often. We look forward to building a team around her, and we expect to have a bright future."

"So much for getting my input and blessing," Carter said.

"Jade," Deecon said. "I had no idea about any of this. I swear."

"I know, Heather. I don't blame you," Carter responded. "Seems to me the owners had already made their decision some time ago."

As the three sat staring at the TV in disbelief, Fargo heard something outside. He left the office, walked down a short hall, and poked his head outside. A few moments later he scurried back into the office.

"Hey," Fargo said. "There's a ton of protestors outside. They sound pretty angry. What should we do now?"

"And so it begins," Deecon muttered. "We've opened a can of worms."

"Wait until my family hears," Jade said shaking her head. "How are we going to coach someone we know is blatantly abusive?"

The three stared at one another, wondering what direction to go now.

Questions for Consideration

1. Who are the stakeholders in this case?
2. What was Carter's first mistake regarding the consideration of having Jo Lupo on the team?
3. Should Carter have had more people involved in his decision-making process regarding Lupo?
4. Regarding how Carter relayed his decision against having Lupo on the team to ownership, do you think it was done correctly? If not, what would you have done? Defend your answer.
5. What should Carter now do in regard to the following groups:

   a. Ownership
   b. The media
   c. The public

6. Place yourself in the position of Heather, the GM. Do you think a story like this is possible without her involvement or knowledge? As a GM, what would you do if this had been done to you by the ownership?

References and Further Readings

Caldwell, D. (2022). Deshaun Watson's reputation is toxic, but do Browns fans care? *The Guardian*. www.theguardian.com/sport/2022/aug/23/deshaun-watson-cleveland-browns-fans-nfl-football

Fainaru-Wada, M. (2015). Documents reveal new details about Hope Solo's actions last June. *ESPN.com*. www.espn.com/espn/otl/story/_/id/12976615/detailed-look-hope-solo-domestic-violence-case-includes-reports-being-belligerent-jail

Gleeson, S. (2015). Britney Griner pleads guilty in domestic violence case, enters counseling. *USA Today*. www.usatoday.com/story/sports/2015/04/28/brittney-griner-plea-deal-guilty-domestic-violence-glory-johnson-wnba/26538559/

Sullivan, B. (2022). Deshaun Watson will be suspended 11 games after allegations of sexual misconduct. *NPR*. www.npr.org/2022/08/12/1117058302/deshaun-watson-controversy-suspension-nfl-preseason

Index

abuse 72, 80–84, 89–92, 169, 172, 185–189
academics 12–15, 54–58, 90, 105, 113
alcohol 77–79, 168–169
assistant coach (key references) 49, 154–157, 174–178
athletic director 3–7, 8–11, 22, 30, 38–39, 45, 49–52, 62–63, 79–80, 83, 85, 106, 111–112, 118–121
athletic trainer 37–40, 123, 169–170, 180–181

baseball 25–28, 89–92, 99–103, 153–157
basketball 22–24, 41–44, 85–88, 104–107, 108–112, 148–152, 185–189
bench players 17–18, 33, 38–39, 46, 62, 65, 82, 85–86, 108, 149–150, 177–179, 186
boosters 29–31, 134

cheating 59–63
cheerleading 74–79
coaching philosophy/styles 5, 19, 22–24, 29, 32, 59, 80–84, 89, 93, 99, 105, 109, 111–112, 122, 140, 153, 167–173, 175–176
code of conduct 17, 29–30, 54
community college 113–116
concussion 33–35

disability 64–68, 80–85
donors *see* boosters
drug use 127–131, 179–184

eating disorder 69–73

facilities 8–11
field hockey 64–68
football 12–15, 37–40, 59–63, 80–84, 93–96, 127–131, 139–147

gymnastics 53–58

hazing 89–92

ice hockey 32–35, 179–184
injuries 32–35, 37–40, 62, 65–68, 106, 123–126, 130–131, 185
international 25–28, 119, 159–166, 181

lacrosse 3–71, 117–121

media 17, 94, 104, 106, 108–112, 114–115, 139, 141, 150, 167–173
mental health 122–126, 132–136, 169
mercy rule 17–18
mixed martial arts (MMA) 115

name, image, and likeness (NIL) 93–96, 131
National Basketball Association (NBA) 108, 112, 148
National Collegiate Athletics Association (NCAA) 12, 99–101, 104–106, 109, 128
National Football League (NFL) 130, 139–147

owners/management 139–147, 148, 151–152, 154–157, 185–189

parents 19–21, 29–31, 42–43, 45–48, 51, 53–58, 64–68, 71–72, 75, 91, 95–96, 100–103, 111–112
personal training *see* strength and conditioning
player contract 54, 141, 145, 153, 159, 185, 188

pregnancy 20
principal 5, 14–17, 22, 42, 45–47, 72, 74, 78–79
private school 16–18
professional development 59

racquetball 158–161
recruiting/recruit 3, 12, 83, 101, 104–105, 118, 122, 124, 132, 167

scholarships 12, 22, 29, 49, 51, 70, 99–103, 122, 133
soccer 16–18, 49–52, 167–178
softball 45–48
strength and conditioning 102, 158–166, 179–184
swimming 29–31, 132–136

team cohesion 25–28, 80–84, 93–96, 108–112, 148–152, 174–178
team selection 25–28, 174–178
tennis 122–126
time management 19–21, 75
track and field 8–11
transfer portal 100, 105, 122–126
transgender 132–136

volleyball, indoor/beach 19–21, 46, 69–73, 122–126

weather 8–11, 172
Women's National Basketball Association (WNBA) 108
wrestling 113–116

Made in United States
Orlando, FL
10 January 2025